Conflict in the Former USSR

Since the collapse of the Soviet Union, conflict in the former USSR has been a key concern in international security. This book fills a gap in the literature on violent conflict, evaluating a region that contains all the modern ingredients for instability and aggression. Bringing together leading experts on war and security, the book addresses current debates in international relations about power, interests, globalisation and the politics of identity as major drivers of contemporary war. Incidents such as the 2008 Russo-Georgian conflict, the wars in Chechnya, and Russia's struggles over national identity and resources with former communist states are all thoroughly examined. With new issues like energy security, terrorism and transnational crime, and older tensions between East and West threatening to deepen once more, this is an important contribution to the international security literature.

DR MATTHEW SUSSEX holds a PhD from the University of Melbourne (2001) and completed his undergraduate and Honours qualifications at the University of Queensland. He is currently Senior Lecturer in the School of Government, University of Tasmania, where he coordinates that institution's international relations programme. His research interests include international security, Russian politics and foreign policy, strategic studies, European politics and international relations theory.

Conflict in the Former USSR

Edited by

Matthew Sussex

CAMBRIDGE
UNIVERSITY PRESS

CAMBRIDGE UNIVERSITY PRESS
Cambridge, New York, Melbourne, Madrid, Cape Town,
Singapore, São Paulo, Delhi, Mexico City

Cambridge University Press
The Edinburgh Building, Cambridge CB2 8RU, UK

Published in the United States of America by Cambridge University Press,
New York

www.cambridge.org
Information on this title: www.cambridge.org/9780521135283

First published 2012

Printed and bound in the United Kingdom by the MPG Books Group

A catalogue record for this publication is available from the British Library

Library of Congress Cataloguing in Publication data
Conflict in the former USSR / [edited by] Matthew Sussex.
    pages   cm
Includes bibliographical references and index.
ISBN 978-0-521-76310-3 (hbk.) – ISBN 978-0-521-13528-3 (pbk.)
1. National security – Former Soviet republics.   2. Security,
International.   3. Political stability – Former Soviet republics.
4. Violence – Former Soviet republics.   5. Ethnic conflict – Former
Soviet republics.   6. Social conflict – Former Soviet republics.
7. Former Soviet republics – History, Military.   8. Former Soviet
republics – Politics and government.   9. Former Soviet republics –
Ethnic relations.   10. Former Soviet republics – Social conditions.
I. Sussex, Matthew, editor of compilation.
UA770.C686   2012
355.020947–dc23   2012016906

ISBN 978-0-521-76310-3 Hardback
ISBN 978-0-521-13528-3 Paperback

For Nicholas

Contents

Maps

Contributors

LESLIE HOLMES has been Professor of Political Science at the University of Melbourne since 1988. He specialises in communist and post-communist politics. He was President of the International Council for Central and East European Studies (ICCEES) from 2000 to 2005, President of the Australasian Association for Communist and Post-communist Studies (AACaPS) from 2005 to 2007, and Co-President of the Contemporary European Studies Association of Australia (CESAA) from 2001 to 2002. He was elected a Fellow of the Academy of the Social Sciences in Australia in 1995. His most recent sole-authored book is *Rotten States? Corruption, Post-Communism, and Neoliberalism.*

ROGER E. KANET is a professor in the Department of International Studies at the University of Miami, where he served as Dean of the School of International Studies, 1997–2000. Prior to 1997, he taught at the University of Illinois at Urbana-Champaign, where he was a member of the Department of Political Science and served as head of that department from 1984 to 1987, and as Associate Vice-Chancellor for Academic Affairs and Director of International Programs and Studies (1989–97). He has published more than 200 scholarly articles and edited more than twenty-five books. Recent publications include: *Russian Foreign Policy in the Twenty-first Century,* 2010; co-edited with Maria Raquel Freire, *Key Players and Regional Dynamics in Eurasia: The Return of the 'Great Game'* (2010); *The United States and Europe in a Changing World* (2009); and *A Resurgent Russia and the West: The European Union, NATO and Beyond* (2009). He is a member of the Council on Foreign Relations, New York.

BEAT KERNEN is a professor and Head of the Department of Political Science at the University of Southwestern Missouri. He holds an MPhil and a PhD from the University of Kansas. Professor Kernen's research and teaching interests include post-Soviet politics, international relations, the European Union and East European politics. He has published articles in *The Soviet and Post-Soviet Review*, *Crossroads*, *Political Chronicle*, *Yearbook of East European Economies* and *East European Quarterly*.

MATT KILLINGSWORTH is an associate lecturer at the University of Tasmania. His PhD on lustration in Eastern and Central Europe was completed at the University of Melbourne in 2007. He has published on opposition and dissent in the former communist countries of Central and Eastern Europe, lustration in the Czech Republic and Poland and the changing nature of war in the former Soviet space. He is Vice-President of the Contemporary European Studies Association of Australia (CESAA) and editor of the *Australian and New Zealand Journal of European Studies*.

NEIL ROBINSON is Senior Lecturer in Politics at the University of Limerick. Prior to his appointment at Limerick he taught at the universities of York and Essex. His research interests focus on Russian and post-communist politics, particularly the political economy of post-communism and post-communist state building. He is the author of *Ideology and the Collapse of the Soviet System: A Critical History of Soviet Ideological Discourse* (1995) and *Russia: A State of Uncertainty* (2002) and co-author (with Karen Henderson) of *Post-communist Politics* (1997). He is the editor or co-editor of *Institutions and Political Change in Russia* (2000), *Reforging the Weakest Link: Global Political Economy and Post-Soviet Change in Russia, Ukraine and Belarus* (with Aidan Hehir, 2004), *State-building. Theory and Practice* (2007) and (with Todd Landman) *The Sage Handbook of Comparative Politics* (2009). He is the author of articles in journals including *Soviet Studies*, *European Journal of Political Research*, *Political Studies*, *The Journal of Communist Studies and Transitional Politics*, *Communist and Post-Communist Studies*, *Demokratizatsia* and *Review of International Political Economy*.

RICHARD SAKWA is Professor of Russian and European Politics at the University of Kent. Sakwa is one of the UK's leading scholars of Russian politics. He has published extensively on Soviet, Russian and post-communist affairs, and has written and edited numerous books and articles on the subject. While completing his doctorate on Moscow politics during the Civil War (1918–21) he spent a year on a British Council scholarship at Moscow State University (1979–80), and then worked for two years in Moscow in the 'Mir' Science and Technology Publishing House. Before moving to Kent he lectured at the University of Essex and the University of California, Santa Cruz. His current research interests include democratic development in Russia, the nature of post-communism and global challenges facing the former communist countries. He is also an Associate Fellow of the Russia and Eurasia Programme at the Royal Institute of International Affairs, a member of the Advisory Boards of the Institute of Law and Public Policy in Moscow, a member of the Eurasian Political Studies Network and a member of the Academy of Learned Societies for the Social Sciences.

MATTHEW SUSSEX is a senior lecturer in the School of Government, University of Tasmania. His PhD on contemporary Russian foreign policy (2001) was completed at the University of Melbourne. His research interests include strategic and security studies, Russian politics and foreign policy, and conflict in the international system. He has been awarded grants from bodies such as the Australian Research Council and the Fulbright Commission, amongst others. His publications include articles and book chapters on globalisation and contemporary war, Russian foreign policy, the foreign policies of great powers and Australian security policy. He is a Fellow of the Contemporary Europe Research Centre, a National Executive member of the Australian Institute of International Affairs and a founding member of the Australian Council for Strategic Studies.

Acknowledgements

This volume grew out of a series of workshops on security and conflict on the territory of the former USSR held in Limerick, Republic of Ireland, and the Australian National University in Canberra. Much excellent scholarship has been done on the politics of former communist states, and there are many detailed evaluations of the often troubled relationship between Russia and the West. But there are few books that examine the topic of war and conflict in the former USSR as their central theme. We therefore offer this contribution to supplement current research.

I owe a particular debt of thanks to Jo Lane and John Haslam at Cambridge University Press for their words of wisdom, encouragement and gentle prodding during this volume's gestation. Their assistance during the preparation of the manuscript was professional, first-rate and understanding. I also thank the copy-editor, Joanna Pyke.

I am also grateful to the Australian Research Council (ARC) for funding my project on globalisation and war in the Caucasus. This grant made it possible to bring together a variety of experts from across the world in the one place, and was the primary impetus for this volume.

There are a number of other people I should acknowledge, but space precludes a more fulsome list. I owe my particular thanks, then, to my fellow contributors, but also to Peter Shearman for his wisdom and long-suffering guidance over the years, to Les Holmes for jumping into the breech, to Matt Killingsworth for being an irreverent kindred spirit, and most of all to my wife, Tracey, whose tolerance of my regular late nights bashing the keyboard made this book possible.

Finally, I would like to dedicate my part in this volume to my young son, Nicholas. He won't be able to read (much less understand) this book for quite a while, but he certainly enjoyed drawing obscure pictures on early drafts and edits. Come to think of it, so did I.

Matthew Sussex
Hobart, Tasmania

Abbreviations

ABM Treaty	Anti-Ballistic Missile Treaty
AO	autonomous oblast
ASEAN	Association of Southeast Asian Nations
ASSR	autonomous Soviet socialist republic
BEEPS	'Business Environment and Enterprise Performance Surveys'
BPI	'Bribe Payers Index'
BTC pipeline	Baku-Tbilisi-Ceyhan pipeline
CFE Treaty	Conventional Forces in Europe Treaty
CHS	Commission on Human Security
CIS	Commonwealth of Independent States
CNPC	China National Petroleum Corporation
COMECON	Council for Mutual Economic Assistance
CPC	Caspian Pipeline Consortium
CPI	'Corruption Perceptions Index'
CSTO	Collective Security Treaty Organization
EaP	Eastern Partnership
ENP	European Neighbourhood Policy
EST	European Security Treaty
EU	European Union
EurAsEc	Eurasian Economic Community
G8	Group of 8
GDP	gross domestic product
GFC	global financial crisis
GSSR	Georgian Soviet Socialist Republic
GUAM	Georgia-Ukraine-Azerbaijan-Moldova
ICC	International Criminal Court
ICISS	International Commission on Intervention and State Sovereignty
ICVS	'International Crime Victims Survey'
IMU	Islamic Movement of Uzbekistan
IO	international organisation

KPRF	Communist Party of the Russian Federation
KSOR	CSTO Collective Rapid Reaction Force
LDPR	Liberal Democratic Party of Russia
MAP	Membership Action Plan
NATO	North Atlantic Treaty Organisation
NGO	Non-Governmental Organisation
NMD	national missile defence (US)
OSCE	Organisation for Security and Cooperation in Europe
PCA	Partnership and Cooperation Agreement
PfP	Partnership for Peace
PRC	People's Republic of China
R2P	Responsibility to Protect
RMA	revolution in military affairs
RSC	regional security complex
SCO	Shanghai Cooperation Organisation
SSR	Soviet socialist republic
TI	Transparency International
TRNC	Turkish Republic of Northern Cyprus
UN	United Nations
UNGA	UN General Assembly
UNSC	UN Security Council
USSR	Union of Soviet Socialist Republics
WMD	weapons of mass destruction

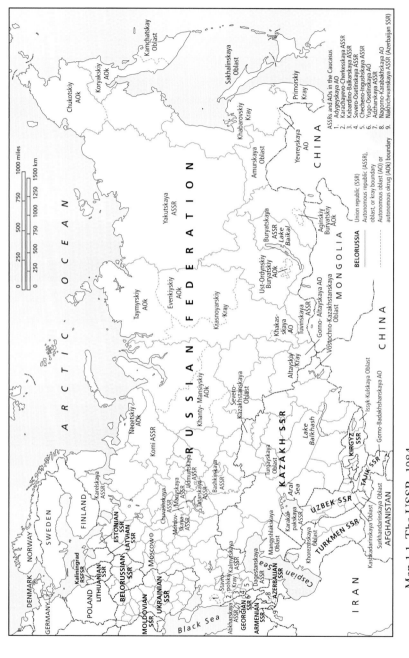

Map 1.1 The USSR, 1984

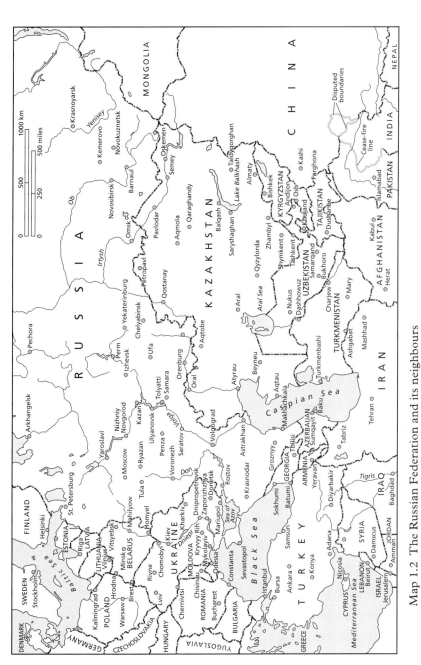

Map 1.2 The Russian Federation and its neighbours

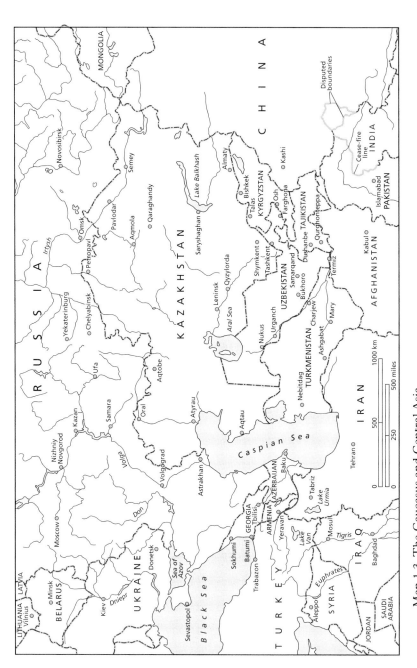

Map 1.3 The Caucasus and Central Asia

1 Introduction: understanding conflict in the former USSR

Matthew Sussex

This book evaluates the nature, causes and implications of conflicts in the geographical space formerly occupied by the USSR. It does so in the context of current debates in the international relations literature regarding the role of power, interests, technological forces, and normative issues as major drivers of contemporary political violence. Since the end of the Cold War, Russia has attempted to maintain a sphere of influence on what was once the territory of the Union of Soviet Socialist Republics (USSR). Whether in the 2008 Russo-Georgian conflict; the wars in Chechnya; struggles over resources with Ukraine; disputes in Central Asia over ethnicity; or in latent conflicts that are aided by terrorism and corruption, the former Soviet space remains an under-evaluated area in the literature on contemporary conflict. With new issues such as energy security and transnational crime gaining in saliency, and older tensions between East and West deepening once more, it is vital that security specialists pay closer attention to this region of the world.

Following the end of the Cold War many specialists on conflict – mistakenly, we argue – shifted their attention away from Russia as a primary area for analysis. At the turn of the twenty-first century George W. Bush suggested upon coming to power that the People's Republic of China (PRC) and Russia would be major focal points of the new Republican Administration's foreign policy.[1] Yet the strategic shock of 9/11 had the immediate impact of redirecting US attention to the 'war on terror', with an increasing focus on the Middle East and the Persian Gulf. Many in the field of international relations also then turned their attention to issues of global terrorism and the threat of rogue or failing states gaining weapons of mass destruction (WMD). Insofar as the former republics of the USSR figured in these new security concerns, it was in relation to their position in the wider war on terror; oil and gas

---

[1] J. Gittings, 'Bush claims Russia and China as allies', *Guardian*, 22 October (2001). Available at www.guardian.co.uk/world/2001/oct/22/china.afghanistan

resources in the Caspian region; pipeline routes; and as potential allies who could facilitate access to bases in Eurasia.

One of the serious consequences of such a narrow focus has been to ignore, or at least to misperceive, Russia's own interests in its immediate geostrategic environment. This can be contrasted with the era of bipolarity, when there was a strong appreciation of Russia's interests and of the importance in Moscow's calculations of relations with its immediate neighbours. The tendency to discount Russia's position occurs despite the many unresolved conflicts in a fragile security environment that threaten the stability of many recently independent states that are now Western allies.

In an attempt to address these issues, this book reveals some unusually common ground amongst its contributors. Certainly, the specific perspectives of each author vary considerably. We are agreed, however, on many of the core challenges facing the former USSR. First, we find that conflict has arisen from problems of state building, sparked by ethnic, economic and structural factors. These are not adequately explained by traditional approaches. Second, we find that institutions are, by and large, poorly equipped to deal with both the traditional and non-traditional conflicts that have broken out on the territory of the former USSR. Third, the region is also experiencing major strategic realignments. Central Asian states, Russia and the Caucasus are all now becoming sites for rivalry. This involves a rising PRC, the West and a resurgent Russia. Finally, while we may disagree on whether conflict has been prevalent or not in specific areas of the former USSR, we are all of the opinion that the triggers for war, whether traditional or transnational, have largely not been ameliorated. Here, rapidly changing patterns of interests and interaction amongst actors in the former USSR compel policymakers to rethink their ideas about conflict and insecurity, and to learn quickly as a result.

Twenty years after the USSR: renewal meets instability

Some two decades after the collapse of the USSR it is difficult to find many commentators prepared to lament the passing of Soviet communism. Of course, this was not always the case. During the mid-1990s rampant inflation within many newly independent states quickly became coupled to the rise of financial oligarchs. Uneven transitions to democracy and the institutionalisation of organised crime became the norm. Many of those in the West who closely studied Russia, the largest of the former Soviet republics, watched with increasing unease as a stalled democratisation effort, the rise of a 'red-brown' axis, and domestic consensus over a more assertive and muscular foreign policy took shape. Russia's two wars in Chechnya, its opposition to North Atlantic Treaty Organisation (NATO) expansion and Western intervention in former Yugoslavia, and its persistent meddling in the affairs of the so-called 'near abroad' – especially in Ukraine, Georgia and Belarus – all seemed indicative of deep structural weaknesses in the Russian state, with worrying implications for those states surrounding it.

Whilst numerous problems remain, it is fair to say that the social and economic malaise experienced across the former USSR during the 1990s was slowly alleviated after the turn of the century. In Ukraine, an economic collapse (that in 1999 had seen United Nations [UN] estimates place some 63 per cent of its population below the poverty line) gradually eased.[2] The 'coloured revolutions' of 2003–5 were seen as flowering symbols of benign Georgian and Ukrainian national identity, which in turn prompted enthusiasm that democracy and free will would become more strongly rooted as the decade progressed.

In Russia itself, democratisation was shunted into a more patriotic and limited form of 'sovereign democracy' under Vladimir Putin, which also empowered a close circle of *siloviki*, much as the old *nomenklatura* system had done under communism. This was accompanied by a massive turnaround in Russia's economic fortunes, built on the back of its burgeoning energy trade, which saw it become an energy superpower.[3] Of course, Russia's use of energy for strategic purposes against former communist states was also an area of concern, especially since it prompted fears of vulnerable European overdependence on Russian gas. But as the countries of the former USSR entered the second decade of the twenty-first century, the crippling internal problems they had experienced just ten to fifteen years earlier had improved in many cases. People living in former Soviet republics were, by and large, better off than they had been toward the end of the Soviet era.

But a puzzling aspect of this is that increased economic security has not translated into enhanced physical security. Indeed, few analysts of security affairs in the former USSR would regard the regional environment as having become more secure since the Soviet collapse. On the contrary, one can make the argument that strategic geography has

---

[2] United Nations Development Program, *Human development report, 1999* (New York: Oxford University Press, 1999).
[3] For a full discussion, see M. Sussex, 'The strategic implications of Russian resource diplomacy' in R.E. Kanet and M.R. Freire (eds.), *Russia and its neighbours* (New York: Routledge, in press), chapter 9.

become much more significant than it was formerly. During its existence the USSR enforced order upon what are today recognised as numerous ethnic, religious and geostrategic trouble spots. Once communism fell, radical terrorism cropped up in the Pankisi Gorge, in Dagestan and in Chechnya; squabbles began between Moscow, Baku and Tbilisi over ownership of energy infrastructure; and the treatment of ethnic Russians in South Ossetia and Abkhazia eventually prompted Russian military intervention in 2008. To the west and south, the 'gas wars' between Russia and Ukraine, Russia and Georgia, and even Russia and Belarus were other permissive factors for conflict. Additional factors included a declining demographic curve in Russia itself as well as social unrest in Central Asia.

In addition to these problems, the former USSR has once again become a site for great power competition. Much of this revolves around what Michael Klare refers to as the 'new geopolitics' shaped by energy,[4] but such notions can be traced back in time to Halford Makinder's notion of the Eurasian Heartland.[5] Far from simple geographic determinism, the region from the Volga to the Yangtze remains fundamentally important to global security, and it is once again deeply affected by economic and strategic balances of power based on material capabilities. With energy, ethnicity and economics decoupled from the controlling order imposed by the USSR, it is not surprising that a rising PRC, European Union (EU), United States and even a growing India have become influential players in the security order of the former Soviet space. For some actors, like Kazakhstan, this has led to new opportunities, giving Astana the chance to launch what is often referred to as a 'multi-vector' foreign policy. This has been based on acquiescing to Russian power via Kazakhstan's participation in the Collective Security Treaty Organization (CSTO), but at the same time it has sought to develop deeper economic relations with the PRC and the United States in its energy sector. Its new flexibility in its foreign policy thus permits a search for external security as well as the prospect of internal economic balancing through cooperation with extra-regional great powers.

For others, however, the search for security has been constraining. In Georgia, the prospects of being locked out of formal NATO membership have presented the (somewhat erratic) Mikhail Saakashvili with

[4] M.T. Klare, *Rising powers, sinking planet: the new geopolitics of energy* (New York: Metropolitan Books, 2008), p. 7.
[5] H. Makinder, 'The geographical pivot of history', *The Geographical Journal*, April (1904).

unpalatable choices: either rely on continued US pressure on Russia, or commit to détente with Russia largely on Moscow's terms. During the presidency of Barak Obama, US diplomacy on the issue of Georgia has fallen under the broad rubric of 'hitting reset' in the bilateral relationship between Washington and Moscow. In this context the United States has used both carrots and sticks. On the one hand it has linked expectations of Russian good behaviour to continued American support for Moscow's accession to the World Trade Organisation. Here, Michael McFaul, who became Senior Director of Russian and Eurasian Affairs at the US National Security Council, has championed that push.[6] But, on the other hand, the United States has also issued an implicit caution that it would not sit idly if Russia attempted to convert its diplomatic recognition of Ossetian and Abkhazian sovereignty into territorial aggrandisement.[7]

Contemporary scholarship on conflict, war and the former USSR

The literature on war has grown exponentially since the end of the Cold War, but especially since the events of 11 September 2001. In many respects 9/11 had a refocusing effect on the discipline of international politics that centred academic attention squarely on the United States, just as it also led to a mad scramble amongst international relations scholars to also become experts on transnational terrorism – much to the consternation of those who had already made it their speciality. To an extent it is understandable that much contemporary writing on war centres upon the power and policy preferences of the United States, given that the symbols of American power were the target of the 9/11 attacks, and the United States enjoys an enviable (if declining) position as the global hegemon. As noted above, however, focusing too heavily on US power neglects other regions where conflict threatens global stability. In this case, the former Soviet territories encapsulate many of the struggles over resources, territory, culture and ethno-religious transnational tensions that are commonly found in studies of contemporary war, but in a region less often acknowledged in the overall literature.

---

[6] P. Craft, 'Stanford Professor Michael McFaul pushes for "Democracy in Russia" proposal', *Stanford Review* 17 April (2009).

[7] F. Weir, 'Hilary Clinton slams Russia over Georgia: why Russia shrugs', *Christian Science Monitor*, 6 July (2010). Available at www.csmonitor.com/World/Europe/2010/0706/Hillary-Clinton-slams-Russia-over-Georgia-Why-Russia-shrugs

More generally, writing on war has been very much informed by Martin van Creveld's *The Transformation of War*, especially concerning the diminished significance of Clausewitzian trinitarian warfare.[8] A similarly important contribution was made soon after the end of the Cold War in the form of Kalevi Holsti's *Peace and War*, which sought to build a typology evaluating how war has evolved over time.[9] This has been extended by the 'new wars' literature epitomised by Mary Kaldor's 2001 book on contemporary conflict in the former Yugoslavia, *New and Old Wars*, with a second edition published in 2006.[10] Also notable in this context is Kaldor's *Human Security*, published in 2007,[11] and the work of Martin Shaw and others concerned with understanding the impacts of globalisation upon war, with particular reference to the role of global norms in resolving conflict.[12]

Yet a consequence of the scholarship on so-called 'new wars' is that – to an extent – it has become captured by a specific normative project: the pursuit of global cosmopolitanism and international law as the most reliable means to legitimately resolve contemporary conflict. This imposes an unnecessary restriction on understanding wars which can arise, unfold and be resolved due to a variety of forces, ranging from pure material factors to cultural and ideational considerations. This book, then, does not extend the 'new wars' literature to encapsulate conflicts in the former USSR for a particular prescriptive purpose. Nor is it our intention to make such a contribution. Instead, the volume offers what we feel is a balanced account of conflict, utilising debates in the theoretical literature as well as new developments in the conduct and nature of conflict as ways to illuminate and contextualise the contributions of individual chapter authors.

In addition to a very large body of scholarship on war, there is an established literature on Russian politics and foreign policy that the chapters in this volume engage with, both in their theoretical foci and their case studies. There were many books on various aspects of Russian foreign policy published during the 1990s and at the start of

[8] M. Van Creveld, *The transformation of war* (New York: Free Press, 1991).

[9] K. Holsti, *Peace and war: armed conflicts and international order*, Cambridge Studies in International Relations (Cambridge University Press, 1991).

[10] M. Kaldor, *New and old wars: organised violence in a global era* (Cambridge: Polity, 2001; 2nd edn 2006).

[11] M. Kaldor, *Human security: reflections on globalisation and intervention* (Cambridge: Polity, 2007).

[12] See, for instance, M. Shaw, *War and genocide: organised killing in modern society* (Cambridge: Polity, 2003); and M. Shaw, 'War and globality: the role and character of war in the global transition', in H. Yeong (ed.), *The new agenda for peace research* (Aldershot, UK: Ashgate, 1999), pp. 61–80.

the twenty-first century, with some providing a general overview, such as Robert Donaldson and Joseph Nogee's *Foreign Policy of Russia*,[13] and others focusing on Russia and the West,[14] as well as Russia and terrorism.[15] Still others deal with Russia's relations with the PRC.[16]

Whilst there are few single volumes dealing with Russia's role in the conflicts in the former Soviet territories, some texts have covered Russia's engagement in the wars in the Caucasus. The best of them include John Russell's *Chechnya: Russia's War on Terror*,[17] Richard Sakwa's edited collection *Chechnya: From Past to Future*,[18] John Dunlop's *Russia confronts Chechnya* and Anatol Lieven's *Chechnya: tombstone of Russian power*.[19] Other books have dealt with Russia's relations with Eurasia with a particular focus on Great Power competition in the Central Asian states.[20] The standout is probably still Karen Dawisha and Bruce Parrot's *Russia and the new states of Eurasia*, published in 1994.[21]

In the wake of the Soviet collapse there was also a large number of books dealing with the unravelling of empire, the role of nationalism

---

[13] R. Donaldson and J. Nogee, *The foreign policy of Russia: changing systems, enduring interests* (New York: M.E. Sharpe, 1999; 3rd edn 2005).

[14] A. Motyl, B. Ruble and L. Shevtsova (eds.), *Russia's engagement with the West: transformation and integration in the twenty-first century* (New York: M.E. Sharpe, 2005).

[15] M. Tsypkin, *Russia's security and the war on terror* (London: Routledge, 2007).

[16] J. Wilson, *Strategic partners: Russian–Chinese relations in the post-Soviet era* (New York: M.E. Sharpe, 2004).

[17] J. Russell, *Chechnya: Russia's war on terror* (New York: Routledge, 2007).

[18] R. Sakwa (ed.), *Chechnya: from past to future* (London: Anthem Press, 2005).

[19] J. Dunlop, *Russia confronts Chechnya: roots of a separatist conflict* (Cambridge University Press, 1998); and A. Lieven, *Chechnya: tombstone of Russian power* (New Haven, CT: Yale University Press, 1998).

[20] Here, for instance, one can identify the two volumes edited by I. Akihiro, *Eager eyes fixed on Eurasia*, vol. 1: *Russia and its neighbors in crisis* (Sapporo: Slavic Research Centre, Hokkaido University, 2007); and I. Akihiro, *Eager eyes fixed on Eurasia*, vol. 2: *Russia and its eastern edge* (Sapporo: Slavic Research Centre, Hokkaido University, 2007).

[21] K. Dawisha and B. Parrot, *Russia and the new states of Eurasia: the politics of upheaval* (Cambridge University Press, 1994). A similar book, also published in 1994, is Kremenyuk, *Conflicts in and around Russia*. See also M. Webber, *The international politics of Russia and the successor states* (Manchester University Press, 1996); and R. Menon, Y. Federov and G. Nodia (eds.), *Russia, the Caucasus, and Central Asia* (New York: M.E. Sharpe, 1999). Still others deal with similar issues such as conflict resolution and peacekeeping. These include, for instance, A. Arbatov et al. (eds.), *Managing conflict in the former Soviet Union: Russian and American perspectives* (Cambridge, MA: MIT Press, 1997); A. Chayes and A. Chayes (eds.), *Preventing conflict in the post-communist world: mobilising international and regional organisations* (Washington, DC: Brookings Institution, 1996); D. Lynch, *Russian peacekeeping strategies in the CIS, 1992–1997: the cases of Georgia, Moldova and Tajikistan* (New York: St Martin's Press, 2000); L. Jonson and C. Archer (eds.), *Peacekeeping and the role of Russia in Eurasia* (Boulder, CO: Westview,1996); and J. Mackinlay and P. Cross (eds.), *Regional peacekeepers: the paradox of Russian peacekeeping* (New York: United Nations University Press, 2003).

and the construction of new nations and states, with some coverage of ethnic conflicts. Perhaps the best of these were the edited volume by Ian Bremmer and Ray Taras, *New states, new politics*,[22] and an edited volume by James Hughes and Gwendolyn Sasse that examined the role of nationalism and the problems of state building.[23] Maria Raquel Freire, meanwhile, has provided an interesting historical evaluation of the engagement of the Organisation for Security and Cooperation in Europe (OSCE) in the immediate aftermath of the collapse of the USSR; at the same time as Ruth Deyermond has assessed the competing conceptions of sovereignty and ownership of post-Soviet assets and territory, focusing upon nuclear weapons, the use of military bases and control of the Black Sea Fleet.[24]

Conflict in the former USSR: five overarching themes

What common analytical threads can be drawn from examining conflicts in the former USSR that might illuminate our understanding of the region, the nature of wars there, and potentially open up ways to chart its future? Whilst many issues can be identified, five interconnected themes recur in this book. They pertain to sovereignty, power and geopolitics – as much as they are important for assessing 'newer' issues like transnational terrorist networks, issues of identity and ethnicity – and structures of patronage and privilege that cut across and between different governance structures.

The first theme is that state building, which was identified immediately after the collapse of the USSR as a core challenge, remains an ongoing process that is centrally important in the region some two decades later. This should not be interpreted as an endorsement of any particular type of political organisation – such as liberal democracy, for instance. Nor is it a prescriptive call to implement any specific polity from the cool remove of a classroom and a whiteboard. On the contrary, some authoritarian regimes – in Central Asia, for example – seem to have been remarkably effective in staving off conflict. But states can change direction rapidly, as demonstrated by the Rose, Tulip and Orange revolutions in Georgia, Kyrgyzstan and Ukraine respectively.

---

[22] I. Bremmer and R. Taras (eds.), *New states, new politics: building the post-Soviet nations* (Cambridge University Press, 1997).

[23] J. Hughes and G. Sasse (eds.), *Ethnicity and territory in the former Soviet Union: regions in conflict* (London: Frank Cass, 2002).

[24] M.R. Freire, *Conflict and security in the former Soviet Union: the role of the OSCE* (Aldershot, UK: Ashgate, 2003); and R. Deyermond, *Security and sovereignty in the former Soviet Union* (Boulder, CO: Lynne Rienner Publishers, 2008).

Even so, 'democratic' revolutions are not immutable, and the history of many former Soviet republics is full of struggles between the prerogative state and the constitutional state, in which the regime (rather than the nation) is often the victor.

A second theme of central importance is that the line between domestic and international politics in the former USSR is extremely blurry. Those students of international relations who seek to make simple 'inside–outside' characterisations based on assumptions about states as unitary actors, the permanency of national interests and the importance of levels of analysis will find it difficult to deliver compelling explanations for state behaviour in the former USSR. The frequency with which leaders and politicians play two-level games, the role of forces associated with globalisation that have facilitated the penetration of the region by business actors, organised criminals and terrorists, and the porous borders of many states in the region make separating the national from the international extremely difficult.

Third, as should be expected, norms and ideas are spongy in Eurasia. When Russia refers to sovereignty it is sometimes using a typical statist model dating back to the Treaty of Westphalia, which discourages outside intervention. On the other hand, when referring to citizenship issues linked to the status of 'ethnic' Russians in former Soviet republics, this becomes a *rationale* for intervention, as the events in South Ossetia during August 2008 demonstrated. Likewise, when the parties to the contest over Nagorno-Karabakh speak of the importance of democracy, peacekeeping and civil institutions, they do not all have in mind the same type of democracy, sources for peacekeeping, or roles for institutions.

Fourth, many of the small and peripheral territories of the USSR – that suddenly became more interesting after the Soviet collapse – have now become fully entrenched as sites of conflict. This has happened for a variety of reasons, from ethnic tension and self-determination campaigns to struggles over material resources. Conflicts in the former USSR also now incorporate a host of new actors previously not present during the communist era. Extra-regional powers have become interested in investing in energy reserves in Central Asia; in playing a role in the mediation of wars; in promoting normative standards relating to human rights and democracy; and in extending their economic and alliance structures to encompass states that Russia regards as falling within its direct geopolitical sphere of interest. So too have institutions and organisations like the EU, which represent the interests of larger states, as well as their powerful normative visions and economic resources.

Fifth, the former USSR represents such a complex mix of temporally shifting alliances, changing power structures and institutions, and contests over ideas – from within and without – that it is difficult to refer to it as a coherent region. To do so would make the mistaken assumption that the actors within the former USSR are more or less static, and that there is relative consensus over the indivisibility of the core problems they face. That each of us in this book uses the term 'region' to refer to the former Soviet space should not be taken as a formal definition. We do so merely for geographical convenience: the term does not reflect any tacit acknowledgments about agents, processes and structures. A mere glance at the different organisations and institutions on the menu in the former Soviet space should be reason enough to question to what extent we can consider the former USSR regionally bounded. For instance, the Commonwealth of Independent States (CIS) may be the largest politico-economic organisation, but not all of the former Soviet republics are members, and not all CIS members participate in the CSTO (as its flagship military-security organisation). The Baltic countries are aspirant EU members, and are alone amongst the former Soviet states in having joined NATO. Ukraine, Georgia, Azerbaijan and Moldova also seek closer ties to the West, but have had to make do with membership of the Georgia-Ukraine-Azerbaijan-Moldova (GUAM) bloc; whilst the PRC is an active player under the auspices of the Shanghai Cooperation Organisation (SCO).

Structure and chapter overview

The themes outlined above are deliberately not examined systematically in this book. Rather, they serve as broad common threads drawing the various contributions together. Instead, the book first traces the role of the main actors and structural processes shaping the former USSR, before moving to evaluate specific case studies of conflict occurring at the national, international and transnational levels. The final part examines the lessons that might be drawn about how we understand war as a result of conflict in the former USSR. It ends by evaluating the potential for future conflicts in the region.

The book therefore begins in what should be fairly logical and familiar territory: the foreign and security policy of the Russian Federation. It is logical because Russia is physically the largest state that emerged from the breakup of the USSR, it has the largest military (including a sizeable nuclear arsenal), and it possesses the largest economy. Russia is also the state that inherited the mantle of regional leadership from the USSR. It is the chief architect of the major institutional arrangements spanning independent nation-states in the region, and regards itself as having special rights and responsibilities in the management of regional security politics. Starting with Russia should be familiar as well, since much attention has recently focused on Moscow's more assertive foreign policy stance. Although this has not emerged overnight – in fact, it can be traced back to the Yeltsin years when Andrei Kozyrev was still foreign minister – the boldness with which Russia began to throw its weight around after Vladimir Putin became president has been regarded as an ominous sign.

In Chapter 2, Roger Kanet evaluates Russian foreign policy and concludes that it has returned to an imperial stance in respect to its neighbours, as well as in its dealings with great powers. Focusing especially on the relationship between Russia and the United States over the conflicts on the former territory of the USSR, as well as on recent contests over energy security, Kanet finds that the West has much to answer for as a result of its neglect of Russian interests before Putin (and then Medvedev) came to power. In spite of the rapprochement between Moscow and Washington under the pretext of 'resetting' their relationship, Kanet finds that the adoption of instruments of military and economic coercion will entrench Moscow's dominance over 'greater Russia' for the foreseeable future.

Chapter 3 – by Matthew Sussex – takes important issues that Kanet raises about Russia's power and interests, and applies them to an evaluation of regional security politics. In an attempt to sketch the shape of regional order, Sussex focuses on the role of security architecture. In contrast to Kanet's arguments about an imperial Russian foreign policy, he argues that the former Soviet space is best characterised as a region of constrained Russian primacy. By tracing the roles played by organisations employed by the Russian Federation to cement its primacy, Sussex shows that Russia has had only limited success in leveraging political, military and economic instruments like the CIS, the CSTO and resource diplomacy. Certainly, it has not attained a position of unquestioned hegemony. Instead, he demonstrates that Russia is constrained in a number of ways: in military-security affairs by NATO; by the growing political clout of the PRC (both within the SCO and as a bilateral partner of Russia and Central Asian nations); and by the normative and economic power of the EU, membership of which remains an attractive proposition for many former Soviet republics. Sussex concludes that despite Russia's constrainment – a position that may well continue to weaken – there is still no robust institutional architecture to resolve the region's security problems, and the conditions for conflict in the former USSR have not been significantly ameliorated.

The book then turns in the next three chapters to examine specific cases of conflict in the former USSR. Richard Sakwa offers a way to understand the ongoing conflict in the Caucasus in the form of a collision between two powerful trends: one related to domestic politics, and the other based on Russia's relations with the West. First, Sakwa argues that the wars in Chechnya between 1994 and 2008 hastened the development of the 'dual' Russian state, in which the legal and normative state increasingly gave way to the prerogative state on issues of Russian security. This has meant not just the securitisation of individual issues, but also the securitisation of the state itself, so that any threat to Russian interests or territory is seen as impeding a strong internal Westphalian order. Second, Sakwa sees the dual state intersecting with a 'cold peace', where Russia has been unfairly branded as the aggressor in the post-Cold War international system. In his critique of Western interference through political, normative and economic means, Sakwa argues that the 2008 war between Russia and Georgia was the product of the cold peace meeting the dual state. The fragile and polarised international order, combined with Russian domestic politics, he concludes, makes regional conflict much more likely.

Issues relating to sovereignty, intervention and identity and human rights have been central features of many conflicts that have taken place in the former USSR. In their chapter dealing with the Russo-Georgian war of 2008, Beat Kernen and Matthew Sussex identify three developments regarding how states might try to legitimate their decisions to use military force. In the conflict over South Ossetia and Abkhazia, both Georgia and Russia attempted to manipulate the politics of identity in order to justify their self-proclaimed rights over the separatist regions. As Kernen and Sussex demonstrate, Russia's approach was especially instructive since it marked a subtle shift in its past legitimation strategies. On the issue of South Ossetia and Abkhazia, Russia came to endorse a hybrid form of norm-entrepreneurship. This modified Westphalian interpretations of sovereignty to focus on diaspora populations, and was tied to a human security rationale for intervention that invoked the doctrine of the Responsibility to Protect (R2P). This approach, which the authors term *adaptationalism*, deliberately used normative arguments to pursue more pragmatic geostrategic objectives, and politically wedged the West between its norms and interests. Georgia, meanwhile, articulated a conventional Westphalian vision of sovereignty based on territory and non-interference. But whereas Tbilisi failed to accomplish its goal of drawing NATO into the conflict – or at least accelerating plans for Georgian membership of that organisation – Russia sent a strong message to its neighbours (and the West) that it was prepared to back up its rhetoric with actions.

Yet given the myriad triggers for war present across the former USSR, one might realistically have expected much greater political violence in the region. This is the context in which Neil Robinson offers a compelling counterpoint to the volume's earlier chapters, identifying Russia and Central Asia as a zone of relative peace. Specifically, Robinson asks, why have there not been more wars in the former USSR? The answer, he argues, can be found in the way that the post-Soviet security order has been mistakenly conceptualised, as well as domestic political trajectories taken by many former Soviet republics. Thus, grim predictions about resource wars, ethnic conflict and state failure have largely not eventuated because expectations of war either focused too heavily on structural causes of violence, or relied too much on seemingly analogous situations in Africa and former Yugoslavia. Moreover, Robinson argues, a preference for regime building rather than state building in Russia and the Central Asian nations has been a key factor in dampening the potential for war. Thus, it is precisely by holding back on state-building practices that would have alienated populations, fractured elites and led to increased social dislocation that regimes have been able to forestall conflict. Even so, Robinson is not sanguine that this will endure, given that significant potential for crises remains unresolved.

Whilst structural forces, Russian foreign policy, the behaviour of the West, nationalism and ethnicity have all been potent sources of conflict in the former USSR, the issue of organised crime and corruption is also salient. As Leslie Holmes points out in Chapter 7, crime and corruption flourish in power vacuums as well as in notionally strong authoritarian states, and can be powerful factors leading to state failure or conflict between groups. Holmes traces the emergence of organised crime in Russia and other states of the former USSR. He demonstrates that globalisation as well as domestic political developments peculiar to the former USSR have been instrumental in facilitating the rise of organised criminal gangs, the pervasiveness of bribery amongst elite groups that include the security services, and the institutionalisation of corruption in Russia and other former republics of the USSR.

The penultimate chapter in the volume turns to examine what, if anything, the conflicts in the former USSR tell us about the nature of war. Matt Killingsworth surveys past and present scholarship on war in order to address this question. His assessment begins with traditional Clausewitzian conceptions before turning to analyse more recent contributions that have seen political violence variously characterised as 'new' wars, or 'frozen' conflicts. He finds that these offer limited insights in the case of the former USSR. Even more limited, he argues, are notions associated with technological advancements such as the revolution in military affairs (RMA) and so-called 'spectator war'. And, by the same token, prescriptive efforts to prevent human suffering through the provision of human security, or regulate conduct through ideas about just war and laws of conflict have made little impact on the international prestige of states participating in armed confrontation in the former USSR.

To conclude the volume, Matthew Sussex discusses some of the future prospects for war in the former USSR. Bringing together the findings of different chapters on great power relations, Russia and its neighbours, regional security and the various frozen conflicts that exist around the region, he examines a number of potential scenarios. Specifically, he argues that renewed Russian imperial conquest, great power war, or conflict between major actors in the post-Soviet space is highly unlikely. However, based on the evidence presented in other chapters, he argues that renewed separatism and state failure, reignited frozen conflicts on Russian territory and in the Caucasus, not to mention resource wars, are altogether possible, if not already taking shape.

2   The return of imperial Russia

Roger E. Kanet

The dissolution of the USSR in 1991 and the emergence of fifteen new states in its place seemingly brought to an end the imperial tradition of Russian domination over various peoples conquered and absorbed into the Russian/Soviet empire over more than half a millennium.[1] Yet as I demonstrate in this chapter, political leaders in Moscow have been committed to returning Russia to the status of a great power since the very creation of the new Russian state. This includes the re-establishment of much of the imperial political order that collapsed in 1991. Before continuing with an examination of the emergence of Russia's more assertive approach to dealing with the world, it is important to note the international environment in which Russian policy developed.[2] To a substantial degree, Western (especially US) policy since the collapse of the former USSR was based on the assumption that Russia's demise as a great power would be permanent. Throughout the 1990s, and even after the turn of the century, Russia's interests and concerns were largely ignored, as both the United States and the Western community more broadly moved to fulfil their own political and security objectives in post-communist Europe; objectives that included the incorporation of most of Central and East European post-Soviet space into Western security, political and economic institutions.

Initially, as the Russian state found itself in virtual political and economic free-fall under President Yeltsin, the objective of re-establishing Russia's great power status seemed little more than rhetoric. Even though Russia did employ its greatly reduced military capabilities in the attempt

---

[1] Obviously this statement does not apply to the twenty per cent of the population of the Russian Federation not composed of ethnic Russians.

[2] For earlier discussions of these issues see R.E. Kanet, 'Zwischen konsens und konfrontation: Rußland und die Vereinigten Staaten', *Osteuropa* 51 (2001), 509–21; R.E. Kanet and Nuray Ibryamova, 'Verpaßte Gelegenheiten? Amerikanisch-Russische Beziehungen in den 90er Jahren', *Osteuropa* 51 (2001), 985–1001; and R.E. Kanet and L. Homarac, 'The US challenge to Russian influence in Central Asia and the Caucasus', in R.E. Kanet (ed.), *Russia: re-emerging great power* (Basingstoke, UK: Palgrave Macmillan, 2007), pp. 173–94.

to play a role in those Soviet successor states challenged by internal conflict (often facilitated by clandestine Russian military interference),[3] the prospect of the Russian Federation rejoining the ranks of major global actors seemed remote. More recently under Vladimir Putin and Dmitri Medvedev, however, Russian self-confidence has been buoyed by the rising price of oil and gas, the revitalisation of other sectors of the economy, and the reassertion of Moscow's administrative control over the vast territory of the Russian Federation itself. As a result, more sophisticated diplomatic and economic instruments, including what amounts to economic blackmail, have become a central component of Russia's reassertion of authority within what Moscow views as its traditional and legitimate sphere of influence.[4]

The general argument of this chapter is as follows. The Russian political leadership's initial commitment to integration into the 'community of civilised states', to use Yeltsin's phrase,[5] and its willingness to follow the Western lead on major international political issues were short-lived. Even before 1995 Yeltsin and Foreign Minister Kozyrev had been forced to redefine Russian foreign and security policy in a much more realistic (and nationalist) direction than they had done initially. With Kozyrev's replacement as foreign minister by Yevgeni Primakov in 1996, Russia proclaimed a formal Eurasian thrust in its policy, one that included active Russian involvement in, and primacy over, the so-called 'near abroad' of former Soviet territory.[6] Closely associated

[3] See A.V. Kozhemiakin and R.E. Kanet 'Russia as a regional peacekeeper', in R.E. Kanet (ed.), *Resolving regional conflicts* (Champaign: University of Illinois Press, 1998) pp. 225–39.

[4] For an excellent discussion of this shift in Russian policy toward the countries of the CIS, and the increasing use of economic and financial instruments of power, see B. Nygren, 'Putin's attempts to subjugate Georgia: from sabre-rattling to the power of the purse', in R.E. Kanet (ed.), *Russia: re-emerging great power* (Basingstoke, UK: Palgrave Macmillan, 2007), pp. 107–23; and B. Nygren, *The rebuilding of greater Russia: Putin's foreign policy toward the CIS countries* (Abingdon, UK: Routledge, 2007).

[5] Boris Yeltsin on Russian television, 14 February 1992; cited in S. Crow, 'Russian Federation faces foreign policy dilemmas', *RFE/RL Research Report* 1:10 (1992).

[6] General discussions of Russian foreign and security policy during the Yeltsin period, including the shift away from a Western-oriented policy, can be found in A. Arbatov, 'Russia's foreign policy alternatives', *International Security* 18 (1993), 5–43; A. Arbatov, 'Russian foreign policy thinking in transition', in V. Baranovsky (ed.), *Russia and Europe: the emerging security agenda* (Oxford University Press, 1997), pp. 135–59; J. Bugajski, *Cold peace: Russia's new imperialism* (Westport, CT: Praeger, 2007); Dawisha and Parrot, *Russia and the new states of Eurasia*; Jonson and Archer (eds.), *Peacekeeping and the role of Russia in Eurasia*; R.E. Kanet and A.V. Kozhemiakin (eds.), *The foreign policy of the Russian Federation* (London: Macmillan Publishers, 1997); B. Lo, *Russian foreign policy in the post-Soviet era: reality, illusion and mythmaking* (Basingstoke, UK: Palgrave Macmillan, 1997); P. Truscott, *Russia first: breaking with the West* (London: I.B. Tauris, 1997); A. Tsygankov, *Russia's foreign policy: change and continuity in national identity* (Lanham, MD: Rowman & Littlefield, 2006); and many other studies.

with this approach was direct and indirect Russian military involvement in regional, mainly ethnically based, conflicts in Azerbaijan, Georgia, Moldova and Tajikistan. Russian support for secessionist activities, which had already begun while Kozyrev was foreign minister, provided Moscow with opportunities for regional influence. This was especially true of Georgia, where in return for Russia's role as a 'peacekeeper' in the secessionist conflicts in Abkhazia and South Ossetia (conflicts that could not have developed as they did without Russian support for the insurgents), the Georgian government finally agreed to join the Russian-sponsored CIS and to grant Russia basing rights on its territory.[7] By the end of the 1990s, with Russia playing the role of 'peacekeeper', most of these conflicts no longer involved active military operations, although they were still far from being resolved. Most importantly, Moscow had successfully reasserted its influence over several other post-Soviet states.

Yeltsin's selection of Putin as his successor and the events of 9/11 led to a short-lived rapprochement between Russia and the United States, and Russia and Europe.[8] However, Putin's commitment to re-establish control over domestic politics and rebuild Russia's great power status, the financial boon resulting from the explosion of oil and gas prices, as well as Washington's short-sighted policies, strengthened and expanded the range of policy instruments available to Russia. These included economic and political leverage across 'Greater Russia', so that the West could no longer ignore Moscow's interests as it had done throughout the 1990s.[9]

This chapter's argument is developed in three steps. First, it summarises Russian policy toward the 'near abroad' in the immediate aftermath of the dissolution of the Soviet state, and tracks those factors that almost immediately resulted in a reassessment of the importance of these regions to Russia's future, as well as the use of military

[7] C. Dale, 'The case of Abkhazia (Georgia)', in L. Jonson and C. Archer (eds.), *Peacekeeping and the role of Russia in Eurasia* (Boulder, CO: Westview, 1996), pp. 121–38; R.E. Kanet 'The Russian Federation', in E.A. Kolodziej and R.E. Kanet (eds.), *Coping with conflict after the cold war* (Baltimore, MD: The Johns Hopkins University Press, 1996), pp. 60–86.

[8] The rapprochement, however, occurred only after continuing deterioration in relations with the United States that had culminated in early 2001 in the mutual expulsion of diplomats in Washington and Moscow. See Kanet and Ibryamova, 'Verpaßte Gelegenheiten?'

[9] See J. Hedenskog et al. (eds.), *Russia as a great power: dimensions of security under Putin* (Abingdon, UK: Routledge, 2005); and V. Rukavishnikov, 'Choices for Russia: preserving inherited geopolitics through emergent global and European realities', in R.E. Kanet (ed.), *Russia: re-emerging great power* (Basingstoke, UK: Palgrave Macmillan, 2007), pp. 54–78.

involvement to re-establish a Russian role. Second, it outlines the overall security objectives, both domestic and foreign, set by Putin at the outset of his administration in 2000, and how he and Medvedev have pursued them. Finally, it tracks the shift from Russia's emphasis on coercion in its relations with its neighbours to a broader set of instruments – especially economic ones – through what Bertil Nygren has termed 'the power of the purse'.[10] This does not mean that Russia has abandoned military intervention and threats as a tool, as developments in Georgia in August 2008 demonstrated.[11] But the reintegration of former Soviet economic space, with Russia playing the dominant role through its control of energy production and distribution, has become the central focus of Moscow's efforts to recreate a 'Greater Russia', and to reclaim its place in that space as a great power.

The Russian Federation and the 'near abroad' under Yeltsin

In the aftermath of the USSR's collapse, Yeltsin and Kozyrev focused Russia's foreign policy efforts almost exclusively on acceptance into the various institutions that comprised the industrialised 'West'. The success of the economic and political reconstruction of Russia was, they argued, tied to joining the various clubs that constituted the capitalist world, and dependent upon Western economic and technological support for that reconstruction. Almost immediately, however, voices in Russia – even among democratic political forces – challenged the feasibility of such an approach. Instead, they called for a new policy that focused on rebuilding Russia's links with (and influence in) the other successor states of the USSR.[12] One aspect of this called for strengthening the CIS, which had initially served mainly as a tool to manage former Soviet military forces after the USSR's dissolution, and in facilitating a programme of economic cooperation.[13] But despite signing a

[10] B. Nygren, 'Putin's attempts to subjugate Georgia', p. 112.
[11] C.J. Chivers, 'UN inquiry concludes that Russian jet downed Georgian reconnaissance drone', *New York Times*, 27 May (2008), p. A6.
[12] Alexei Arbatov provides two excellent reviews of the growing criticism of Russian policy and of the gradual shift that occurred during 1992–6. See Arbatov, 'Russia's foreign policy alternatives', and Arbatov, 'Russian foreign policy thinking in transition'.
[13] P.G. Roeder, 'From hierarchy to hegemony: the post-Soviet security complex', in D.A. Lake and P.M. Morgan (eds.), *Regional orders: building security in a new world* (University Park: Penn State University Press, 1997) p. 223; *Agreements on the Creation of the Commonwealth of Independent States Signed in December 1991/January 1992* (London: Russian Information Agency/Novosti, 1992), p. 3, cited in R. Sakwa and M. Webber, 'The Commonwealth of Independent States, 1991–1998: stagnation and survival', *Europe-Asia Studies* 51 (1999), 381.

number of general agreements on security, the members of the CIS were unwilling to commit themselves to effective integration of their security forces.[14] Moscow soon viewed the CIS as an instrument to help cement its hegemonic position over the other former Soviet territories. Already in February 1993 Yeltsin, who had maintained that Russia had no intention of resurrecting its imperial past, responded to domestic complaints about the plight of the 25 million ethnic Russians 'stranded' outside Russian borders and to the growing disorder in a number of post-Soviet states. He noted that 'the time has come for authoritative international organisations (IOs), including the UN, to grant Russia special powers as guarantor of peace and stability in this region'. In other words, Yeltsin was seeking a specific Russian zone of influence on the territory of the former USSR.[15]

By then Russia was already fully involved in a whole series of regional conflicts – from Moldova in the west to Tajikistan in Central Asia – in which Russian forces were playing an important role.[16] Russian involvement exhibited a number of objectives. First, there was the desire to fill the power vacuum that had resulted from the collapse of the USSR, and to ensure Russia's regional dominance. Second, at a time when the Russian military was in rapid decline, the military leadership sought a way to impose unity on the remnants of the collapsed union. Third, Russia needed the CIS as a way to preserve existing links of inter-republic cooperation, mainly in the economic sphere. Finally, Russian military involvement in those conflicts was justified by the desire to protect the interests of the ethnic Russians and the Russian-speaking population in the CIS.[17] By the middle of the 1990s this final objective had become an important rhetorical issue in Russian politics.[18]

Despite numerous efforts throughout the second half of the 1990s to turn the CIS into a meaningful integrative organisation, in particular in the security area, virtually no progress was made prior to the

---

[14] D.S. Papp, 'The former Soviet Republics and the Commonwealth of Independent States', in D.J. Murray and P.R. Viotti (eds.), *The defence policies of nations: a comparative study* (Baltimore, MD: Johns Hopkins University Press, 1994), p. 211.

[15] B. Yeltsin, 'Speech of Boris Yeltsin to members of Civic Union', ITAR-TASS, 1 March (1993).

[16] See Arbatov et al. (eds.), *Managing conflict*; Jonson and Archer, *Peacekeeping and the role of Russia in Eurasia*; Kremenyuk, *Conflicts in and around Russia*; Lynch, *Russian peacekeeping strategies in the CIS*; and Sakwa and Webber, 'The Commonwealth of Independent States'.

[17] See Kozhemiakin and Kanet, 'Russia as a regional peacekeeper'.

[18] Among the best of the many studies of the importance of the Russian diaspora in Russian politics see P. Kolstoe, *Russians in the former Soviet republics* (Bloomington: Indiana University Press, 1995); and D.D. Laitin, *Identity in formation: the Russian-speaking populations in the near abroad* (Ithaca, NY: Cornell University Press, 1998).

transfer of political authority from Yeltsin to Putin.[19] On paper, the Commonwealth was a forum for significant cooperation. In reality, it witnessed a diminishing base of collaborative activities.[20]

As part of the effort to reduce its focus on the West in the second half of the 1990s Russia also pursued policies aimed at strengthening ties with countries throughout Asia, several of which had been important clients of the former USSR. This occurred despite strong opposition from the United States. Central to this effort was the 'strategic partnership' with the PRC, whose leaders shared Russia's growing concerns about global US dominance. A number of high-level meetings between the two countries during 1997 and 1998 emphasised the threat of US global hegemony and condemned NATO expansion, as well as the pressure NATO was bringing to bear against Yugoslavia. By early 2001 George W. Bush's decision to develop a national missile defence (NMD) system catalysed Russo-Chinese policy collaboration. Moreover, an important part of the improving relationship between the two countries was the growth of Russian exports, especially of military equipment.[21]

Simultaneously, in the late 1990s, Moscow expanded relations with Iran and rebuilt its ties with India, both of which represented important markets for Russian military equipment and nuclear technology.[22] These initiatives, which had the dual objective of generating additional exports and strengthening Russia's position as an independent global actor, brought Russia into direct conflict with Washington's policy objectives.

---

[19] See S. Blank, 'Putin's twelve-step program', *The Washington Quarterly* 25 (2002), p. 150; and D. Lynch, *Russian peacekeeping strategies in the CIS*, p. 89. See also Jonson and Archer (eds.), *Peacekeeping and the role of Russia in Eurasia*; and Kremenyuk, *Conflicts in and around Russia*.

[20] Sakwa and Webber, 'The Commonwealth of Independent States'; and see Blank, 'Putin's twelve-step program', p. 150. The Russian 'security concept' approved in 2000 stated that Russian security interests mandate the permanent stationing of forces abroad: Blank, 'Putin's twelve-step program', p. 146. See M. Dobbs, 'Doktrina informatsionnoi bezopasnosti Rossiiskoi Federatsii', *Rossiiskaia gazeta*, 28 September (2000), pp. 3–4, available at www.scrf.gov.ru/Documents/Degree/2000/09–09. html; and P. Kolstoe, 'Kontseptsiia natsional'noi bezopasnosti Rossiiskoi Federatsii', *Nezavisimoe voennoe obozrenie*, 11 July (2000), available at http://nvo.ng.ru/ concepts/2000–01–14/6_concept.html

[21] Information on the SCO is available at the official website: www.sectsco.org/EN/ brief.asp

[22] On Russian policy in Asia see G. Rozman et al. (eds.), *Russia and East Asia: the twenty-first century security environment* (Armonk, NY: M.E. Sharpe for East/West Institute, New York, 1999); Truscott, *Russia first*, pp. 54–8; J.M. Conley, *Indo-Russian military and nuclear cooperation: lessons and options for US policy in South Asia* (Lanham, MD: Lexington Books, 2001).

The gap between US and Russian policy goals grew significantly during the latter half of the 1990s. For example, Russia opposed the use of largely US-initiated UN sanctions against a number of countries viewed in Moscow as potential partners. Russia sought an end to sanctions against both Yugoslavia and Iraq. In the former case Russia was concerned both about a former long-term ally, and in the latter about Iraq's inability to repay the substantial debts that had accrued in the Soviet period. At the time of US and British military strikes in retaliation for repeated Iraqi refusals to cooperate with UN weapons inspectors in late 1998, Yeltsin referred to 'gross violations of the UN Charter' by the two Western states.[23] When the West began to bring pressure on Yugoslavia once again in 1998 over the issue of Kosovo, the Russians supported the Yugoslav right to do virtually anything to protect its territorial integrity, and threatened various forms of retaliation if the West bombed Yugoslavia.

The issue that raised the most serious response in Moscow in this period was the eastward expansion of NATO and the incorporation of former Warsaw Pact allies into the Western security system.[24] Prior to NATO's Madrid meetings of July 1997, at which the decision was to be made about possible expansion, Moscow orchestrated a multifaceted campaign that included pressure on applicant countries and threats that the expansion would initiate a new Cold War. In fact, when NATO decided to invite the Czech Republic, Hungary and Poland to join the alliance, Russia accepted the decision without retaliating. Yet it was clear in the approach that Washington and its allies took to Moscow's objections that Russia was not viewed as a serious player in the restructured European security environment.

Once it became obvious that it had failed to forestall NATO expansion, Russia accepted reality and attempted to gain whatever it could out of that acceptance. It shifted the focus of its opposition to NATO expansion to the Baltics. On 27 May 1997 Moscow signed the NATO-Russia Founding Act that was supposed to provide clear parameters for the relationship between Russia and the Western alliance. In return, Russia was granted membership in an expanded Group of 8 (G8). During the rest of the year Russia participated in a US-led military exercise in the Baltic Sea, and continued to cooperate with Partnership for Peace (PfP) activities.

[23] Boris Yeltsin, cited in A. Kreutz, *Russia in the Middle East: friend or foe?* (Santa Barbara, CA: Praeger Security International/Greenwood Press, 2006) p. 89.

[24] For a discussion of NATO expansion see R.E. Kanet and N.V. Ibryamova, 'La sécurité en Europe centrale et orientale: un système en cours de changement', *Revue d'Études Comparatives Est-Ouest* 33 (2002), pp. 179–203.

In fact, neither of these relationships really met Russian objectives. Moscow was excluded from full participation in those G8 meetings at which meaningful decisions concerning international financial matters were likely to occur. Moreover, given the disastrous state of Russia's economy there was little hope of exercising any real influence within the group. At the same time the NATO-Russia Founding Act also proved unsatisfactory. While the act did not provide Russia with anything approximating veto power over NATO decisions, it did call for effective consultation on important security issues. In fact, over the next two years NATO largely ignored Russia's increasingly vehement complaints about its refusal to consult on issues ranging from the former's attempts to arrest Serbs as war criminals, to the implementation of the Dayton peace accords.

Another issue of great importance complicated US-Russian relations by the end of the 1990s. Ever since President Reagan had begun the development of an anti-missile defence system, the Soviet (and then Russian) governments had voiced their serious concern that such a system would have major destabilising effects. Although modest research continued on the project in the late 1980s and through the 1990s, it was not until the final years of the Clinton presidency that the matter became prominent in US-Russian relations. By then, key conservative members of the Republican-dominated Congress had begun to push for missile defence. Clinton first seemed willing to go forward with the programme but reversed his position in the face of strong opposition, as well as worryingly high cost projections and evidence of likely technical limitations. During the election campaign of 2000 George W. Bush and his spokespeople made it clear that if he were elected the United States would move ahead with development of what became known as NMD. Simultaneously, it would withdraw from the 1972 Anti-Ballistic Missile (ABM) Treaty precluding the testing and deployment of such a system. This is precisely what the new administration did.

In 2000 and 2001 Putin had stated Russia's clear opposition to US policy and gained support from the PRC (which perceived a similar threat from NMD). Later, in 2009 and 2010, President Medvedev also generated some interest in Europe with alternate proposals for a regional missile defence system, as well as tentative endorsements by the Obama administration that such a proposal was worthy of consideration. Even so, concerns remained in Moscow – which were ignored during the Bush Jnr era – that the development of a small US system would be the first step in undermining Russia's nuclear arsenal, which serves as its sole remaining claim to great power status.[25] Under George W. Bush, the United States proceeded with the process of building a radar system and establishing interceptor missile sites in the Czech Republic and Poland. Whilst Obama subsequently cancelled that project in a gesture designed to reach out to Russia under the rubric of 'resetting' the relationship, Bush's policy had previously caused significant anger in Moscow.[26]

By the summer of 2001, then, little more than one and a half years into Putin's presidency, US-Russian relations were on a collision course.[27] The leaderships of both countries had established objectives that were in direct conflict with one another. Russians were increasingly frustrated by Washington's apparent disregard for their role in world affairs, and by the seeming US lack of concern for Russian interests – as in the NATO bombing of Yugoslavia, and US efforts to restrict Russian involvement in the development of oil and gas reserves in the Caspian Basin.[28] The mutual diplomatic expulsions of early spring 2001, initiated by Washington, were an especially visible indication of the tensions in bilateral relations.

Before I turn to a discussion of Russian policy in the Putin era, it is important to refer to the Chechen war because of its overall impact on many other aspects of Russian policy. The decision by President Yeltsin in the mid-1990s to suppress the demands for an independent state in Chechnya, and the ensuing defeat of the Russian army, initiated more than a decade of internal warfare that influenced Russian foreign policy significantly. At one level, the ferocity with which Russia attempted to suppress Chechen opposition, both prior to and after Putin's rise, has had an important negative impact on Russia's relations with the United States and the countries of the EU. Russian abuses of human

[25] V. Solovev 'Moskva ustupila Vashingtonu', *Nezavisimaia gazeta*, 3 November (2001). Available at http://ng.ru/politics/2001–11–03/1_moscow.html

[26] After the Polish and US governments signed an agreement on the emplacement of US missiles on Polish territory, Russian president Medvedev noted: 'This will create additional tension and we will have to respond to it in some way, naturally using military means' ('Russian PM threatens to review relations with EU', *RIA Novosti*, 23 March 2008). The deputy chief of the Russian general staff, General Anatolii Nogovitsyn, noted that Poland was 'exposing itself to a strike – 100 percent'. See C. Philip and T. Halpin, 'Russia in nuclear threat to Poland', *The Times*, 16 August (2008). Available at www.timesonline.co.uk/tol/news/world/europe/article4543744.ece

[27] See the excellent article by A. Kassianova, 'Russia: still open to the West? Evolution of the state identity in the foreign policy and security discourse', *Europe-Asia Studies* 53 (2001), pp. 821–39.

[28] See R. Ebel and R. Menon (eds.), *Energy and conflict in Central Asia and the Caucasus* (Lanham, MD: Rowman & Littlefield for The National Bureau of Asian Research, 2000); and Kanet and Homarac, 'The US challenge to Russian influence'.

rights became an important factor in the deteriorating relationship with the West. Moreover, the ongoing Russian struggle to maintain control over Chechnya brought Moscow into regular conflict with Georgia, whose government the Russians regularly accused of harbouring and supporting Chechen separatists. So the war in Chechnya became much more than simply an internal challenge to central authority within the Russian Federation. It also had a visible impact on relations with both near neighbours and with the West.

The issue of Russia's relations with the 'near abroad' thus evolved in an environment in which the Russian Federation's relations with the West, especially the United States, were increasingly conflictual. Russia was no longer taken seriously in world affairs, and its views and concerns ignored, based on the assumption that it was no longer an important actor.[29] Even in its immediate geopolitical environment Moscow could not control developments that it viewed to be of central importance to Russian security. This was the situation inherited by Putin at the turn of the millennium.

Putin and the return of Russia as a great power

Once Yeltsin plucked Vladimir Putin from political obscurity in August 1999, several developments were especially relevant for Russian policy. The first was the renewed challenge from Chechen separatists. This provided Putin, as the new prime minister, with the opportunity to present himself as a forceful leader who would destroy the terrorist challenge and stabilise the chaotic political and economic situation. After the bombing of an apartment building in Moscow, Putin initiated a massive military campaign in 1999 that brought Moscow *de facto* control over most of Chechnya. This generated support among the Russian population and played an important role in Putin's resounding electoral victory in spring 2000 – even though the brutality of the policy raised serious Western criticism, including censure by the Council of Europe.

---

[29] Senator Jesse Helms, then the powerful chair of the Senate Committee on Foreign Relations, was especially outspoken on this question. In introductory remarks before the committee he dismissed Russian objections to US changes in the ABM Treaty. See US Senate, Committee on Foreign Relations, 'Ballistic missiles: threat and response: hearings before the Committee on Foreign Relations United States Senate', One Hundred Sixth Congress, First Session, 15 and 20 April, 4, 5, 25 and 26 May, and 16 September 1999 (Washington, DC: Government Printing Office, 1999); and J. Helms, Senator, 'Amend the ABM Treaty? No, scrap it', *The Wall Street Journal*, 22 January (1999).

The general parameters of Russian policy, including toward the United States, were set early in Putin's presidency and derived directly from the policy lines already established in the mid-1990s. Putin made clear his commitment to re-establishing Russia as the pre-eminent regional power and an important global actor. Essential preconditions for the fulfilment of these objectives, as the 2000 Foreign Policy Concept indicated, were the internal political stability and economic viability of Russia.[30] According to the document, Russia had to overcome separatism, national and religious extremism, and terrorism. Putin moved forcefully and, in most cases effectively, in reasserting central control in Russia. The economy, while still not flourishing, had turned around, with growth rates of 4.5, 10.0 and 5.0 per cent in the years 1999–2001.[31]

These political and economic gains, however, occurred with little or no regard for the civil liberties and democratic processes to which Putin's government was nominally committed. His anti-corruption campaign soon become a catch-all that targeted those who in any way challenged his position. This was especially the case for those associated with the independent media. In the foreign policy arena Putin continued to seek allies who shared Russia's commitment to preventing the global dominance of the United States that represented, in the words of the 2000 Foreign Policy Concept, a threat to Russia's goal of serving as a major centre of influence in a multipolar world.

In other words, up until 9/11 there was little evidence that the seemingly enduring issues that divided the two countries throughout the 1990s would soon disappear – in particular since they derived from core elements of their respective foreign policy commitments. In fact, after a very brief hiatus immediately after 9/11, those issues resurfaced and continue to plague Russo-US relations today. Russia's invasion of Georgia, the formal recognition of the sovereignty of South Ossetia and Abkhazia, and the *de facto* incorporation of the two territories into the Russian Federation have exacerbated that relationship, as has Russia's penchant for aggressive resource diplomacy with its neighbours.

However, Putin's success in dealing with the major problems challenging the Russian state at the beginning of the decade has meant that Russia now faces the United States and the West from a position

---

[30] See 'The Foreign Policy Concept of the Russian Federation', approved by the president of the Russian Federation, V. Putin, 28 June (2000), reprinted in *Johnson's Russia List*, no. 4403, 14 July (2000); and P. Kolstoe, 'Kontseptsii natsional'noi bezopasnosti', *Rossiiiskaya gazeta*, 26 December (1997), 4–5.

[31] Central Bank of the Russian Federation, 'Main macroeconomic indicators' (2000). Available at www.cbr.ru/eng/statistics/credit_statistics

of increased strength. Putin's reassertion of central control by elim-
inating the election of provincial governors, by suppressing domestic
opponents and critics, and by playing on fears of domestic terrorism,
crime and general chaos played an important role in strengthening the
Russian state.[32] Putin also benefited greatly from the exponential rise
in global demand for gas and oil and the ensuing revitalisation of the
Russian economy. This, in turn, has contributed to Russia's ability to
pursue a much more active and assertive foreign policy.[33]

Thus, Putin was quite successful during the eight years of his presidency in establishing the economic and political foundations for a strong
centralised state as the prerequisites for Russia returning as a major
player in international politics. While the voices calling for Russia to
resume its role as a major power in the 1990s were strident but not realistic, today under Medvedev they hold the dominant position in Russian
domestic debates. They are also now based upon realistic expectations
of Russian policy objectives. This began with former president Putin's
statement to the Russian Duma that 'the collapse of the USSR was
the greatest geopolitical catastrophe of the century'.[34] These comments

---

[32] Several excellent discussions of domestic political developments during the Putin
years can be found in L. Shevtsova, *Russia: lost in transition* (Washington, DC:
Carnegie Endowment, 2007); D. Trenin, *Getting Russia right* (Washington, DC:
Carnegie Endowment, 2007); and B. Taylor, 'Putin's "historic mission": state-building and the power ministries in the North Caucasus', *Problems of Post-Communism* 54
(2007), 3–16.

[33] However, as many analysts have argued, the revived role of Russia as a regional and
global political actor is based extensively on the wealth generated by oil and gas production and exports. See, for example, K.J. Hancock, 'Russia: great power image versus
economic reality', *Asian Perspectives* 31 (2007), 71–98; M. McFaul and K. Stoner-
Weiss, 'The myth of Putin's success', *Foreign Affairs* 87 (2008), 68–84; and R. Menon
and A. Motyl, 'The myth of Russian resurgence', *American Interest* 2 (2007), 96–101,
available at www.the-american-interest.com/ai2/article.cfm?Id=258&MId=8

[34] V. Putin, 'President's speech to the Federal Assembly', BBC Monitoring, Former
Soviet Union, April (2005); 'Putin focuses on domestic policy in state-of-nation
address to Russian Parliament', RTR Russia TV, Moscow, 25 April (2005), BBC
Monitoring, Former Soviet Union, trans. in *Johnson's Russia List*, no. 9130, 25 April
(2005). For recent discussions of the commitment of Russia's political elites to regaining great power status see I. Oldberg, 'Foreign policy priorities under Putin: A *Tour
d'Horizon*', in R. Hedenskog et al., *Russia as a great power: dimensions of security under
Putin* (Abingdon, UK: Routledge, 2005), pp. 29–56; I. Oldberg, 'Russia's great power
ambitions and policy under Putin', in R. Kanet (ed.), *Russia: re-emerging great power*
(Basingstoke, UK: Palgrave Macmillan, 2007), pp. 13–30. Public opinion surveys
in Russia indicate that a majority of Russians support the return of Russia to great
power status. Fifty-one per cent expect Putin's successor to return Russia to a pre-
eminent global role, while only nine per cent expect the next president to establish
good relations with the West. See Angus Reid Global Monitor, 'Half of Russians
yearn for superpower status', 4 February (2008), reprinted in *Johnson's Russia List*,
no. 2008–24, 4 February (2008). In August 2008, at the time of the Russian invasion of Georgia, opinion in Moscow strongly supported the reassertion of Russian

were followed early in 2006 with Putin's broad attack on virtually all aspects of US policy at the Munich Security Conference, and marking Russia's new assertive approach to foreign policy, beginning with its relations with the United States.[35] As Mark Beissinger notes, Putin's comments implied that the 'persistence of the Soviet empire would have been preferable to the East European democracies or to the current fifteen states that now cover former Soviet space'.[36] Putin's – and also Medvedev's – commitment to the re-establishment of 'Greater Russia' is their reaction to the collapse of those old imperial relationships.

From military intervention to economic coercion

As we have already noted, despite the rhetorical commitment of Russian leaders to deal with the former republics of the USSR as sovereign equals, from almost the very creation of the Russian Federation, Moscow has been directly and indirectly involved in the internal affairs of its new neighbours. Throughout the 1990s the major instruments used to re-establish Russia's influence were various types of *de facto* military intervention and attempts to turn the CIS into a meaningful organ of economic and political reintegration. Since the year 2000 Russian policy toward its neighbours has relied increasingly on the use of Russia's dominant position in the energy field and its growing economic leverage vis-à-vis its generally much weaker and economically dependent neighbours. Most important has been the Russian government regaining almost total control over Russian energy production and distribution and increasingly dominating the energy sector of neighbouring countries – often through semi-coerced purchase of their energy distribution and processing infrastructure.[37]

Oil, gas and the revival of Russian political dominance

Other authors have documented in substantial detail the fact that the exponential increase in global demand for energy has been the single most important factor contributing to the revival of the Russian economy.[38]

influence. See A. Barnard, 'Russians confident that nation is back', *New York Times*, 15 August (2008): www.nytimes.com

[35] See Trenin, *Getting Russia right*; and S. Wagstyl, 'The year Russia flexed its diplomatic muscle', *Financial Times*, 17 December (2007).

[36] M. Beissinger, 'The persistence of empire in Eurasia', *NewsNet: News of the American Association for the Advancement of Slavic Studies* 48 (2008), 1–8.

[37] See Nygren, *The rebuilding of greater Russia*, esp. pp. 238–45.

[38] The dominant narrative in analyses of Russia's economic revival attributes it almost exclusively to Russian gas and oil exports, and to the rise in global demand (and

In fact, almost from the very inception of the new Russian Federation Moscow has used its control of energy as a means to 'influence' other former Soviet republics to change political positions that they had taken or to follow Moscow's policy lead. This has been especially true in Russia's relations with the Baltic republics, with Ukraine, Georgia, and more recently even with Belarus, all post-Soviet states with which Russia has had serious policy differences. Moscow has in all cases put the blame for the cut-off of energy flows on the other side, or explained them as the result of technical problems. It has also argued that the policies of its oil and gas companies were dictated solely by economic (and not political) considerations.[39]

All of these countries are energy poor and almost totally dependent on supplies of petroleum, natural gas and, in some cases, electricity imported from the Russian Federation. Russia has pursued what Nygren refers to as the 'tap weapon'[40] – by stopping the delivery of oil and/or gas to these countries – on various occasions in the past decade as a means of strengthening its position in policy disputes and negotiating situations. The dispute with Ukraine in 2005–6, which resulted in Russia cutting off exports of gas in the middle of winter – resulted from Gazprom's decision to more than triple the price of gas. This decision, however, emerged only in the aftermath of the 'Orange Revolution' that reversed the 'victory' of Russia's preferred candidate in the Ukrainian presidential elections. Until that time, Putin's policy toward Kiev had been based on pragmatic long-term political and economic considerations. However, with the collapse of pro-Russian political forces in Ukraine, Russia initiated a new, more coercive approach, to demonstrate to the Ukrainians that assertions of independence from Moscow's influence would have real costs.[41]

The 'gas war' of 2005–6 between Russia and Ukraine was 'resolved' by a complicated settlement in which a majority Russian-owned Swiss company, Gazprom, sold gas originating supposedly from Central Asia to Ukraine at subsidised prices which increased gradually over several

---

thus, prices). This has been increasingly challenged by those who point to vibrant growth in other sectors of the Russian economy. See World Bank in Russia, *Russian Economic Report* 16 (2008).Available at http://siteresources.worldbank.org/INTRUSSIANFEDERATION/Resources/rer16_Eng.pdf

[39] With the collapse of the USSR the Russian Federation decided to continue to supply gas and oil to other former republics – now, new sovereign states – at prices substantially below the world market price.

[40] B. Nygren, 'Putin's use of energy resources with respect to CIS countries'. Unpublished paper presented at the Seventh International CISS Millennium Conference, Buçaco, Portugal, 14–16 June (2007).

[41] Bugajski, *Cold peace*, pp. 80–9.

years to world market levels.[42] Ukraine was in a position to bargain with Gazprom and Moscow because Russia depended upon the secure flow of gas through pipelines across Ukraine in order to fulfil its export obligations to customers in Central and Western Europe. In other words, Ukraine was not totally helpless in responding to Russian pressures, as was evident from the fact that the Ukrainians had, in fact, 'illegally' tapped supplies of gas destined for Europe during the height of the confrontation. And, to a substantial degree, the reaction of the EU to the reduction of gas supplies in January 2006 was an important factor in Russia's willingness to reach a settlement with Ukraine.

At the root of the renewed Russo-Ukrainian confrontation over gas deliveries in January 2009 was the issue of Ukraine's defiance of Moscow's preferences across a broad range of issues, and not simply the disagreement over the price of gas exported to Ukraine. For example, Ukraine had insisted on the Russian removal of its Black Sea fleet from its bases in Sevastopol, currently scheduled for 2017. Moreover, its government had made clear its interest in joining NATO and George W. Bush had pushed for Ukrainian and Georgian membership.[43]

Ukraine is by no means the only post-Soviet state to have experienced the effects of the 'tap weapon'. Belarus, which for most of the post-Soviet period pursued a slavishly pro-Russian policy, angered Putin's government in 2002, thereby leading to four years of confrontation between the two countries, with Gazprom taking the lead role in the dispute. Because pipelines to the West crossed Belarusian territory, Belarus had some bargaining power. Eventually, however, the government of President Lukashenko was forced to capitulate or face the cutoff of Russian gas supplies. Prices were to be increased over a five-year period. Gazprom briefly gained direct control over the pipelines across Belarus,[44] until backing out of the deal in 2010.

Until the August 2008 Russian invasion, the gas weapon, as well as that of electricity, had been the most important instrument in Russian pressures brought against Georgia, in order to coerce Tbilisi into policies more in line with Moscow's interests. These pressures have

---

[42] Nygren, *The rebuilding of greater Russia*, pp. 61–2.

[43] For more detail on the areas of disagreement between Russia and Ukraine, see J. Berryman, 'Russia, NATO enlargement and the new "lands in between"', in R.E. Kanet (ed.), *A resurgent Russia and the West: the European Union, NATO and beyond* (Dordrecht, The Netherlands: The Republic of Letters Press, 2009), pp. 161–85. On the January 2009 gas war, see M-A. Eyl-Mazzega, 'The gas crisis between the Ukraine and Russia: one crisis too far that obliges a humiliated Europe to react', *European Issues* 125, *Les Policy Papers de la Fondation Robert Schuman*, 26 January (2009), available at www.robert-schuman.org/question_europe.php?num=qe-125

[44] Ibid., pp. 76–9.

been employed along with traditional threats of military intervention in support of Abkhaz and South Ossetian separatists, and the latter were finally realised in August 2008.[45] Russia has acquired substantial ownership of energy production and distribution facilities in Georgia to cover the costs of outstanding debts, and as a precondition for continued discounted prices on Russian gas.[46] This control, however, did not cow the Georgian government into accepting Russian dominance in the region, or accepting the *de facto* autonomy of the Russian-backed secessions in South Ossetia and Abkhazia. This resulted in military hostilities in August 2008 that in effect wiped out Georgian military capabilities, developed over several years with US military assistance and training.[47]

Russia's *de facto* control over the energy supplies of other post-Soviet states – Armenia, Moldova and the Baltic states – has also been used in similar ways.[48] However, there is another part of Russia's use of its domination over energy production and distribution that is significant for the drive to re-establish Greater Russia and the Russian Federation as a major world power: namely, attempting to gain control over the distribution of oil and gas from Central Asia in Western markets.

Pipeline politics, from Central Asia to the Baltic Sea

Since the mid-1990s the United States has been actively involved in efforts to ensure alternative distribution routes to Europe and the West for gas and oil from Azerbaijan and Central Asia, in order to prevent

---

[45] 'Georgia and Russia: gather round the gorge', *The Economist*, 17 May (2008), p. 20.

[46] See R. Giragosian, 'Shifting security in the South Caucasus', *Connections: The Quarterly Journal* 6 (2007), 100–6; and A.N. Pamir, 'Energy and pipeline security in the Black Sea and Caspian Sea regions: challenges and solutions', in O. Pavliuk and I. Klympush-Tsintsadze (eds.), *The Black Sea region: cooperation and security building* (Armonk, NY: M.E. Sharpe, 2003), pp. 123–55. In 2003 the Russian firm UES obtained 75 per cent ownership in a Georgian electricity distribution company and management control over several power plants, as well as 50 per cent ownership of a nuclear power plant. See H. Khachatrian, 'Russian moves in Caucasus energy and power sectors could have geopolitical impact', *Eurasia Insight*, 25 September (2006); and I. Torbakov, 'Russian policymakers air notion of "liberal empire" in Caucasus, Central Asia', *Eurasia Insight*, 27 October (2003); and I. Torbakov, 'Russia seeks to use energy abundance to increase political leverage', *Eurasia Insight*, 19 November (2003).

[47] See R. Giragosian, 'Georgian planning flaws led to campaign failure', *Jane's Defence Weekly*, 15 August (2008); M. Dobbs, '"We are all Georgians"? not so fast', *Washingtonpost.com*, 7 August (2008), p. B01; and J. Galloway, 'A bad neighbour in a bad neighbourhood', *Miami Herald*, 17 August (2008). See also G. Friedman, 'Georgia and the balance of power', *New York Review of Books*, 25 September (2008).

[48] Nygren, *The rebuilding of greater Russia*.

Russia from strengthening its semi-monopoly position in the distribution of Eurasian energy resources. Washington has pushed for the development of oil and gas pipelines that would skirt Russian territory and, therefore, reduce the potential of Russia's gaining further leverage over either Central Asian exporters or Western clients.[49] Yet Russia has effectively outmanoeuvred the United States in its relations with the oil- and gas-producing countries of Central Asia. Although several pipelines have been completed that avoid Russian territory, Moscow has been successful in establishing solid political and economic relations with the authoritarian regimes of Central Asia. It signed new agreements with Kazakhstan, Uzbekistan and other major energy producers that will result in expanded supplies of gas and oil destined for European consumers through the existing and planned pipeline networks that cross Russian territory,[50] rather than via southern pipelines favoured by the United States.[51] This is all part of a Russian effort to increase control over the flow of oil and gas to Europe so as to influence key European governments on issues such as the status of secessionist regions of Moldova and Georgia, as well as Russian policy on separatism within its own borders.[52]

Russia and important Western partners have also put into place plans for the future distribution of oil and gas to Europe that will eliminate the possible interference of current transit states such as Ukraine and Belarus, as well as Poland, by avoiding them altogether. The planned North Stream pipeline under the Baltic Sea directly from Russia to the

[49] A. Sultanova, 'Pipelines to speed flow of Caspian oil to West', *Miami Herald*, 25 May (2005), p. 18A; E.E. Arvedlund, 'Pipeline done, oil from Azerbaijan begins flowing to Turkey', *New York Times*, 26 May (2005), p. C6; 'Oil over troubled waters', *The Economist*, 28 May (2005), p. 54; A. Lantier, 'US oil pipeline politics and the Russia–Georgia conflict', *World Socialist Web Site*, 21 August (2008), available at www.wsws.org/articles/2008/aug2008/pipe-a21.shtml; C.E. Ziegler, 'Energy in the Caspian Basin and Central Asia', in R.E. Kanet (ed.), *The new security environment: the impact on Russia, Central and Eastern Europe* (Aldershot, UK: Ashgate, 2005), pp. 210–18; and Kanet and Homarac, 'The US challenge to Russian influence'.

[50] M. Hahn, 'Moscow achieves success with Kazakh oil deal', *Power and Interest News Report*, 29 May (2007); A.E. Kramer, 'Central Asia on front line in energy battle', *New York Times*, 20 December (2007), pp. C1, C6. On the PRC's role, see M. De Haas, 'SCO summit demonstrates its growing cohesion', *Power and Interest News Report*, 14 August (2007); B. Pannier, 'Central Asia: Beijing flexes economic muscle across region', Radio Free Europe/Radio Liberty (RFE/RL), 29 May (2008); and 'China/Russia: focus on pipelines during Medvedev visit', Radio Free Europe/Radio Liberty (RFE/RL), 29 May (2008).

[51] M.K. Bhadrakumar, 'Russia takes control of Turkmen (world?) gas', *Asia Times*, 30 July (2008). Available at www.atimes.com/atimes/Central_Asia/JG30Ag01.html

[52] This statement and others that emphasise the political aspects of Russian energy exports and policy should not be interpreted to mean that economic benefits are not also an important factor that influences policy decisions.

coast of Germany,[53] as well as the South Stream pipeline that will run under the Black Sea from Russia directly to Bulgaria,[54] will expand Russia's domination over the gas markets of Europe, while reducing the possibility of countries such as Ukraine, Belarus or Poland disrupting those flows.[55] Overall, Russia has positioned itself effectively to control the production and distribution of energy across almost the entirety of former Soviet space and to Europe as well, as part of former president Putin's commitment to establish Greater Russia as a major global actor. The dependence on external sources for virtually all gas and oil needs of some countries in the EU and their willingness to cut bilateral deals with Russia outside the context of a common EU policy (notably Germany), has greatly aided Russia in its attempt to employ energy as a foreign policy tool.

Toward the future

The broader project to which this chapter contributes focuses on new and old armed conflicts in post-Soviet space. The 'frozen conflicts' in Moldova, Georgia (until the Russian intervention of August 2008), Nagorno-Karabakh and Chechnya are clear examples of those armed conflicts. Here I have emphasised the non-military but still largely coercive aspects of Russia's policy, as Moscow has expanded its efforts at establishing a Greater Russia. By no means does this indicate that Russia has abandoned its use of military capabilities in relations with its neighbours. Military coercion remains an important tool in Moscow's efforts to dominate the former Soviet space. Its ongoing military pressure and threats against Georgia (that culminated in the August 2008 partial occupation) and its official recognition of the two breakaway enclaves in Georgia are illustrative of this. So too are its continuing support for secessionist forces in Moldova and Nagorno-Karabakh, and the continued suppression of potentially autonomous power centres in Chechnya.

It is important to recognise, however, that this policy has been partly a response to what Russian leaders view as a systematic attempt by the United States and the EU to take advantage of past Russian

---

[53] 'Intelligence brief: Poland fumes over Russian-German projects: meeting in Lithuania to counter Russian influence in FSU', *Power and Interest News Report*, 2 May (2008); 'Poland wants talks with Russia, Germany on pipeline', *RFE/RL Newsline*, 8 January (2008).

[54] V. Isachenkov, 'Russia strengthens gas grip', *MiamiHerald.com*, 19 January (2008).

[55] 'Eastern Europe, America and Russia: pipedreams', *The Economist*, 26 January (2008), p. 50; 'Poland wants talks with Russia, Germany on pipeline', *RFE/RL Newsline*.

weakness. The expansion of NATO and the EU in the past two decades has occurred almost exclusively in areas that – until the demise of the USSR – were part of the Soviet sphere. Much of the planned future expansion of both organisations would incorporate former Soviet republics into these Western institutions. In Moscow's current view, a continuation of the expansion of Western institutions eastward is simply not acceptable.

Since the 2008 war with Georgia, Russia has primarily returned to using economic levers, which have become the most reliable instruments for Russia in its campaign to reassert control over its neighbours.[56] Efforts within the CIS to expand security cooperation in 2010, as well as to effect formal economic integration, have been largely unsuccessful. Meaningful agreements have been difficult to reach and almost impossible to implement. The Single Economic Space 'has encountered basically the same fate as the CIS as a whole. [In other words] it has started as an agreement on general principles which has been followed by negotiations on details which have failed and stalled the process.'[57] It has been primarily through the manipulation of oil and gas prices, the coerced purchase of neighbouring states' energy infrastructure, and agreements reached with key European customers such as Germany that Russia has been able to reassert its dominant role in Eurasia. This does not mean that Moscow does not face competition, because the PRC represents for the states of Central Asia an alternative to total dependence on Russia[58] and the West continues to compete for influence in Ukraine, Georgia and elsewhere in Eastern Europe and the Caucasus.[59] However, during the past decade Russia has expanded its ability to influence, even dominate, the policymaking of most of its neighbours who depend on Russian sources of energy.

Given the extensive support in Russia among political elites (as well as among the general population) for the reassertion of Russia's role as a great power, and given the limited likelihood of alternative energy sources for most of Russia's neighbours, one can assume that energy

---

[56] Nygren, *The rebuilding of greater Russia*, p. 232ff. In 2005 Herman Prichner also emphasised the place of economic instruments in the revival of Greater Russia: H. Prichner, Jr., *Reviving greater Russia? The future of Russia's borders with Belarus, Georgia, Kazakhstan, Moldova and Ukraine* (Lanham, MD: University Press of America, 2005).

[57] Nygren, *The rebuilding of greater Russia*, p. 238.

[58] C.E. Ziegler, 'NATO, the United States and Central Asia: challenging sovereign governance', unpublished paper presented at the II WISC Conference, Ljubljana, Slovenia, 5–6 July (2008); H. Chun, 'Russia's energy diplomacy toward Europe and Northeast Asia', unpublished paper presented at the II WISC Conference, Ljubljana, Slovenia, 5–6 July (2008).

[59] Berryman, 'Russia, NATO enlargement and the new "lands in between"', chapter 8.

supply and infrastructure will remain a central tool in Russian policy, even though recent events demonstrate that Moscow is able and willing to use its military power in situations where the West is unable to counter that use.

In the longer term – but here we are speaking of decades, not years – Russia's position, both in relations with neighbouring states and as a refurbished great power, is likely to erode, as Russian oil and gas reserves are depleted and dependent states shift to alternative energy sources.[60] Moreover, there is the important issue (seldom discussed seriously) of the impact of Russia's impending demographic disaster on its ability to maintain its economy or pursue its foreign policy objectives.[61] Yet, for the foreseeable future the Russian Federation will likely continue to exert major influence over Greater Russia, based heavily on its domination of the energy lifeline essential for most of its neighbours. But ominously, as the events of 2008 demonstrated, Russia has also exhibited a willingness to exert other pressures, up to and including military intervention.

---

[60] On the issue of the weakness of the overall Russian economy, see Hancock, 'Russia: great power image versus economic reality'.

[61] See W. Laqueur, *The last days of Europe: epitaph for an old continent* (New York: Thomas Dunne Books, 2007).

3 The shape of the security order in the former USSR

Matthew Sussex

It is symptomatic of the uncertainty surrounding contemporary international politics that two decades after a 'New World Order' was proclaimed, key questions about sources of insecurity remain unanswered.[1] With that uncertainty in mind, this chapter examines the security order emerging in the territory of the former USSR, with a specific focus on the roles played by different institutions and organisations. It finds that the former Soviet space is best characterised as a zone reflecting what I call Russian 'constrained primacy'.[2] There are several reasons for this. To begin with, the prospects for the development of an overarching form of security architecture that satisfies the strategic objectives of regional and extra-regional powers remain bleak. The primary political and military-strategic organisations shaping the former USSR still have fundamentally divergent purposes, with those championed by Moscow acting as vehicles for bloc consolidation, while those reflecting Western interests undermine Russia's attempts to cement its hegemony. Moreover, it is unlikely that institutions promoting economic interdependence can quickly be leveraged to build greater trust and reciprocity, due to the simple fact that actors both within the region and outside it continue to use trade strategically. Finally, recent attempts to propose new types of architecture to manage the post-Soviet space (and European security in general) have fallen prey to fundamental disagreements. As a consequence, the region faces a continued complex balance between a Russian state with rising power but declining centrifugal pull, and the use of primarily economic incentives by external actors to encourage smaller states into multi-vector foreign policies.

---

[1] The use of the term in its post-Cold War context was popularised by a speech given by former president George Bush Snr to a joint session of Congress in 1990. See G.H.W. Bush, 'Toward a new world order' (Washington, DC: US Government Printing Office, 1990).

[2] I borrow this term from the late Gerald Segal. See G. Segal, 'East Asia and the "constrainment" of China', *International Security* 20 (1996), 107–35.

To examine this I ask three questions. First, what are the strategic preferences of Russia, as the largest power after the collapse of the USSR, and how has Moscow gone about embedding its regional eminence? Second, is there evidence that regional actors are learning to live with the constraints of interdependence, or are economic institutions largely instruments for relative gains? Third, I examine the effects of external pressure on Russia, and ask: to what extent is Russia regionally constrained?

Before answering these questions I briefly survey the scholarly literature on regional security, and conclude that whilst there are many (often complex) ways to explain evolving security orders, none are completely useful in the case of the former USSR. Instead, I adopt a simpler approach that investigates how the preferences of regional actors are played out. I examine instruments of Russia primacy in three areas: political organisations like the CIS; military-security alliances such as the CSTO; and economic instruments. The rest of the analysis considers those areas in which Russian primacy is constrained. I consider the growing economic role of the SCO, reflecting the PRC's increasing influence in regional affairs, which has a number of political consequences for Russia. Next, I evaluate the role of the EU, which has exhibited little desire to get involved in conflicts on the former territory of the USSR, but nonetheless holds important potential power to draw states such as Ukraine and Georgia even further away from Russia's orbit. Finally, I examine the role of military-security pacts, and demonstrate that while NATO may appear increasingly rudderless, it is nonetheless an important counterweight to Russian preferences for a strengthened CSTO. This is especially the case given Russia's frequent attempts to promote alternatives such as Dmitry Medvedev's stalled idea to replace the Conventional Forces in Europe (CFE) process with a new European Security Treaty (EST).

Regions, power and security architecture in the former USSR

Various attempts have been made to explain how geopolitical regions emerge and begin to cohere. Most of them differ markedly in their basic assumptions about the main variables that are responsible for creating and maintaining regional order. For those focusing on notions of power balancing – concert-based systems or regions where the status quo is upheld by a great power – the primary factor shaping that order is material power. Historically, one can locate numerous examples where regions coalesce due to an external threat or the imposition of hegemony.[3] Conversely, for those writing about security complexes, communities or regimes, normative factors such as ideas and identities, as well as domestic and regional discourses, can also play a formative role.

This has produced significant disagreement within even well-established schools of international politics about the most stable type of regional order. Realists disagree about the relative utility of balance-of-power systems – in which major powers manage security affairs along clearly delineated spheres of influence.[4] Conversely, hierarchal approaches[5] favour regional orders in which a single great power takes on the functional tasks of managing security affairs, in a geopolitical space populated by largely satisfied second-tier actors with few incentives to become peer competitors.[6] And while this may seem like hair-splitting to the casual observer, the sources of disagreement are fundamental: on the one hand is the assumption that stability obtains when power is balanced; whilst on the other it is assumed that power transitions (when power moves from hegemony to balance through competition) are actually the least desirable outcome.

Similar problems can be found in other ways of evaluating regional security dynamics. For the enthusiastic supporters of the Copenhagen School,[7] the best way to understand security is through the interactions within and between different regional security complexes (RSCs).[8] Through sectoral analysis – identifying social, political, economic, environmental and

---

[3] See J. Mearsheimer, *The tragedy of great power politics* (New York: W.W. Norton, 2001).

[4] For instance, R. Jervis, 'From balance to concert: a study of international security cooperation', *World Politics* 38 (October 1985), 58–79; and C.A. Kupchan and C.C. Kupchan, 'Concerts, collective security and the future of Europe', *International Security* 16 (1991), 114–61.

[5] On the contest between hegemonic stability and balance of power, see, for instance, C. Layne, 'The war on terrorism and the balance of power: the paradoxes of American hegemony', in T.V. Paul, J. Wirtz and M. Fortmann (eds.), *Balance of power: theory and practice in the twenty-first century* (Stanford University Press, 2004), pp. 103–27. See also D. Kang, 'Why China's rise will be peaceful: hierarchy and stability in the East Asian region', *Perspectives on Politics* 3 (2005), 551–4; and R. Powell, 'The inefficient use of power: costly conflict with complete information', *American Political Science Review* 98 (2004), 633–48.

[6] D. Kang, 'The theoretical roots of hierarchy in international relations', *Australian Journal of International Affairs* 58 (2004), 337–52.

[7] For a good early introduction to the Copenhagen School see B. McSweeney, 'Identity and security: Buzan and the Copenhagen School' (review essay), *Review of International Studies* 22 (1996), 81–93.

[8] On RSCs, see the primary tomes by B. Buzan and O. Waever, *Regions and powers: the structure of international security* (Cambridge University Press, 2003); and B. Buzan, O. Waever and J. de Wilde, *Security: a new framework for analysis* (Boulder, CO: Lynne Rienner Publishers, 1997).

military spheres in which the discursive practice of securitisation occurs –
RSC theorists claim to have identified a rich vein of scholarly inquiry.
Here, they claim, process-tracing can help establish why particular issues
make it on to the agenda of regional security, how they do so, and what the
implications are for the actors within and outside the complex. Hence in
the former USSR one can notionally find a 'centred'[9] great power complex
dominated by Russia, in which Moscow cements its regional authority
through a neo-imperial foreign policy and an exclusionary group of nested
institutions and organisations. Yet here one can raise the obvious criticism
of how homogeneous a region is, especially – to abuse a cliché – in a world
affected significantly by factors of globalisation. Equally, regions are frequently sites of competition from external actors, particularly when there
are good reasons for it (e.g., strategic resources). On this basis, similar
criticisms can also be levelled at the security community literature.[10]

More recently there has been a renewed focus on security 'architecture': put simply, the building blocks for regional stability. This appetite for construction has been visible amongst both policy practitioners
and analysts. Broadly speaking, there are three goals that a region-wide
platform for cooperation can serve: security, prosperity and transparency. First, regional architecture requires some kind of mechanism for
regulating security cooperation. Often the most appropriate means of
organisation is through consensus, with equal multilateral participation
by actors.[11] However, this is not to say that multilateralism is a necessary condition. On the contrary, there is no reason why security needs
to be regulated by a specific form of collective apparatus. Indeed, in
some regional power configurations it could be imposed by a hegemon,
split between competing camps, or regional cooperation could occur in
response to a shared external threat.[12]

A second important component of regional architecture is some form
of vehicle – or series of vehicles – to promote regional prosperity.[13] This

---

[9] Buzan and Waever, *Regions and powers*, pp. 428–9. For a more critical perspective see
R. Allison, 'Regionalism, regional structures and security management in Central
Asia', *International Affairs* 80 (2004), 463–83.

[10] On security community see especially A. Acharya, *Constructing a security community in
Southeast Asia: ASEAN and the problem of regional order*, 2nd edn (New York: Taylor &
Francis, 2009); E. Adler and M. Barnett, *Security communities* (Cambridge University
Press, 2008); and A. Acharya, 'The Association of Southeast Asian Nations: "secur-
ity community" or "defence community"', *Pacific Affairs* 64 (1991), 159–78.

[11] See, for example, J. McMillan et al., 'Toward a new regional security architecture',
Washington Quarterly 23 (2004), 161–75.

[12] See J. Mearsheimer, 'The false promise of international institutions', *International
Security* 19 (1994/5), 5–49.

[13] G.J. Ikenberry, *After Victory: institutions, strategic restraint and the rebuilding of order
after major wars* (Princeton University Press, 2001), pp. 3–4.

may take the form of a free trade area linked to a customs union and a highly institutionalised regulatory framework such as the EU. It may be an instrument for 'open' regionalism like the broad-based Asia Pacific Economic Cooperation grouping, or it could be used as an exclusively 'closed' trading arrangement, creating benefits of free trade only for a select group of members.

A third requirement commonly cited by regional security specialists is for a coordinated effort to increase transparency and build confidence amongst members of a security grouping. This may consist of dialogues or forums between policymakers or bureaucrats. Thus, there is differing weight and purpose between summits, for instance, and gatherings of officials meeting to discuss a particular security challenge.[14] Such meetings may be highly formalised (through 'Track 1' diplomacy), they may be looser discussions between invited academics, public servants and experts ('Track 2'), or they may be a hybrid with both governmental and non-governmental participants ('Track 1.5'). There are numerous examples of fora such as these, from the Munich Security Conference and the Shangri-La Dialogues to the Association of Southeast Asian Nations (ASEAN) Regional Forum.

Yet it is instructive that the geopolitical space of the former USSR defies explanation either by established academic approaches for understanding regional security politics, or by recent attempts to focus on the need for new architecture for new realities. Unlike the EU, the former USSR lacks a universally accepted and overarching institutional vehicle for cooperation. Unlike ASEAN, the states that make up the former USSR have no clear overriding sense of common economic interest. And, contrary to the claims of RSC theorists, a coherent security complex is manifestly absent from the territory of the former USSR.

Instead of representing a hegemonic order underpinned by Russia exercising control over its post-imperial space, the former USSR resembles a melange of competing interests, strategic priorities and influences. Following the collapse of the USSR, which had managed the area simply by virtue of its existence as a cohesive state, the area has once again become a site for renewed great power competition over strategic resources, with the EU, the United States and the PRC all seeking to secure safe and reliable access to energy and minerals. It is certainly true that Moscow has attempted to recreate a buffer zone amongst the newly independent states, utilising both the rhetoric of great power status as well as more formal arrangements. However, much of this has consisted of responding from a position of weakness rather than

---

[14] J. McMillan et al., 'Toward a new regional security architecture', 172.

proactive policy from a position of strength; a situation that a number of commentators believe will only continue to worsen.[15] Perceiving itself to be surrounded by fragile actors (a condition Russia itself experienced during the 1990s), the primary security challenges Russia has faced have been local and internal. They pertain to economic frailty, ethnicity, the rise of organised crime and militant ideologies that accompanied the power vacuum left by the USSR's dissolution. Responding to its loss of an empire, Russia also needed to construct a new unifying national idea, which only recently has begun to coalesce around Putin's notion of 'sovereign democracy', and more recently Medvedev's urgings for 'modernisation'.

Any notion of robust Russian regional hegemony is therefore challenged by the fact that Moscow has only recently re-emerged from a period of significant structural decline. Although it has become customary to declare that the 'bear is back', as a result of Russia's emergence as an energy superpower in the first decade of the twenty-first century,[16] the preceding years were marked by serious decline. This included rampant inflation and corruption, the emergence of a privileged and much detested gang of financial oligarchs, national humiliation in the form of the ageing and frequently ill President Yeltsin, revolutions in the Caucasus, and the progressive demodernisation of Russian society, especially in rural areas.

The problems that Russia experienced internally have been mirrored by other states in the region. Georgia in particular finds its strategic choices constrained. It is sandwiched between Russia (which sees Tbilisi as a vital part of Russia's post-communist sphere of influence), and the West, which remains leery of extending full NATO membership to a state in the Caucasus. Ukraine, too, has emerged from massive poverty and unemployment in the 1990s to find itself the target of aggressive Russian resource diplomacy.[17] Kiev's rediscovered sense of national pride after the Orange Revolution provided little real ability to seek greater foreign policy enmeshment with the West. And, unlike other regional environments like Asia or the Middle East, where the sources of

---

[15] See, for instance, D. Trenin, 'Russia reborn: reimagining Moscow's foreign policy', *Foreign Affairs* 88 (2009), 64–78; and S. Blank, 'Toward a new Chinese order in Asia: Russia's failure', *National Bureau of Asian Research, Special Report* 26 (March 2011).

[16] See P. Dibb, 'The bear is back', *American Interest* 2 (2006), 78–85.

[17] In addition to an economic contraction, other indicators of decay included poverty, which UN estimates put at 47 per cent in 2001, declines in fertility rates (down to 1:1 in 2001 from 2:0 in 1991) and declining spending on health in real terms. See *Ukraine country economic memorandum* (New York: World Bank, 2009), pp. 7–9; and I. Kalachova, 'Poverty and welfare trends in Ukraine over the 1990s', *UNICEF Country Papers*, UNICEF Innocenti Research Centre (Florence: UNICEF, 2002).

competition are relatively clear, this is less obvious in the former USSR. It is hard, for instance, to untangle the networks of ethnic, nationalist and geopolitical strife that led to the 2008 Russo-Georgian war, the frozen conflict that came out of two wars in Chechnya, instability in Kyrgyzstan, ongoing concerns over terrorism and organised crime, and resource politics in the Caucasus.

This makes mapping the shape of the regional security order problematic, much less trying to divine how to manage it. Yet one potential way to shed light on this is to examine how actors have attempted to shape the various institutions and organisations in the regional space of the former USSR. To do this, however, it is necessary to ask first which organisations matter in the former USSR. Two asymmetrical organisations are obviously significant. First, the CIS is important as Russia's main apparatus for encouraging regional unity. The extent to which CIS membership represents an attractive option to different states in the former USSR is highly variable. But as a political and economic instrument of Russian attempts to solidify a sphere of influence in its direct region of vital interest, the CIS merits attention. Second, it is important to identify where the CSTO belongs in regional security dynamics, since it is the primary vehicle to secure Russian military-security interests in the post-Soviet space. Third, one may consider how Russia pursues economic primacy through multilateral channels like the CIS and the Eurasian Economic Community (EurAsEc), as well as bilaterally.

In addition to organisations that help advance Russian regional interests, there are others that curtail them. At the broadest level of engagement, the SCO is a conduit for enhanced Sino-Russian cooperation, as well as a means to develop coordinated policy over both states' agreement that a multipolar world order is preferable to US unipolarity.[18] But with Chinese power growing, the key question that analysts ask now is whether Russia can live with a Chinese partner that outstrips it considerably in relative power terms. As the analysis below shows, it may indeed have to do just that.

A number of other extra-regional bodies are important in constraining Russia. The first of these is NATO. Although often described as virtually moribund, Russia still identifies NATO as its major security challenger. The history of Russia's rejection of the alliance, not to mention the fact that several of Russia's neighbours remain aspirant

---

[18] The text of the Shanghai Charter refers to the parties' desire to see the 'strengthening of peace and ensuring of security and stability in the region in the environment of developing political multipolarity'. See www.sectsco.org/EN/show.asp?id=69

members, merits its consideration. So too does the EU. Later in this chapter I argue that its role in the former USSR has not been through direct influence, but rather to indirectly constrain Russia by creating potential opportunity structures for those countries seeking to diversify their interests away from Moscow.

Political instruments of Russian regional primacy

Russia's preferences for regional order are clearly visible in the CIS, which was created even before the USSR was dissolved. It formed after a meeting between the leaders of the main three Soviet socialist repub-lics in a forest north of the Belarusian city of Brest on 8 December 1991. This led to the Belavezha Accords that formalised Ukraine, Russia and Belarus's status as sovereign entities. Membership of the CIS was enlarged when eight more Soviet republics signed the Alma-Ata Protocol on 21 December. By 1993, when Georgia acceded, the CIS encompassed twelve of the fifteen former republics of the USSR, with only the Baltic states of Lithuania, Estonia and Latvia choosing not to participate. But rather than representing a strong multilateral body, even leaders like Alexsandr Lukashenko and Vladimir Putin have said that its original intention was to facilitate a 'civilised divorce' from the USSR.

Russian policymakers left the door open at an early stage for the CIS to become a basic building block for regional integration. The CIS Charter (which in January 1993 replaced the original Creation Agreement) foresaw the need for a common economic order that permitted the free movement of goods, services and people, and the harmonisation of economic policies so as to create favourable direct production links between member-states.[19] Initially the CIS had the goal of unifying members' military forces as well. The formal com-ponents of military-strategic cooperation within the CIS were first codified in the Cooperative Security Treaty of 1992 (also known as the Tashkent Treaty). But its joint headquarters dwindled amid Russia's internal power struggle that saw Boris Yeltsin enshrined under a 'super-presidential' constitution after obtaining the support of the military to put down his own rebellious parliament. It was not until October 2002, three years after the Tashkent Treaty had notionally lapsed, that the Cooperative Security Treaty reformed as the Collective Security Treaty Organisation (CSTO).[20]

---

[19] For the CIS Charter see the United Nations Treaty depository, no. 31139, with declar-ations and decisions: http://untreaty.un.org/unts/120001_144071/6/8/00004863.pdf

[20] The Charter of the CSTO is available at http://untreaty.un.org/unts/144078_158780/5/9/13289.pdf

Aside from a general drift toward a collective security pact that only became more urgent for Russia once NATO expansion was put on the agenda in 1994, the main operations of the CIS in the 1990s revolved around the limited extent to which its members were prepared to cooperate. The organisation took tentative steps towards the coordination of policies to combat drug trafficking and organised crime in 1995, and announced a customs union in 1996 that only five of the participating members (Belarus, Kazakhstan, Kyrgyzstan, Russia and Tajikistan) decided to join. As a way to manage disputes between members and to preserve order, the CIS endorsed Russian-led peacekeeping missions in Tajikistan, and held limited discussions about the conflict in Abkhazia at Heads of Government and Heads of State meetings in 1997.

Once Vladimir Putin became chairman of the CIS Council of Heads of State in 2000, the CIS took a number of important steps in relation to regional security. It adopted a Declaration on Maintaining Strategic Stability in June of that year, revolving around Russia's signing of the START II Agreement and ratification of the Comprehensive Test Ban Treaty.[21] But it also issued a blunt condemnation of US attempts to press ahead with ballistic missile defence. In a joint statement the CIS noted that American plans to abrogate the ABM Treaty would 'undermine steps towards further reductions in strategic nuclear armaments'.[22] At subsequent meetings it created a joint counter-terrorism centre and deepened cooperation over a common air defence system. In the economic field, an agreement to coordinate tariff, transport and customs legislation was signed between Ukraine, Russia, Belarus and Kazakhstan in 2003, laying the groundwork for the future extension of the EurAsEc to Kiev. But in 2011 Ukraine was still outside EurAsEc, which had become the main organisation for Russia to press for a common energy market in the CIS space.

Despite numerous statements of purpose on the need for harmonisation and a free trade area, the CIS had effectively split its focus between economic integration and security by 2004, when it identified the fight against terrorism as the main priority for CIS activities at its March meeting of foreign ministers. This allowed Moscow to wedge Georgia on the issue of insurgency close to Chechnya in the Pankisi Gorge,[23] and

---

[21] 'The Commonwealth of Independent States', *Inventory of international non-proliferation organisations and regimes* (Washington, DC: Center for Nonproliferation Studies, 2008), p. 4.

[22] Ibid.

[23] For more on Russia's policy in Chechnya, see P. Shearman and M. Sussex, 'Globalisation, "new wars" and the war in Chechnya', in R. Sakwa (ed.), *Chechnya: from past to future* (London: Anthem, 2005), pp. 199–221.

also on human rights issues related to the treatment of ethnic Russians in the enclaves of South Ossetia and Abkhazia. Repeated threats by Georgia and Ukraine to withdraw from the CIS during 2006 led to Tbilisi stating its preference for a 'slow exit', which was hastened by the Russo-Georgian war of 2008. Kiev, meanwhile, used its decision not to ratify the CIS Charter (which made Ukraine officially a member-participant) to justify remaining involved in CIS activities.

Perhaps the clearest manifestation of weakness in the CIS came when the representatives of the organisation's southern flank (Uzbekistan, Tajikistan and Turkmenistan) all chose not to attend the October 2009 Heads of Government meeting. Each state had its own concerns, but their collective absence served as a warning to Moscow that the CIS did not equate to *de facto* Russian dominance. Uzbekistan scaled back its participation in CSTO peacekeeping activities and implemented laws deliberately targeted at Russian companies that dealt with the transport of Uzbek gas, imposing a 25 per cent excise tariff on non-Uzbek participants in production-sharing agreements.[24] Turkmenistan, for its part, was annoyed at the time taken by Gazprom to rebuild a gas pipeline that had exploded in April that year. Tajikistan used its non-attendance to highlight its desire for Russia's 201st Division to pay rent on military bases it had used since the end of the Second World War,[25] and was simultaneously embroiled in a spat with Moscow over its decision to drop Russian as an official language.

How do we assess Russia's use of political institutions to embed its regional primacy? From the discussion above it is clear that Russia has not always had it all its own way in the CIS. Indeed, it could be inferred that Russia has missed an opportunity to cement its leadership in the former Soviet space by not generating a clear political framework for cooperation. However, to make such an argument misunderstands the point of Russian strategy. In this context it is important to consider the scope and purpose of the organisation, the differing agendas of its participants, and their expectations about further collaboration.

First, Russia has deliberately avoided promoting the CIS as an integrative vehicle underpinned by the spirit of compromise needed for consensus politics to function effectively. Instead, it permitted the CIS to serve as an umbrella organisation for broad intergovernmental

---

[24] These figures are available in Global Legal Group, 'International comparative legal guide to gas regulation 2011' (2011), www.iclg.co.uk/khadmin/Publications/pdf/4183. pdf. See also Price Waterhouse Coopers, 'Guide to doing business and investing in Uzbekistan' (2010), available at www.pwc.com/uz/en/assets/pdf/UZ_DBG_2010.pdf

[25] 'Tajikistan wants Russia to pay for military base', *RIA Novosti*, 30 July (2009). Available at http://en.rian.ru/world/20090730/155672919.html

statements of common purpose, beneath which it pursued a classic divide-and-rule approach. This took the form of numerous bilateral deals coupled to preferential 'minilateral' arrangements. As a result, the scope and purpose of the CIS was repeatedly reshaped to take on the flavour of core Russian activities. This permitted flexibility in policymaking since Moscow could tailor the CIS to suit changing circumstances, rather than being tied to a broad multilateral agenda that must – by definition – move at the pace of the slowest member.

It should not be surprising, therefore, that in the first years of its existence, with Russia focused on joining what Mikhail Gorbachev had called the 'common European home',[26] the CIS was not seen as a major priority. By the time the 1993 Russian Foreign Policy Concept was published, amid domestic concerns about the fragility of the Russian democracy and the weakness of the 'near abroad', it was logical that non-traditional security threats such as organised crime were prioritised.[27] Once a consensus on Russian national interests was reached, around the time Yevgeni Primakov launched the strategy of multipolarism, it also followed that greater attention to economic union in the face of the threat of NATO expansion received closer attention. With the stabilisation of Russian politics and the 'restoration of the vertical' under Putin and then Medvedev, the emphasis of the CIS turned to counter-terrorism following 9/11, solidifying the CSTO under the Putin strategy of foreign policy pragmatism, and then to energy as the region experienced a boom in oil and gas prices.

A second point, linked to the first, is that Moscow sees the CIS as an asymmetrical organisation, and expects the right to have the leading voice in managing its activities. Thus, the former Soviet space is unlike the EU, in which powerful actors like France and Germany (and to some extent the UK and Italy) must juggle their agendas, making compromise more commonplace and hence more accepted. Nor is it like South East Asia, which is comprised of aspiring middle powers, and lacks the asymmetry of the former USSR. In fact, Russia's 2008 Foreign Policy Concept noted starkly that those regional states seeking

---

[26] For his address, given at the Council of Europe, see M. Gorbachev, 'The common European home', 6 July (1989) available at www.coe.int/aboutcoe/index.asp?page=no sInvites&sp=gorbachev

[27] The 1993 Foreign Policy Concept was loosely based on the Council on Foreign and Defence Policy's 'Strategiya dlya Rossii', published in August 1992 in *Nezavisimaya gazeta*. For the draft concept, see 'Strategiya dlya Rossii', *Nezavisimaya gazeta*, 22 April (1993), pp. 1, 3. The full text of the Concept can be found in 'Russia's Foreign Policy Concept', *International Affairs* 40 (Moscow) (1993).

alternative modes of integration would be granted no special treatment due to their proximity to Russia, but would instead be subjected to normal threat assessments:

> Russia's attitude towards subregional entities and other bodies to which Russia is not party in the CIS area is determined by their assessed real contribution into ensuring good neighbourly relations and stability, their eagerness to take into account Russia's legitimate interests in practice, and to duly respect existing cooperation mechanisms such as the CIS, CSTO, EurAsEc and the Shanghai Cooperation Organisation.[28]

Finally, it is worth noting that Russian expectations of CIS members and the attitudes of their populations have not been completely divergent. Russia's National Security Concept of 2000 identified the weakening of the integration process in the CIS as a key threat, and strengthening the security of CIS members was listed as a priority. When Russia's Foreign Policy Concept was updated in 2008, CIS integration was referred to in the context of realising the organisation's 'true potential', and revolved primarily around trade issues.[29] More dramatically, the identification of areas of 'privileged' Russian interest in the Medvedev Doctrine of September 2008 was a clear reference to the former Soviet space. Yet despite the public reassertion of Russian expectations about its right to a sphere of influence, enthusiasm for the CIS continues even amongst some of Russia's more difficult partners. In December 2010, the notionally pro-Russian (but generally centrist) Ukrainian president, Viktor Yanyukovych, spoke publicly about the importance of Ukraine extending its participation in the CIS, potentially even to the point of joining a customs union, which Kiev had hitherto resisted.[30] More surprisingly, a Gallup poll on Georgian attitudes to Russia after the 2008 war (and the withdrawal of Tbilisi from the CIS) saw respondents indicate strongly that bilateral trade with CIS members was important. More than 80 per cent were in favour of deeper CIS integration.[31] Only 18 per cent of respondents thought that the CIS should not take steps toward full economic union.

---

[28] 'The Foreign Policy Concept of the Russian Federation: 30/07/2008' (2008). Available at www.maximsnews.com/news20080731russiaforeignpolicyconcept10807311601.htm
[29] Ibid.
[30] I. Adyasov, '2010: a milestone for CIS', *RIA Novosti*, 29 December (2010).
[31] S. Crabtree and N. Esipova, 'Georgians favour ongoing cooperation among CIS countries', *Gallup News*, 25 August (2009).

Military-security instruments of Russian regional primacy

The main military-security instrument for the maintenance of Russian regional primacy is the seven-member CSTO. Like the CIS, it serves as a weak form of local coordination rather than a robust institution. Whilst its primary documents are the 1992 Tashkent Treaty and the CIS Charter, the associated *Basic Guidelines for Deepening Military Cooperation among the Collective Security Treaty States* suggest that a member of the CSTO is forbidden to join any other security alliance.[32] For this reason, a number of former Soviet republics are not CSTO members. The list includes Georgia and Ukraine, both of which have repeatedly stressed a preference for joining NATO, and Azerbaijan, which declined the opportunity to recommit to the Tashkent Treaty when it lapsed in 1999. Turkmenistan, which officially lists itself as a neutral country, changed its membership in 2005 to 'associate' status in order to reflect its stance, and Uzbekistan only rejoined the CSTO in 2006, having flirted with membership in the GUAM group from 1999 until its formal withdrawal from that bloc in 2005.

The division of the CSTO into three military groupings – a Western sector, the Transcaucasus and Central Asia – allows participants to hold joint exercises in their own distinct (but overlapping) strategic theatres. The Tashkent Treaty was boosted by the events of 9/11, with the April 2003 summit formally incorporating the CSTO, and establishing a Joint Staff in 2004. The CSTO's Collective Rapid Reaction Force (KSOR) of 20,000 personnel was established in June 2009 and was deployed to Russia's Kant base in Kyrgyzstan.[33] In the same year, Medvedev signed three documents ratifying previous agreements amongst CSTO members: a stipulation that the headquarters of the CSTO must be on Russian soil; an agreement on the preferential exchange of material and supplies for members' law enforcement and intelligence organisations; and a document codifying the operation command and support structure for KSOR.[34] This dovetailed with earlier enhancements to the CSTO's role in 2007. These included a deal for the use of a contingent of 3,500 personnel from the organisation's forces in UN-mandated or local peacekeeping operations (with members eligible to purchase arms

[32] For the text, see www.ssoar.info/ssoar/files/swp/analysen/AA95_65.pdf
[33] J. Kucera, 'The CSTO, forthcoming as ever, on Kyrgyzstan', *Eurasianet*, 6 May (2010). Available at www.eurasianet.org/node/61003
[34] Ibid.

at Russian prices); and an agreement reached in Dushanbe to deepen security cooperation with the SCO.[35]

The CSTO's first major exercise (with some 4,000 troops participating) was codenamed 'Rubezh'. Held in 2008, it was intended to test the interoperability of CSTO forces in a response 'to protect the sovereignty and territorial integrity' of a member-state.[36] Subsequent exercises almost doubled the number of participants to over 7,000 personnel at the strategic, tactical and operational levels during 'Interaction 2009', held in Kazakhstan after the 'West 2009' exercises in Belarus. The next year, 'Interaction 2010', held in Russia's Chelyabinsk oblast, was designed to simulate how CSTO forces might contain an armed conflict in the CIS region.[37]

However, the CSTO has noticeably failed initial tests of its capacity to function as an effective regional instrument for collective security. This was especially clear during the 2010 ethnic clashes that broke out around the Kyrgyz city of Osh in the Fergana valley.[38] Both the Kyrgyz and Uzbek governments called for CSTO peacekeepers, but the initial response from Moscow was that the conflict was a domestic matter. It was only after a meeting of CSTO representatives that the organisation pointed the blame at unspecified external 'incitement'. Even so, the CSTO response was limited to material and technical assistance to Kyrgyzstan, working with the Red Cross and the International Organisation for Migration to provide assistance to refugees who had fled to Uzbekistan.[39] A further meeting in Moscow between CSTO secretary-general Nikolai Bordyuzha and the Kyrgyz national security chief, Alik Orozov, also resulted in little more than expressions of support.

In spite of its relative incoherence, Russia has attempted to use the CSTO as a political instrument. Medvedev made a failed effort in 2008 to have its members recognise the independence of South Ossetia and Abkhazia. Russia had also raised the idea of dialogue on an equal basis between NATO and the CSTO in 2007, but received no official

---

[35] 'The Commonwealth of Independent States', p. 3.
[36] 'Rubezh 2008: the first large-scale CSTO exercise', *Partnership for Peace Information Management System*, 24 July (2008). See www.pims.org/news/2008/08/06/rubezh-2008-the-first-large-scale-csto-military-exercise
[37] 'CSTO launches situation containment exercises', *Russia Today*, 25 October (2010).
[38] For details, see R. Orange, 'Death toll in southern Kyrgyzstan violence mounts to 23', *The Telegraph*, 11 June (2010), available at www.telegraph.co.uk/news/worldnews/asia/kyrgyzstan/7820518/Death-toll-in-southern-Kyrgyzstan-violence-mounts-to-23.html
[39] 'CSTO to rush aid to Kyrgyzstan', 17 June (2010). Available at www.natomission.ru/en/security/article/security/artnews/99

response. The NATO secretary-general, Fogh Rasmussen, had apparently warmed to the idea in 2009, and the long-time US foreign policy insider Zbigniew Brzezinski had endorsed closer ties in a prominent article published in *Foreign Affairs* that year.[40] But Washington stymied any prospect of dialogue, recommending instead that bilateral relations were preferable to engagement with the CSTO, which would potentially legitimate what it regarded as a waning organisation.[41]

Moreover, while it is true that CSTO membership has been promoted as a positive-sum incentive to former Soviet republics (as well as external actors such as Iran), the consequences against either a member or non-member that threatens Russian interests have also been clearly communicated. A prominent example of this was Putin's programme of military renewal and modernisation, articulated in the 2003 update of Russia's 2000 Military Doctrine, which identified several contingencies whereby Russia might use pre-emptive force in the post-Soviet space.[42] One such contingency was threats to ethnic Russians, a deliberate warning to Ukraine, Moldova and Georgia over the situation in Trans-Dniester, South Ossetia and Abkhazia. Other contingencies included reduced Russian access to areas of financial or security interest (viewed in the Transcaucasus and Central Asia as a pointed hint), instability in the former USSR and direct threats to Russian sovereignty. The 2006 Military Doctrine update went further, formally stating that Russia would 'defend its citizens' rights abroad', and participate in armed conflict on its borders 'where principles of international rights are violated and can thus be classed as aggression against [Russian] citizens'.[43] This was viewed with such alarm in Europe that a special report on Russian military modernisation, commissioned by the West European Union's Security and Defence Assembly, expressed concern that Russian moves had 'direct consequences for European and international security'. It went on to recommend greater EU efforts to encourage membership in NATO and the EU for former Soviet states.[44]

---

[40] Z. Brzezinski, 'An agenda for NATO', *Foreign Affairs* 88 (September–October 2009), 2–20.

[41] J. Kucera, 'US blocking NATO–CSTO cooperation', *Eurasianet*, 12 February (2011). Available at www.eurasianet.org/node/62882

[42] B. Nygren, *The rebuilding of greater Russia*, p. 131.

[43] 'Russia's new military doctrine declares USA and NATO key potential enemies', trans. D. Sudakov, *Pravda.ru*, 19 September (2006). Available athttp://english.pravda.ru/russia/kremlin/19-09-2006/84521-russia_doctrine-0/

[44] European Security and Defence Assembly, Assembly of WEU, 'Russia's defence policy', 5 June (2008). Available at www.assembly-weu.org/en/documents/sessions_ordinaires/rpt/2008/2008.php

Russian policy in relation to military-security aspects of its regional primacy is therefore a story of regular impressive pronouncements that paper over institutional weaknesses. The limited nature of CSTO exercises demonstrates that the organisation is far from having a realistic capability to balance against large external alliances such as NATO. The development of limited interoperability at the medium-sized unit level between Russia and small powers is a far cry from the massed divisions the Warsaw Pact was able to field during the Cold War. When one considers that CSTO forces possess military equipment that is often antiquated and in poor repair, coupled to training practices that are limited by the capabilities of participating states, it is difficult to see how the CSTO can transcend its capability gap relative to the West. By the same token, the inability and/or unwillingness of the CSTO to respond to local emergencies suggest that it has only limited utility as a collective security organisation. The disagreements that prevented a common position on key Russian concerns during the 2008 war with Georgia further underscored this sense of institutional underdevelopment.

That said, Russia has not forced CSTO membership on those states – especially Ukraine and Georgia – that it perceives as leading the anti-Russian bloc in the former Soviet space. Apart from encouraging Uzbekistan to come into the fold, official statements by Russian representatives on future enlargement have been relatively circumspect, tending to express the hope that Ukraine will join rather than demanding it does so. This suggests that Moscow has been relatively content to maintain the CSTO as a nucleus for regional security cooperation, in which its primacy is generally (but not always) accepted by its closest allies in Belarus and Central Asia. Arguably, it does not need to build consensus, since it has explicitly reserved the right to involve itself in conflicts within its sphere of influence, using pre-emptive force if necessary.

Economic instruments of Russian regional primacy

It has been extensively documented that energy is the primary economic instrument of Russian regional dominance. Taken together, energy sales accounted for over 20 per cent of Russia's gross domestic product (GDP) in 2007, and 25 per cent by 2010. In 2009 some 81 per cent of exported Russian gas was consumed in Europe and the CIS.[45]

---

[45] EIA (US Energy Information Administration) report on Russia (last updated November 2010), available at www.eia.doe.gov/cabs/russia/Full.html. See also A. Goldthau, 'Resurgent Russia? Rethinking Energy Inc', *Hoover Institution Policy Review* 147, 26 January (2008).

Russian moves to employ energy both in terms of carrots and sticks were most visible in the 2006 and 2009 gas wars between Ukraine and Russia, which raised fears in the EU about vulnerable overdependence on Russian energy. Even in Belarus, Russia's formerly close ally, gas supplies flowing through its territory were interrupted by Gazprom in June 2010, after direct intervention by Medvedev during a row over gas prices and debts. The relationship soured further with an outpouring of vitriol from Moscow in August over the repeated failure of Aleksandr Lukashenko to recognise the independence of South Ossetia and Abkhazia. Medvedev's aide, Sergei Prikhodko, labelled Lukashenko 'inconsistent', and threatened to release CSTO memos apparently proving the Belarusian leader had supported independence, while another Kremlin insider branded Lukashenko 'dishonourable'.[46] However, whilst Russia has certainly used energy as a weapon, and has stated that it will continue to do so, it is also the case that it has employed access to energy as an inducement to other CIS members through the negotiation of preferential trading arrangements.

In assessing the second question posed at the outset of the chapter – whether Russia was learning to live with the constraints of interdependence – the answer is clearly no. As Dmitri Trenin has argued, Russian strategy is an odd mix of geo-economics and old-fashioned realpolitik, as if it had 'exited the twentieth century through two doors at the same time: one leading to the globalised market of the twenty-first century, and the other opening onto the Great Game of the nineteenth century'.[47] But this is only part of the picture. What remains significant is in understanding how Moscow has leveraged its position in the economic sector – especially the energy market – in order to deepen its position of primacy. In sum, Russian strategy has three components: the reassertion of control over oil and gas on its territory; bullish rent-seeking directed at energy-rich neighbours to ensure energy is transported across Russian territory; and efforts to establish a 'gas caliphate' across the CIS.

Russia has taken drastic steps to shut out potential foreign control over its energy resources. In fact, Western interest in Russian energy predates the collapse of the USSR. In 1990 Chevron launched the joint Tengizchevroil venture in Kazakhstan's Tengiz oil field, in a deal finalised in 1993. In the Far East, companies like Texaco, Mobil, BP and Exxon all invested heavily in attempts to tap the estimated 700 million

---

[46] 'Russia's Medvedev attacks Belarus President Alexander Lukashenko', *BBC News*, 4 October (2010). Available at www.bbc.co.uk/news/world-europe-11469027

[47] D. Trenin, 'Russia reborn', 65.

tons of oil and 2.5 trillion cubic metres of natural gas off Sakhalin Island. Yet Russia came to interpret this as a risk to its sovereign assets. Under Putin, Russia signalled its intention to lower the threshold for what it considered to be energy assets of strategic value by effectively renationalising its oil and gas industries between 2003 and 2006. It did so by hollowing out energy giants and selling them off at bargain-basement prices to state-owned shelf companies. This was exemplified by the 'Yukos affair' that saw Yuganskneftegaz (Yukos's main subsidiary) liquidated in 2006 to recoup alleged tax debts, and its high-profile CEO, Mikhail Khodorkovsky, imprisoned for fraud. Since then, Western firms have been reticent about reinvesting significantly in companies that may once again be stripped of their assets by retroactive Russian legislation.

In addition to its renationalisation programme, Russia outpositioned Western efforts to encourage oil and gas source diversification in Central Asia, primarily by signing up former Soviet states to use Russian infrastructure for transit purposes. This began with the Caspian Pipeline Consortium (CPC) that took an export route from Kazakhstan to the Black Sea. The CPC competed directly with the Baku–Tbilisi–Ceyhan (BTC) pipeline owned by BP, designed to get oil to Turkey without transiting Russia. By 2005 Russia had also diversified its gas network away from Europe by announcing the 'Blue Stream 2' pipeline agreement with Turkey to take Russian gas as far away as Israel. Two years after that, in 2007, it was seeking to rival the Nabucco pipeline (which bypassed Russia) after signing a series of agreements to create the 'South Stream' pipeline that would transport gas to Italy and Austria by 2015.

The second part of Russian energy strategy has been to ensure it is a framework partner in all deals with CIS member-states that are often bilateral, designed to produce relative gains, and are undertaken outside institutional mechanisms. This rent-seeking behaviour has been ongoing at least since the early days of the Putin presidency. An agreement in 2003 between Russia and Turkmenistan, for instance, saw Russian companies secure the rights to all the gas produced by Turkmenistan for 25 years.[48] Likewise, the Russian decision in 2005 to abandon gas subsidies for former communist states helped boost Gazprom's profits. Russia also offered states unable to accommodate price jumps of up to 68 per cent annually[49] the option of paying for gas by selling off their

---

[48] V. Socor, 'Russia resumes gas imports from Turkmenistan', *Asia Times Online*, 6 January (2010). Available at www.atimes.com/atimes/Central_Asia/LA06Ag02.html

[49] R.B. Anders and M. Kofman, 'European energy security: reducing volatility of Ukraine–Russia natural gas pricing disputes', *Strategic Forum*, Institute for National Strategic Studies (Washington, VA: National Defence University, 2011).

domestic pipeline networks. In this way, Gazprom initially secured a controlling stake in the Belarus pipeline operator, Beltransgas. Ukraine, which resisted entreaties to sell off its pipeline networks, instead negotiated a deal to exclude its pipelines from bilateral gas agreements and obtain heavy discounts on gas bought from Russia. For its part, Moscow received highly preferential transit tariffs for gas destined to Europe, which increased by some 65 per cent in 2010.[50] To further increase pressure on Kiev, in early 2009 Gazprom also secured a memorandum of understanding with the Azerbaijani company SOCAR, allowing it to bypass intermediary transport businesses, and forcing Ukrainian consumers back to reliance on gas resold by Gazprom.[51]

However, many deals have also fallen through. Gazprom's 2009 offer of no-interest loans to Turkmenistan in order to fund joint energy infrastructure projects totalling around US$5 billion was cancelled as the global financial crisis began to chip away at Gazprom's profits. And although pursuing a unified energy market through EurAsEc became a priority after 2008, with increased ties between its members and the PRC, little progress was made on tariff harmonisation or freedom of movement for labour, beyond agreements already made by the framework members in Central Asia and the Russian Federation. EurAsEc's attempts to increase energy efficiency – the former USSR is the most energy-intensive economic sector in the world – have also amounted to little due to the prohibitively high cost of infrastructure conversion.

Finally, Russia has attempted to corner the market for gas in the strategically important subregion of Central Asia. In a deliberate effort to court Kazakhstan and Uzbekistan, Moscow vowed to 'pay European prices' for Central Asian gas. The move was consistent with Russia's Energy Security Strategy of 2003, which stipulated that Russia should rely on Central Asian gas until technological advancements made extraction from Siberia more feasible. It also helped to avert a buyer's market, which would have allowed European companies to goad Russian and Central Asian suppliers into a bidding war for supply contracts. But in 2009 Russian GDP fell roughly 8 per cent as a result of the global financial crisis.[52] This, coupled to lower global gas prices and the decline

[50] See D. Bochkarev, 'European gas prices: implications of Gazprom's strategic engagement with Central Asia', *Pipeline and Gas Journal* 236 (June 2009), 15–22.
[51] See the company's press release: Gazprom, 'Gazprom and SOCAR sign agreement on Azerbaijani gas purchase and sale terms', 29 June (2009). Available at www.gazprom.com/press/news/2009/june/article66713
[52] See the roundtable with Aslund et al., 'Russia's response to the Financial Crisis', Carnegie Endowment for International Peace, 4 May (2010). Available at www.carnegieendowment.org/events/?fa=eventDetail&id=2895

in the value of the ruble, meant that the high watermark amount of US$340 per cubic metre of gas offered by Gazprom to Kazakhstan, Uzbekistan and Turkmenistan was unsustainable. This was especially the case since it was more than double the average price of US$150 per cubic metre that it had previously paid.[53] Late in 2009 Russia declined to buy any gas from Turkmenistan, forcing it not only to look for new customers, but also to keep paying Russia rents for pipeline access.

Russian primacy constrained: political, economic and military-security dimensions

The above analysis demonstrates that whilst Russia retains a position of primacy in the regional security order comprising the territory of the former USSR, this does not equate to the ability to act entirely as it desires. Even Russia's closest CIS partners, those comfortable in choosing the full package of integration via membership in the CSTO and EurAsEc, have refused to accept being relegated to mere Russian satrapies. Indeed, they have had regular disagreements with the Kremlin. The lesson here is that Russia enjoys a privileged position in the former Soviet space, but its neighbours have gone to some lengths to ensure a degree of independence. Moreover, there is evidence that even though Russian power has expanded after the calamitous decade of the 1990s, its ability to dictate regional order is being diminished. Indeed, despite public triumphalism at the West's inaction over its war with Georgia, since 2008 Moscow has been cautious in assuming it has a free hand on the territory of the former USSR.

In fact, one could make the argument that Russian regional primacy is significantly constrained by a range of external actors in the political, military and economic spheres. In military-security affairs, NATO represents the dominant check against Russian power. Moscow has found it difficult to renegotiate NATO's position as a building block of European security, given that many of its members still regard Russia as a threat. Moreover, on the political and economic level, both the SCO and the EU act as implicit constraints on Russian primacy. It is true that the SCO is the framework organisation reflecting the global security aspirations of Russia and the PRC, primarily geared around assisting the emergence of a multipolar world order. On this issue the two have found significant common ground, even though the power disparity between NATO and the SCO makes any attempt at hard balancing an asymmetrical prospect for the time being. But while the

---

[53] Bochkarev, 'European gas prices', p. 18.

SCO symbolises the significant warming in the relationship between Moscow and Beijing, it also serves as an instrument of Chinese power in the Far East and Central Asia. It does so in two ways: as a check against Russia; and as a vehicle for the entrée of Chinese interests into the regional security order. Already the SCO has facilitated Chinese business opportunities in laying the groundwork for enhanced bilateral relationships, especially with Kazakhstan and Uzbekistan.

To Russia's west, the EU may not be an entirely cohesive supra-national actor, but it has nonetheless had an effect on the security order in the former USSR. It has done so by providing an aspirational alternative to membership in a Russian-led regional order. Like the SCO, the EU has paved the way for bilateral deals with individual states. Unlike the SCO, it has also attempted to project an alternative set of values that contrast with the primacy of state sovereignty favoured by Moscow and Beijing. And although its condemnations of human rights abuses during conflicts in the former USSR have been generally ineffectual, its 'soft power' approach has at least added to the expectation that states participating in conflict should justify their actions with respect to broad international norms and standards of behaviour.

Political and economic constrainment: the SCO and the EU

The SCO is effectively a vehicle for bilateral diplomacy between Russia and the PRC conducted at the multilateral level. Yet it also reveals divergent agendas that have effectively reduced Russia's strategic options. Russia has seen the SCO primarily as a way to deepen security cooperation, emphasising the importance of joint military exercises. Its 'Peace Mission' manoeuvres in 2005 and 2007 (masquerading as counter-terrorism cooperation) reflected increasingly large-scale military cooperation. Russia has also viewed the SCO as a potential venue for negotiating arms sales, and both Russia and the PRC have used the organisation to press the international community to respect long-established principles of state sovereignty.

The PRC, on the other hand, has sought to turn the SCO into a framework for economic cooperation, seeing an opportunity to embed itself in the energy sector after Putin's campaign against Yukos saw Western firms largely ejected. This, in itself, does not run contrary to Russian interests. But Moscow initially resisted Beijing's urgings to develop a common market, even though it was prepared to accept an 'energy club' amongst its members. This was due to the concern that the introduction of the PRC on a level playing field in Central Asian markets could crowd Russia out, especially given that the volume of trade between the PRC and Central Asian states had tripled between 2002 and 2007.[54] This saw increased activity by Chinese state-owned enterprises in Central Asian energy businesses. In particular, Chinese investment in Kazakhstan – as a potential competitor to Russia – had risen to prominence as early as 1997, when the China National Petroleum Corporation (CNPC) bought a 60 per cent stake in the Kazakh company controlling the Aktobe oil fields. In 2007 the CNPC increased its share to 85 per cent.[55]

In 2009, with the global financial crisis beginning to bite, Russia had no option but to acquiesce in the face of Chinese offers to inject capital into its own energy sector, and Medvedev agreed to a joint development plan for the Russian Far East. Whilst Moscow had made repeated statements about the vital importance of building energy infrastructure in Siberia and the Far East, projects to accomplish this were lagging well behind schedule, and had fallen prey to chronic corruption. The agreement, which was essentially a 'loans for oil' deal that saw Chinese capital flowing into the Central Asian states, was accompanied by a Chinese investment drive in core Russian energy producers. It acquired a controlling stake in Russian companies with licences to develop Siberian oil fields, and in 2010 announced that it would increase its investment in the Russian economy by 600 per cent over four years.[56]

The PRC's success in nudging the SCO toward an economic organisation has significant political implications for Russia. According to one analyst, the Central Asian nations have increasingly begun to follow the PRC's lead rather than Russia's.[57] This is because Chinese investment allows Central Asian states to adopt 'multi-vector' foreign economic policies: to pick and choose between Russian and Chinese investment, and play one nation off against the other. By the same token, the PRC also has the ability to choose where it invests in the Far East and Central Asia. This gives it strategic influence over the former Soviet space as well as direct influence over Russia itself through its large-scale investments in the Russian energy sector. This means that through the SCO Russia needs the PRC more than the PRC needs Russia, and by signing up to joint development of the Far East it has committed itself to

[54] S. Ibraimov, 'China–Central Asia trade relations: economic and social patterns', *China and Eurasia Forum Quarterly* 7 (2009), 47–59.
[55] China National Petroleum Corporation (CNPC), 'CNPC in Kazakhstan' (n.d.). Available at www.cnpc.com.cn/eng/cnpcworldwide/euro-asia/kazakhstan
[56] 'China, Russia to enhance mutual investment', *China Daily*, 27 March (2009). Available at www.chinadaily.com.cn/china/2009–03/27/content_7625216.htm
[57] S. Blank, 'Towards a new Chinese order in Asia', p. 15.

providing long-term supply to its Asian ally.[58] This in turn helps guard against the prospect of Moscow drifting to the West and becoming captured by the EU's orbit.

Although it has deliberately distanced itself from wars in the former USSR, preferring instead to call for the OSCE to have a greater oversight role in monitoring and mediation, the EU itself has nonetheless had an impact on regional security affairs. This has been most notable through its European Neighbourhood Policy (ENP). Designed to coordinate the EU's ten Partnership and Cooperation Agreements (PCAs) with individual states in Eastern Europe and Eurasia,[59] and lay a cross-pillar basis for potential accession agreements in later years, the ENP notionally offered 'everything but institutions' to former Soviet states. In doing so it also served the objective of creating concentric circles of multilateral cooperation outlined in the first European Security Strategy of 2003. Consisting of a number of action plans spelling out what those seeking closer access to the single market must do in exchange for deeper engagement, the ENP is more than just a 'good neighbour' policy. As Karen E. Smith has noted, it contains an emphasis on political issues – especially human rights and democracy – as well as a significant dose of EU self-interest.[60] This includes, for instance, a stipulation that Ukraine should seek to deepen cooperation with the EU on long-range air transport (a missing link in the European Defence and Security Policy), as well as an insistence that Moldova and Ukraine conduct readmission agreements with the EU.[61] This puts the responsibility on 'outsider' states to readmit any foreign nationals expelled from the EU, even if those nationals had only crossed the territory of the state in question while en route to the Schengen area.

A further function of the ENP is that it has shifted the emphasis of the EU's dealings with states in the former USSR away from broad-based multilateralism. Instead, it encourages deepening bilateral ties, especially with aspirant members.[62] Rather than join the ENP, Russia has insisted on 'equal partnership' with the EU. Progress on this front has been slow, with little concrete action on the 2005 agreement conducted in Moscow for a roadmap to implement the four common EU–Russia

[58] See R. Maksutov, 'The Shanghai Cooperation Organisation: A Central Asian perspective', SIPRI Project Paper, August (2006). Available at www.sipri.org/contents/worldsec/Ruslan.SCO.pdf/download

[59] The ten are Armenia, Azerbaijan, Georgia, Kazakhstan, Kyrgyzstan, Moldova, Russia, Ukraine, Uzbekistan and Tajikistan.

[60] K.E. Smith, 'The outsiders: the European Neighbourhood Policy', *International Affairs* 81 (2005), pp. 757–73.

[61] Ibid., p. 763.   [62] Ibid.

spaces of economics; freedom, security and justice; external security; and research, education and culture. At the press conference following the 2007 Samara summit between EU leaders and Russia, Putin's aide, Sergei Yastrzhembsky, was unable to play down the rift that had emerged between Brussels and Moscow over Russian decisions to ban Polish food, launch an oil embargo against Lithuania, and conduct negotiations with Moldova on Trans-Dniester outside the '5+2' consultative processes.[63] In 2009, when Russia's energy minister, Sergei Shmatko, complained that Russia was being shut out of negotiations on the extension of Ukrainian gas pipelines, Putin threatened that Russia would 'review the fundamentals' of its relationship with the EU if its interests were ignored.[64]

The EU's role in the former USSR has thus not reflected an ability to directly exert pressure on Russia. In fact, its efforts to do so have been largely symbolic. They have included the tokenistic suspension of Russian participation in the Council of Europe over its conduct of the war in Chechnya. In addition the EU decided in 2008 to delay negotiations over a new PCA until Moscow had implemented all six conditions of the Sarkozy ceasefire plan following its war with Georgia. In the event the negotiations went ahead anyway in November that year, with Lithuania the only nation in the twenty-seven-member bloc voting against their resumption. More recent developments, such as the 2010 Meseberg Initiative between Medvedev and Angela Merkel for a Russia–EU Commission on Foreign Policy have been similarly symbolic, with no clear purpose or binding effect on either party. Yet where the EU has been a significant actor is in the implicit threat that it will negotiate deeper economic and political agreements with those states that Russia considers lie within in its sphere of geopolitical interest. And while the EU has been criticised as weak or ineffectual in its rapid shifts from condemning Russia to 'business as usual', it nonetheless has a powerful carrot in the form of its accession agreements, which are more attractive to Georgia, Ukraine and Moldova than a Europe managed by an EU–Russia duopoly. In this context Russia may be able to ignore small-scale rival organisations such as GUAM, but only if its members remain outside the EU itself.

---

[63] The 5+2 format consists of Moldova, Trans-Dniester, Russia, Ukraine and the OSCE as framework participants, while the EU and United States are observers. See A. Reitman, 'EU and Russia tackle thorny issues at Samara summit', *EU Observer*, 18 May (2005). Available at http://euobserver.com/9/24088

[64] 'Russian PM threatens to review relations with EU', *RIA Novosti*, 23 March (2009). Available at http://en.rian.ru/russia/20090323/120699757.html

Military-security constrainment

The military-security sphere is the most obvious arena in which Russian regional primacy is constrained. Chief amongst these barriers is the NATO alliance. Russian attitudes towards NATO expansion have been well documented, but when he was foreign minister in the mid-1990s Yevgeni Primakov summed up Moscow's position with a neat counterfactual.[65] Primakov asked his audience to imagine that the Cold War had ended with the USSR victorious, and Germany unified under a communist banner. Suppose, said Primakov, the USSR promised an anxious United States that while it was not ready for Washington to come into the Warsaw Pact, it had no intention of expanding its alliance systems. Then it admitted Germany, France and Italy into the organisation, and began talking openly of the possibility of Mexico and Canada joining. Surely, Primakov asked, the United States would feel as though it was being contained under similar circumstances?

The NATO expansion issue has been used for domestic political purposes in Russia, especially during the interventions in Bosnia, and then in Kosovo during 1999. Political parties across the spectrum from the far right to the pragmatic liberal Yabloko movement all condemned the enlargement of a military-security organisation to Russia's borders. There was consensus on the need for firm Western recognition of a Russian sphere of influence in the former Soviet space and in Eastern Europe as well. Thus, Russia's participation in the various dialogue forums launched by NATO, such as the PfP programme and the NATO–Russia Council, has been lacklustre. This is because of Russia's (arguably legitimate) concerns that it was being offered second-class NATO membership, with a voice in NATO affairs but no veto power over its decisions. In formal documents on foreign and security policy Russia has consistently expressed its opposition to NATO, noting in the 1993 Foreign Policy and 1996 Security Concepts that NATO expansion was a threat to Russian *interests*. Its tone became more blunt in the 1998 Military Doctrine, which identified NATO as a threat to Russian *security*. Moscow has reiterated this position in more recent policy strategies, as well as in Medvedev's dramatic statement of Russian resurgence at the Munich Security Conference in 2008, which prompted some excitable commentators to raise the spectre of a new Cold War.[66]

---

[65] Y. Primakov, 'Russia, the West and NATO', *Obschaya gazeta* 37, 22–7 September (1996).

[66] This was evident in the 2000 Foreign Policy Concept, the 2005 update to the Military Doctrine, and the new Foreign Policy Concept and National Security Strategy of 2008.

Russia has also sought to break out of the idea that the end of the Cold War simply shifted the boundaries of bipolarity eastwards by proposing a new security architecture. Soon after the collapse of the USSR, the Russian Ministry of Foreign Affairs under Andrei Kozyrev championed a reconstructed Conference on Security and Cooperation in Europe as the best way to deepen security cooperation and ensure full implementation of the CFE Treaty. However, the West was disinclined to see what was essentially a talking shop transformed into the premier organisation for the management of European security affairs. The Visegrad Three (Poland, Hungary and the Czech Republic), which were invited to join NATO in 1997, still clearly saw Russia as a threat, and sought NATO membership as a means of collective defence. Worries about Russian intentions amongst the Visegrad states did not abate after they joined NATO, and there was particular public concern about the Bush Jnr administration's controversial plan – later cancelled by Barack Obama – to create ten interceptor and monitoring stations on Polish and Czech soil as part of its NMD programme.

Following the war in Iraq, which revealed deep fissures in what was previously assumed to be a strong and stable Western alliance, Russia made fresh attempts to exploit Western discord by articulating a less NATO-centric vision for European security. Initially, under Putin, Russian proposals consisted of a vague suggestion that the Helsinki Process should be revived. Issues of common interest, including counter-terrorism and non-proliferation, would be placed into a 'basket' of cooperation. Energy security was mooted as a theme for a second basket, while issues of disagreement – like human rights – would effectively be quarantined in another. Yet the suggestion came on the heels of the gas wars with Ukraine, a unilateral Russian moratorium on participation in the force limits imposed by the CFE Treaty, trenchant Russian criticism of US foreign and security policy, and a concerted push by Moscow to have US forces evicted from the Central Asian bases it had helped Washington gain access to after 9/11. Hence it is little wonder that Putin's proposal received little serious attention.

Subsequent Russian proposals, announced by Medvedev, were more detailed. In 2008 he suggested a new EST as a diplomatic catalyst for improving Russo-Western dialogue.[67] Yet the response from the West was similarly muted, with various EU leaders merely expressing polite support for new ideas. The proposal received no response at all from the United States until Secretary of State Hillary Clinton rejected the notion outright in February 2010. Instead, Clinton argued that

---

[67] For Russia's draft text of the treaty, see http://eng.kremlin.ru/news/275

good faith negotiations between Russia and NATO were necessary to strengthen stability in the former USSR, and stated that the United States saw no reason to replace existing arrangements for European security. Russia's ambassador to NATO, Dmitri Rogozhin, retorted that Clinton's position 'sounded like a belch of the Cold War', and was particularly critical of what he regarded as 'cosmetic' alterations to the OSCE.[68] In fact, there was some truth to Rogozhin's frustrations. Given that its observers have been denied access to many sites of conflict on the territory of the former USSR, the OSCE has become little more than an advocacy network for human security issues rather than a robust vehicle for closer Russo-Western ties.

Despite 'resetting' relations with Russia, negotiating the New Start Agreement on strategic nuclear forces, and opening the door for potential US-Russian cooperation, the Obama administration has been reluctant to wind back an increasingly troubled NATO. Soon after taking office Obama found out first hand that the divisions amongst alliance partners ran deeper than simple hostility towards his predecessor, when he toured NATO capitals to call for increased burden-sharing from Washington's allies in Afghanistan. The response was disappointing, especially from Germany, which refused to extend its commitment. Yet for the United States as well as the UK a strong NATO is the bedrock of Euro-Atlantic security. It keeps the United States engaged in Europe as a balancer, and it is not unreasonable to suggest that 'soft power Europe' has been made possible by continued US willingness to bear the responsibility for hard power security commitments.

More importantly, the presence of NATO constrains Russian primacy in the former Soviet space considerably. For other states in the former USSR, NATO membership remains an important goal to strive for. It brings with it the binding commitment of assistance under Article 5 of the NATO Charter, and it is still seen by Georgia and Ukraine as a stepping stone to EU membership. After the 2008 war with Georgia, Russian foreign minister Sergei Lavrov claimed in an interview with *Echo Moskvy* that Russia would 'do everything possible to prevent the accession of Ukraine and Georgia to NATO'. Lavrov went on to note that this would lead to the 'worsening of relations with the alliance, its leading member states and our neighbours'.[69]

---

[68] 'Hilary Clinton's invitation to Russia sounds like a belch of the Cold War', *Pravda*, 24 February (2010). Available at http://english.pravda.ru/world/americas/24–02–2010/112349-russia_nato-0

[69] 'Moscow to prevent Ukraine's, Georgia's NATO accession', *RIA Novosti*, 8 April (2010). Available at http://en.rian.ru/russia/20080408/104105506.html

Conclusions: the former USSR as a region of constrained Russian primacy

The security order in the former USSR is best characterised as a region of increasingly constrained Russian primacy. It is clearly not a centred regional security complex, or a closed system of Russian hegemony. Political and military-security instruments have certainly been employed by Moscow since the collapse of the USSR to exert some degree of control. The CIS and the CSTO are asymmetrical organisations, hence they primarily reflect Russian preferences rather than the consensual agreement of all participants. They have also not achieved objectives that they profess to be fundamentally concerned with. Key issues such as a free trade zone and a customs union await resolution by the CIS, and it is not surprising that it is frequently referred to as the place where 'everyone talks but nothing happens'. For its part, the CSTO is still largely a paper tiger. It has a rapid reaction force that not all members participate in, divides its area of oversight into three separate zones to accommodate the wide space and diverse nations it encompasses, and efforts by Russia to use it for instrumental purposes, especially over recognition of South Ossetian and Abkhazian independence, have come to naught.

But, paradoxically, the weakness of the CIS and the CSTO has itself assisted Russian attempts to construct a loose position of primacy in the regional security order. It has not pushed too hard for formal political or economic integration, and it has not sought to impose CSTO membership on those who do not want to participate. Indeed, the foreign policy independence of Ukraine, Georgia, Azerbaijan and Moldova has been generally tolerated (if grudgingly) by Moscow. But the willingness of even its closest allies in Central Asia and Belarus to spurn it indicates that Russian primacy over the regional security order is not unquestioned. As a result, Russia's main mechanisms for control have been economic, and thus far it has not shown that it is constrained by interdependence. Instead, its energy policy has all the hallmarks of realpolitik.

This, however, may be changing. The emergence of the PRC as a major player in the Central Asian economic space represents a challenge for Russian economic policy in the same way that it provides new options for Kazakhstan, Uzbekistan, Tajikistan and Turkmenistan. To its West, Russian ambitions remain checked by a NATO alliance that Moscow has been unable to persuade European and North American members to abandon, in favour of a new and broader security arrangement.

Understanding the constrained nature of Russian primacy has important implications when evaluating the conflicts that have occurred in the former Soviet space. The future of the security order in the former USSR is likely to hinge on the outcome of complex struggles for power in which a variety of subnational, international and institutional actors are locked in competition over resources, territory, influence and ideas. In this context, it is tempting to conclude that the status quo – local Russian dominance constrained by external political and economic forces to the west and east – may be preferable to either a power transition that causes Russian primacy to fragment, or a strengthening of Moscow's ability to dominate the former USSR. But the weak stability at the macro-level of interstate interaction that has defined the ex-Soviet space since 1991 appears tenuous at best.

4   Great powers and small wars in the Caucasus

Richard Sakwa

In this chapter I outline a model for understanding Russian and international politics against the background of conflicts in the Caucasus, beginning with Russia's internal wars in Chechnya and culminating in the interstate five-day Russo-Georgian war. Both conflicts exposed an impasse at the global and regional levels, and reflected the fact that the international political order established after the disintegration of the Soviet bloc between 1989 and 1991 had failed to deliver a viable and inclusive international system of security and development. This has been most apparent in the Caucasus, which has become the epicentre of a new series of confrontations.

As I argue in this chapter, two of these confrontations are crucial. The first is the clash between two principles of authority within the Russian state itself: between the prerogative and the constitutional state. The war in Chechnya, the longest and arguably the most bitter conflict on the territory of the former USSR, has now ended in some sort of resolution based on a despotic regime in a clientelistic relationship with Moscow, entrenching the powers of the arbitrary state in the Caucasus, and reinforcing arbitrariness in the Russian political system as a whole. In particular, the Chechen war(s) from 1994 to 2008 intensified the emergence of a Russian 'dual state', in which the state as a normative/legal entity increasingly gave way to the prerogative state on issues of vital interest, such as territorial integrity and access to resources.

The second confrontation occurred when an expanding Western hegemony encountered a rival system in the Caucasus with hegemonic aspirations of its own. These two conflict systems – the Russian and the global, each with its own dynamics – overlap and interact in a region where rival imperial systems have historically fought for pre-eminence. Geopolitical rivalry exacerbates regional conflicts, and expectations that great powers and regional organisations would act as 'honest brokers' has only partially been fulfilled. And whilst a variety of transnational forces may have contributed toward the emergence of so-called 'new' wars in Chechnya, any new type of peace in the Caucasus will be determined by continuing developments in Russian domestic politics, which in turn are a response to changing power relations in the international system. The conflicts within and between Russia and outside powers are linked, but the nature of this relationship remains contested.

War, peace and state building in the former USSR

The character of war is constantly changing, and so too is the nature of state building. The shifting pattern of international interactions modifies the context in which wars are fought. States have never developed in isolation: indeed, they are shaped by their relations with others. It is when the two processes come together that both war and state building become part of a single process determining the fate of nations and the geopolitical contours of an era. In the Russian case, the first war in Chechnya between 1994 and 1996 revealed the *fragility* of the whole state system and its permeability to social corruption, quite apart from its demonstrable lack of coherence. The second war, however, from 1999 to its formal conclusion a decade later, and the withdrawal of the bulk of Russian regular forces, was characterised by the *restoration* of Russian state capacity, although in highly ambivalent forms. By the time of the war with Georgia over South Ossetia and Abkhazia in 2008 internal reconstitution began to spill over, or so it appeared to many observers, into greater assertiveness abroad.

While this narrative of successive stages of Russian state weakness, consolidation and then external expansiveness conveys part of the truth, it leaves out of account the external context: the evolving character of international politics. Paradoxically, the moment of greatest Russian weakness in the 1990s was accompanied by the greater readiness of the international community to accept that country as a partner. But as the trajectory of Russia consolidation rose, the ability of Russia and the West to find an adequate institutional and political form to regularise their relationship entered a declining curve. The two movements are related and were evident in the Russo-Georgian war of 2008, which marked a turning point in Russian state development and its international stance. Not only did Russia – for the first time since the disintegration of the USSR in 1991 – engage in interstate conflict, but the war also exposed the underlying logic of confrontation between the former Cold War protagonists.

The asymmetrical end of the Cold War and the coming of the cold peace

The twentieth century, according to a powerful study by Alain Badiou, 'unfolded *under the paradigm of war*' (italics in original throughout), with the endless invocation of the view that only war could put an end to war.[1] This was the case during the 'interwar' period of 1918–39, in which peace was effectively the same as war. The much-heralded 'reset' in the relationship between Russia and the US, prompted by the Obama administration in 2009, has not altered this fact. Instead, we once again find ourselves in a type of interwar period in the former USSR of no war and no peace, that is nonetheless pregnant with renewed conflict. At the height of the post-war peace in 1968 Anatol Rapoport had argued that 'war seems to have disappeared as a major item on the agenda of *European* politics. Europe seems to have unlearned the lessons taught by Machiavelli and Clausewitz.'[2] This may well have been true during the Cold War, but instead a harsh competitive dynamic has emerged in the post-Cold War era. War is thus back on the agenda as the accompaniment to state building in the Balkans and the Caucasus.

Mikhail Gorbachev, who had done so much to transcend the logic of bloc politics during perestroika (1985–91), stressed that 'new political thinking' in the USSR had put an end to the bipolar world order, noting that 'the Cold War was contrary to the interests of humanity'.[3] However, he was well aware that on its own, 'the abrogation of ideological conflict did not lead automatically to a general, definitive peace'.[4] Since then, new threats have emerged and old ones have returned. As Gorbachev put it, 'the Cold War froze numerous geopolitical, national, and ethnic conflicts, not all of which were connected to the Cold War itself [...]. The Cold War quasi-stability created a reassuring impression that the post-conflict world order was predictable.'[5] In his view the end of the Cold War did not equate to more stability. Today, he argued, 'many people are beginning to look on total Westernisation as they once did on the threat of total, forcible communalisation [sic]'.[6] The reason for this, according to Gorbachev, was that the West 'is incapable of dealing in a reasonable way with the results of the new thinking that freed the world from bloc politics and total confrontation'.[7] He lamented the

---

[1] A. Badiou, *The Century*, trans. A. Toscano (Cambridge: Polity, 2007), p. 34.
[2] A. Rapoport (ed.), 'Introduction', in C. von Clausewitz, *On War* (London: Penguin, 1968 [1832]), p. 51.
[3] M. Gorbachev and D. Ikeda, *Moral lessons of the twentieth century: Gorbachev and Ikeda on Buddhism and Communism* (London: I.B. Tauris, 2005), p. 57.
[4] Ibid.   [5] Ibid.   [6] Ibid.   [7] Ibid.

fact that the fruits of the new thinking were 'withering away before our eyes'.[8] Even though Russia had 'rushed towards the West with open arms and the best possible will', the West had not reciprocated.[9] It had been incapable of 'working out either a new doctrine of collective security or a new ideology of peaceful development. Today the fate of the world is in the hands of institutes [sic] formed during the Cold War.'[10] The European process was sacrificed, in his view, to the eastward expansion of NATO, and the 'possible untoward consequences of this mechanistic approach to the problem of European and global security are overlooked'.[11]

A customary view about the end of the Cold War is that Western pressure forced the USSR to launch its reforms during perestroika, and that in some way Western powers 'won' the Cold War. This reflects a totally inappropriate triumphalism. As a 'Reaganite' reading of post-Cold War international history this has had malignant consequences. Soviet reforms were launched as a response to domestic developments and normative concerns, and outside powers were at best marginal in the process.[12] The West did, however, miss the opportunity to build a lasting relationship of trust with Russia at the end of the Cold War from 1988 to 1992, failing to offer sufficient intelligent economic and moral assistance and support, and instead began the process of NATO enlargement and other actions to isolate Russia. The asymmetrical end of the Cold War, in which one side claims victory that the other side sees as a common achievement, generates tensions in the form of a 'cold peace', which assumes a traditional geopolitical form.[13]

This is also reflected in the contemporary institutional makeup of European and Eurasian security politics. The institutions that had embodied the Cold War in the West, primarily NATO, and those that had developed in its shadow, such as the EU and the Council of Europe, prospered and expanded their reach in the post-Cold War era. After 1989–91 they claimed a hegemonic position in Europe, couching their particularistic interests in universal terms that invoked democracy, law and human rights in more or less equal measure. On the 'other side of the barricades', however, the Soviet-sponsored structures of the Cold War were swiftly abandoned. These included the Warsaw Treaty Organisation (the Warsaw Pact) and the Council for Mutual Economic

---

[8] Ibid.   [9] Ibid.   [10] Ibid.   [11] Ibid.

[12] A. Brown, *The Gorbachev factor* (Oxford University Press, 1996), chapter 7; A. Brown, 'Perestroika and the end of the Cold War', *Cold War History* 7 (February 2007), 1–17.

[13] R. Sakwa, '"New Cold War" or "twenty years' crisis?" Russia and international politics', *International Affairs* 84 (2008), 241–67.

Assistance (COMECON), and their pretensions to some sort of hegemonic status. The OSCE was a common construct of all European
states (plus the United States and Canada). For that reason, much hope
was placed on the Vienna follow-up conference during perestroika, but
this turned out to be less universal than Russia had hoped. The new
thinking in foreign affairs, developed by Gorbachev and his reformers,
had been premised on the idea that the European system would be able
to combine unity through security with a diversity of regime types,
but this fundamental premise of the new political thinking proved
unfounded. As Russia found itself in a position of structural weakness during the 1990s, pursuing an effectively reactive foreign policy
agenda, it encountered an expanded and exclusionary NATO and EU
rather than a broad and inclusionary system of cooperation.

This experience came to influence both Putin and Medvedev after
the turn of the century. Russia's shift to become a proclaimed agenda
setter in the first decade of this century was accompanied by greater
economic nationalism. Russia was accused of leveraging its energy
resources in a way that other countries do not, as a reflection of great
power self-identity. This is despite the fact that the use of economic
strength as an instrument of great power ambition has certainly not
been lacking elsewhere. Russia is more than Saudi Arabia with nuclear
weapons and great power ambitions. It seeks full membership in the
international community, but on its own terms. The fundamental question is whether these terms were acceptable to others.

Russian state building and international behaviour are closely linked,
but so are they in other states. Sheldon Wolin notes the process of 'anti-
communism as mimesis: the character of the enemy supplied the norm
for the power demands that the democratic defender of the free world
chose to impose on itself'.[14] A 'superpower' is defined by Wolin 'as an
imaginary of power that emerges from defeat unchastened, more imperi-
ous than ever'.[15] The 'war' in the abstract has been declared, while the
reality of great power rivalry is occluded.[16] From this perspective war
is inevitable: the only question is the form in which the conflict will
become manifest. Thus, the end of the Cold War only prepared the way
for a new era of conflict. The Russo-Georgian war in 2008 suggested
that the mimetic character of the cold peace was turning into something akin to the great power confrontations of the pre-Cold War era.
But here there is an important difference: today, Russia must contend

---

[14] Cf. S. Wolin, *Democracy incorporated: managed democracy and the spectre of inverted
totalitarianism* (Princeton University Press, 2008), p. 37.
[15] Ibid.   [16] Ibid.

also with factors relating to globalisation, with important dynamics of their own.

Globalisation and (new?) war: Russia and the Caucasus

If war is back on the agenda, both in the post-Soviet space and more broadly between major powers, it is necessary to understand the nature of contemporary conflict. War was certainly constitutive of the twentieth century too, but it has changed over time. Does globalisation transform the nature of warfare? This certainly is the argument of Mary Kaldor, who insists that 'the new wars have to be seen in the context of the process of globalisation', and by globalisation she means 'the intensification of global interconnectedness'.[17] The definition of a new war, however, is less clear. According to Kaldor it 'brings together diffuse conflicts, low intensity struggles, the privatisation of violence and the American-style revolution in military affairs', based above all on the application of digital technologies to military equipment and techniques.[18] A key characteristic is the interpenetration of domestic and international agencies, including a whole raft of non-governmental agencies, accompanied by the erosion of the state's alleged monopoly on organised violence. Also important are new economics, and new objectives in which identity politics becomes more salient.

However, all of this is highly contentious. In fact, it could be argued that the major novelty is the changed *rationale* for state action, not the *behaviour* or role of sub-state actor. Thus the 'war on terror' can be seen to be the logical outcome of the ideology of globalisation, elevating a local conflict into a global crusade while delegitimating various forms of struggle against the hegemony of the dominant powers. The concept of globalisation itself has been used instrumentally, as a way of embedding hegemony in an unchallengeable discourse that takes on mythic – and uncontestable – dimensions. The notion of 'war' in this context is indeed redefined, but not in the way suggested by Kaldor. War is organised violence, but the military side is only one aspect of a broader conflict involving ethnic mobilisation, economic resources and physical coercion of various types. This is accompanied by broader security policy focusing on pre-emptive strategies. The purpose of warfare is to enhance the power of the state, embedded in a narrative about globalisation that reduces belief in the efficacy of its power. Institutionalised globalisation thus also makes state building harder, depriving a state of the autonomous capacity to exert decision-making functions over

---

[17] M. Kaldor, *New and old wars*, p. 3.   [18] Ibid.

swaths of the domestic economy. At the same time, the ideology of humanitarian intervention raises the sword of Damocles over recalcitrant states.

The result of this is that war has become internalised into the operative codes of society. This is more than the dominance of the 'military-industrial complex' and even deeper than the reflexive confrontation of the Cold War. A profound militarism became apparent in the crusader mentality revealed by the 'war on terror', which changed to 'the long war' in the late Bush Jnr years. This was a war without end, formless and pervasive, but constitutive of Anglo-American societies and their allies. The EU geared up to supplement its much-heralded 'soft power' with strengthened disciplinary techniques, encouraged by the revanchist sentiments of its post-communist members.[19] This militancy is diffuse but generates enemies as required. Russia's resistance to incorporation as a subaltern element of the new hegemony singled it out as a potential enemy. The structures that fought the Cold War have therefore generated a behavioural pattern that reproduces axiological contestation at the global level.

A key characteristic of the new wars taking place with the Caucasus as the battleground is that they are asymmetrical. The blurring of the boundary between combatants and 'civilians' and the generalisation of warfare to encompass the whole population has intensified, and marks a move away from the era of 'high warfare' in the modern age. This, of course, was a feature of the Thirty Years War, and various guerrilla and liberation struggles. The asymmetrical wars of third world insurgencies also mobilised civilian populations. States have never enjoyed a total monopoly on violence, and in areas such as the Caucasus, where modern forms of statehood are limited, the quality of 'civilianness' remains weakly defined.

Philip Bobbitt agrees with Kaldor that a new type of war is emerging, but he interprets this in a very different way. For him 'the long war' of the twentieth century, 1914–90, focused on industrial, national and positional enhancement, accompanied by various anarchist, national-liberation and terrorist movements. In contrast, the wars of the

---

[19] See, for example, P. Demes et al., *Why the Obama administration should not take Central and Eastern Europe for granted*, Policy Brief, The German Marshall Fund of the United States, 13 June (2009); and its accompanying 'Open letter to the Obama Administration from Central and Eastern Europe', signed by the original authors plus a number of politicians, including Valdas Adamkus, Alexander Kwasniewski, Vaclaw Havel and Lech Walesa: Radio Free Europe/Radio Liberty (RFE/RL), 16 July (2009), available at www.rferl.org/content/An_Open_Letter_To_The_Obama_Administration_From_Central_And_Eastern_Europe/1778449.html

twenty-first century, in his view, are concerned with three main threats: globalised, networked terrorism; the proliferation and 'commodification' of weapons of mass terrorism (which enhance the dangers of the first threat); and the increased vulnerability of civilian populations to various humanitarian crises. The three may combine to create a sustained crisis, provoking an epochal confrontation along the lines of the Thirty Years War, accompanied by the transformation of the traditional state into the market state.[20]

If in the epoch of revolutions 'all wars have been transformed into civil wars',[21] today civil wars retain intense local resonance but little universal significance. Hence they are increasingly protracted and intractable. One act of violence succeeds the other, but the IOs established at the end of the Second World War lack the power or mandate to intervene effectively, while the former superpowers are each preoccupied with new problems of their own. In this way, the era of the emancipation of classes has given way to a permanent crisis whose transformative capacity appears limited. The novelty of the new conflicts lies precisely in their return to an early modern form in which the motives of the age of revolution have given way to traditional elite-driven preoccupations. Here, even nationalism is marginalised by various forms of identity politics, and pre-modern clannism. It is reinforced by postmodern networks and clientelist associations, provoking amorphous conflicts of the type that have now become endemic in the republics of the North Caucasus.

Russia is particularly resistant to cosmopolitanism and has become wary of a universalism rooted in Western-dominated institutions. The notion of 'sovereign democracy' advanced after 2004 was an expression of Russia's ambivalence, and reflected a shift from the norm-taking stance predominant in the 1990s to the growing ambition to be a norm entrepreneur. This was reflected in resistance to the internationalisation of Russia's problems, and in particular the Chechen war. Vladimir Putin claimed to be fighting 'international terrorism' in Chechnya, yet he resolutely refused to accept outside assistance.[22]

At the same time, it is important to distinguish between the radicalisation of the resistance, on the one hand, and the ideology of jihad, on the other. Although there were supranational factors at play in the

---

[20] P. Bobbitt, *Terror and consent: the wars for the twenty-first century* (London: Allen Lane, 2008).

[21] R. Koselleck, 'Historical criteria of the modern concept of revolution', in R. Koselleck (ed.), *Futures past: on the semantics of historical time*, trans. Keith Tribe (Cambridge, MA: MIT Press, 1985 [1979]), p. 54.

[22] For a discussion of this, see Russell, *Chechnya*, chapter 8.

various conflicts in the North Caucasus, the regional and demographic dimensions are constitutive.[23] In the early nineteenth century the great Caucasian war was provoked by Russia's attempts to consolidate its hold over the North Caucasus to ensure security and supply lines to the South Caucasus. Today a new great Caucasian war is in the making, once again characterised by the restless aspirations of the people of the Caucasus, and accompanied by the retreat of ethnic Russians from the region. The ethnic Russian population in the North Caucasian republics between the two censuses of 1989 and 2002 fell by 31 per cent from 1.3 million to 0.9 million, while the indigenous Caucasian population of those republics grew by 51 per cent from 3.5 million to 5.3 million.[24] Russian social modernisation and state-building projects have petered out in the mountains and valleys of the Caucasus, and Russia is increasingly being drawn into a 'long war' of its own in the region.

The dual state meets the cold peace in the Caucasus

The war in Chechnya was the longest and most intense conflict on the territory of the former USSR.[25] The conflict from the first revealed the emergence of a dualism in Russian state development. The adoption of the constitution in December 1993 sought to provide a robust normative/legal framework in which Russia's new statehood could be institutionalised, but the road to genuine constitutionalism was far from complete. The drafting of the constitution had been a traumatic process, accompanied in the end by bloodshed in October 1993. The constitutional limbo between 1991 and 1993 can be characterised as a period of phony democracy, where declared aspirations failed to find an adequate institutional form. This provoked a prolonged political crisis, accompanied by a secession bid in Chechnya.

Elsewhere I have called this a *regime system*, in which a power network was interposed between the formal institutions of the constitutional state from above and the party-political representative system from below.[26] This took the form of tension between the constitutional state and the administrative regime. The former was the institutionalised

---

[23] E. Souleimanov and O. Ditrych, 'The internationalisation of the Russian–Chechen conflict: myths and reality', *Europe-Asia Studies* 60 (September 2008), 1199–222.

[24] See the website of Valery Tishkov, Director of the Institute of Ethnography of the Russian Academy of Sciences: www.valerytishkov.ru

[25] For an overview of arguments, see R. Sakwa (ed.), *Chechnya*.

[26] R. Sakwa, *Russian politics and society*, 4th edn (London: Macmillan, 1997), pp. 466–70; R. Sakwa, *Putin: Russia's choice*, 2nd edn (London: Routledge, 2008), chapter 5; see also R. Sakwa 'The regime system in Russia', *Contemporary Politics* 3 (1997), 7–25.

normative order accompanied by the rule of law and political pluralism, while the latter embodied the tutelary powers claimed by the ruling elite, and was accompanied by informal practices within which intra-regime factionalism took place.[27] It is this dualism that shapes the character of Russian state building, where prerogative powers come into contradiction with constitutional processes. The adoption of the constitution did not put an end to the phony democracy, which was already becoming deeply entrenched as a mode of governance in the Russian polity, but provided a normative counterpoint that created a dual state.

Dualism and the war in Chechnya: the securitisation of the Russian state

While the institutional choices of Russian democracy had been made, notably in the form of a strong presidency in what was formally a semi-presidential system, this was embedded in a set of relationships that were far from constitutional. In other words, even without Chechnya the development of Russian constitutionalism would have been highly ambiguous and retained 'phony' elements. But the Chechen conflict reinforced the salience of the administrative regime and impeded attempts to bring the prerogative state within the ambit of constitutional politics. A degree of 'Chechenisation', defined as the subordination of law to power, was inherent in the Russian political system from the early 1990s, and this exercise of prerogative powers weakened the contrary drive for genuine constitutionalism.

Rather than Chechnya, in Anatol Lieven's words, becoming the 'tombstone' of Russian power,[28] Chechnya served as the crucible for the restoration of that power. Yet that power was deeply flawed and the dual character of the Russian state was exacerbated by the conflict. As Dmitri Trenin and Aleksei Malashenko put it, 'owing equally to the government's weakness and corruptibility, Russia failed to respond to the Chechen challenge'.[29] This, in turn, sent 'a clear message to neighbouring countries and beyond that a power vacuum existed inside Russia from the Caucasus to the Kremlin'.[30] This was a situation that

---

[27] See R. Sakwa, *The dual state in Russia: factionalism and the Medvedev succession* (Cambridge University Press, 2010).

[28] A. Lieven, *Chechnya: tombstone of Russian power.*

[29] D. Trenin and A. Malashenko, with A. Lieven, *Russia's restless frontier: the Chechnya factor in post-Soviet Russia* (Washington, DC: Carnegie Endowment for International Peace, 2004), p. 11.

[30] Ibid.

Putin would not tolerate. In his book of interviews soon after becoming acting president Putin stressed:

> [T]he essence of the situation in the Caucasus and Chechnya was a continuation of the collapse of the USSR. It was clear that we had to put an end to it at some point [...] My evaluation of the situation in August [1999] when the bandits attacked Dagestan was that if we don't stop it immediately, Russia as a state in its current form would no longer exist. Then we were talking about stopping the dissolution of the country.[31]

In a television statement on 23 January 2000 he noted: 'the active public support for our actions in the Caucasus is due not only to a sense of hurt national identity but also to a vague feeling [...] that the state has become weak. And it ought to be strong.'[32] For Putin, the war in Chechnya was about preventing the disintegration of Russia, and the associated horrors that would entail.[33] Certainly, the second Chechen war provided Putin's springboard to the presidency, but of far greater significance was the clear assertion that the era of Russian state disintegration and international retreat was over. As a consequence, the practices of dualism became enmeshed in a process of state consolidation and intensified the great power stance that had been built into the self-definition of Russian statehood from the beginning.

The character of the Chechen 'insurgency' remains contested. Was it a national liberation struggle pursued through traditional means of a guerrilla war and thus part of familiar patterns of anti-colonial struggles? Was it a genuine 'new war' as described by Kaldor? Or was it part of an Islamic jihad to overcome Western structures in their entirety, and thus best understood within the framework of political Islam? Elements of all three are present. According to James Hughes, what began in the early 1990s as a secular nationalist struggle for some type of independence had by the late 1990s become radicalised and transformed into a conflict over religious and national identity.[34] This may be true, but Putin's Chechenisation strategy effectively de-radicalised Islam in Chechnya and brought the republic back into the mainstream of Sufi traditions and the depoliticised Islam that is seeing such a revival in

---

[31] V. Putin, *First person: an astonishingly frank self-portrait by Russia's President Vladimir Putin*, with N. Gevorkyan, N. Timakova and A. Kolesnikov, trans. C.A. Fitzpatrick (London: Hutchinson, 2000), p. 140.

[32] Quoted by P. Rutland, 'Putin's path to power', *Post-Soviet Affairs* 16 (2000), 324.

[33] Henry Hale and Rein Taagepera analyse the degree to which Russia's disintegration really is a serious possibility: H.E. Hale and R. Taagepera, 'Russia: consolidation or collapse?', *Europe-Asia Studies* 54 (2002), 1101–25.

[34] J. Hughes, *Chechnya: from nationalism to jihad* (Philadelphia: University of Pennsylvania Press, 2007).

the rest of Russia, especially in Tatarstan.[35] Chechenisation entailed not only the co-optation of moderate nationalists, those willing to drop secessionist aspirations in favour of what in effect became 'systemic separatism' within the Russian Federation, but also a repudiation of Salafist Islam in favour of traditional Sufi forms. Contrary to some of the more alarmist expectations, Islam in Russia has reverted to some of its pre-revolutionary Jadidist traditions, although a radical current certainly exists and has become the main driver of the continuing insurgency in the North Caucasus.[36] This, however, was accompanied by a pan-Caucasianism that used the instruments of insurgency to address the social backwardness, high unemployment and civic exclusion endemic in the region.

In national politics the formal constitutional state was balanced by an arbitrary power system based on prerogative right. This evaded the formal constitutional system but did not repudiate the principles on which the constitution was based. Parliamentary powers were relatively low, and even those stipulated in the constitution were flouted in the first Chechen war. For instance, the Federation Council should have sanctioned the use of the armed forces in 1994. Later, although clearly there was no time to secure its approval in the Georgian war in 2008, the deployment of forces beyond Russia's borders should again have been sanctioned by a house of review. These conflicts demonstrated the profound duality of the Russian state. This applied to domestic politics, particularly during elections, but when it came to matters of vital interest – such as territorial integrity, the defence of an allied regime and Russian citizens, and access to resources – the prerogative state predominated. The accentuation of executive dominance is not unusual in times of war, but in the Russian case took blatant forms that undermined the credibility of the constitutional order in its entirety.

This is more than the securitisation of a specific policy arena. It can be considered part of the securitisation of the state itself. The concept of securitisation, developed in particular by the Copenhagen school, focuses on security as a speech act. It envisages a two-stage process whereby an issue is declared to be an existential threat to the survival of the naming party, and that party then seeks to have the terms of this declaration accepted by the audience. If it is successful, subsequent

---

[35] For an excellent study, see A. Malashenko, *Islam dlya Rossii*, Carnegie Endowment for International Peace (Moscow: Rosspen, 2007). For a contrary view, stressing the rising radicalisation of Islam in Russia, see G.M. Hahn, *Russia's Islamic challenge* (New Haven, CT: Yale University Press, 2007).

[36] G.M. Hahn, 'The *Jihadi* insurgency and the Russian counterinsurgency in the North Caucasus', *Post-Soviet Affairs* 24 (January–March 2008), 1–39.

emergency measures to deal with the declared existential threat are thus considered legitimate.[37] Securitisation operates at the global and regional levels, and is no less deeply entrenched in the practices of the great powers. American experience suggests that state terrorism is applied in the global south when neo-liberalism fails.[38] In Russia's case, state terrorism was turned inwards, reflecting the incomplete nature of state formation. The most spectacular aspect of this was the conflict in Chechnya, which in one form or another has continued since 1991, and has now taken pan-Caucasian forms.

The dual state is characterised by factionalism, with a broad division between economic liberals and the power forces known as the *siloviki*. When it came to Chechnya, the factions were divided but on the whole the *siloviki*, the group that had done so much to assert the powers of the arbitrary state at the national level, distrusted the most extreme manifestation of the prerogative state at the regional level. Ramzan Kadyrov emerged as an independent actor, and although his form of Chechenisation represented the most extreme manifestation of the prerogative state, his lack of subordination to Moscow rankled with the power ministries.

The Chechen insurgency from 1991 and Russia's counter-insurgency operations accentuated the powers of the prerogative state. Securitisation in this context becomes extremely partial, and is characterised by the same duality that affects the state as a whole. In the Russian case, the prerogative state is a condition of institutionalised securitisation, whereby its practices are given permanent form. It is thus no longer an emergency or extraordinary situation but becomes entrenched as part of the operative code of the power system. It is countered only weakly by the partisans of the constitutional state, which in terms of our model means the restoration of the rule of law, and the priority of procedures and due process over arbitrariness and personalised rule.

The war in Chechnya was part of Russian aspirations to build a Westphalian state, conventionally described as one in which the sovereignty of the centre runs unimpeded across the whole territory. But the effect was to demonstrate just how far Russia was from becoming a bounded sovereign state with a single source of domestic sovereignty. Equally, in Chechnya civilians turned not to the law to protect

---

[37] For an interesting application to the Chechen case, see A. Snetkov, 'The securitisation versus post-structuralist debate in post-conflict environments: the Chechen case study'. Paper presented to the CREES Annual Conference, Cumberland Lodge, 8 June (2008).

[38] This argument is made by R. Blakelely, *State terrorism and neoliberalism: the north in the south* (London: Routledge, 2009).

themselves, but to a neo-feudal leader in the form of Ramzan Kadyrov, whose power was drawn from the authority sanctioned by the arbitrary state. This was pre-modern state development with a vengeance, and demonstrated once again how far new-style old wars undermine the Westphalian order.

The cold peace and Caucasian conflicts

If in the 1990s the centre of conflict in Europe was found in the Balkans, by the 2000s the source of division and tension had moved to the Caucasus. The geographical shift also represents a fundamental change in the nature of the conflicts, although there are elements of continuity. The Balkan wars were concerned with the decay of a supra-national state, Yugoslavia, and the creation of successor nation-states. The borders of nations and states did not coincide, and thus 'new' wars were provoked. The conflicts in the Caucasus today share this charac-teristic of the legacy of a decayed multinational state, but the difference lies in the fact that we are dealing with both nation building and the state-building stages rolled into one. A number of separate nations are looking for ways to affirm their political identity, and this comes into conflict with the struggles of other nations to create their own political communities. In addition, in the Balkans, while the competing inter-ests of the former great powers (Germany, France, Britain) were not absent, the battles on the whole remained regional in focus, whereas the conflicts in the Caucasus today are intensely bound up with great power rivalries and geo-religious contestation.

Political events in the Caucasus region have had an inherent inter-national and local resonance. On the one hand, the logic of develop-ments in Georgia, Abkhazia, South Ossetia, Nagorno-Karabakh and any number of other trouble spots has its local dynamic, which must be studied on its own terms. On the other hand, each of these conflicts has a global dimension (and often more than one) that has little to do with globalisation but reflects the classic multidimensionality of conflict at the borders of competing empires. It is always easy to blame the global powers for local problems, and there has been no lack of this in discus-sion of the Russo-Georgian war. In certain respects the practices of the Cold War have returned, when the superpowers did not enter into direct conflict but fought numerous proxy wars in Asia and Africa. The smaller states became victims of the larger conflict. A similar process is at work today.

In the original Cold War the battle lines were clear, and included an ideological dimension: the struggle between two systems of social organisation – capitalism and communism. The question today is whether the emerging struggle between the Anglo-American West and Russia has anything more to it than a naked struggle for power and influence. Geopolitics is certainly back, described sometimes as a continuation of the old 'great game' by other means. The notion of 'values' is inserted into the debate, but too often in an instrumental and self-serving manner. There is no effective compass to assess the legitimate interests of the United States or Russia in the Caucasian region – but we have to assume that both do have legitimate concerns there. The typical asymmetrical understanding – for or against one side or the other – is simply inadequate in trying to assess the processes going on in the region.

Just as the boundary between combatants and civilians is blurred, so is the line between war and peace. In Chechnya the war is over, but like the end of the war in Serbia/Kosovo, this does not mean peace. The notion of securitisation conveys the ambivalent in-between status of a conflict or an issue, where politics and processes shift from the 'normal' regime to one where security considerations trump others. However, the process whereby normal politics become securitised is not clear, and neither is it clear when an issue has become desecuritised. Against the background of increased threats from across the region, Chechnya is no longer seen as quite the existential threat it once was. Indeed, under Kadyrov Chechnya aspired to become the gendarme of the Caucasus. Forces were sent into South Ossetia during the five-day war, into Ingushetia following the assassination attempt against President Yunus-Bek Yevkurov on 22 June 2009, and on several occasions into Dagestan.

From Chechnya to Georgia: the five-day war and its implications

While Clausewitz argued that war was a rational instrument of national policy, the five-day war met none of the criteria of rationality, instrumentality or the advancement of national interests that he stipulated.[39] Nevertheless, it was still probably necessary in that a failure to respond to the Georgian assault against Tskhinvali, the capital of South Ossetia, on the evening of 7 August 2008 would have reduced Russia to the state it had found itself in during the first Chechen war. It would also have opened the prospect for a major geopolitical shift in power, with NATO forces in due course using a reunified Georgia as the strategic centre

---

[39] Rapoport (ed.), 'Introduction', in C. von Clausewitz, *On War*, p. 13.

to influence the whole Caspian and Black Sea region, and to influence developments in Iran. In other ways, too, this war did not conform to classic Clausewitzian principles, since the main actors were not the clearly delineated sovereign states acting as persons that he envisaged. Instead, numerous sub-state actors were involved, including an irregular formation from Chechnya and the South Ossetian volunteer militias. The armies involved revealed themselves to be little better than irregulars, with a rapid collapse on the Georgian side and some major inadequacies in terms of command, control and communications on the Russian side.

The road to war

The post-Cold War peace in the Caucasus has been fragile. Even without Russia, Georgia faced some intractable issues in attempting to build a state and a nation, all of which were exacerbated by the confrontational policies of its first president, Zviad Gamsakhurdia, and its third, Mikhail Saakashvili. It is wrong to argue that Russia always had neo-imperial ambitions in regard to the two regions. From 1990, when South Ossetia sought to join Russia, and throughout the period thereafter there is no evidence to suggest that Russia was seeking to incorporate them, and South Ossetian requests to this effect were rebuffed. In 2004, moreover, Russia sought to ensure the integrity of Georgia through some sort of federal solution, and hence its attempts in Abkhazia to ensure the election of someone amenable to this plan.

This is not the place to enter into the history of the development of the Georgian state and the relationship of South Ossetia and Abkhazia with it.[40] South Ossetia has its own narrative of national survival and interaction with Russia that sharply separates it from the rest of Georgia.[41] Abkhazia had maintained a treaty relationship with Georgia from 1917 until its incorporation in 1931. It was this status that the republic aspired to restore throughout the Soviet period. With the disintegration of the USSR, however, ambitions shifted from autonomy to independence. The Abkhaz Supreme Soviet in August 1990 voted in favour of independence, a resolution immediately annulled by the Georgian Supreme Soviet. In April 1991 Georgia declared independence, and

---

[40] For an excellent overview, see B. Coppieters and R. Levgold (eds.), *Statehood and security: Georgia after the rose revolution* (Cambridge, MA: MIT Press, 2005).

[41] For the most developed version of this narrative, see V.D. Dzidzoev and K.G. Dzugaev, *Yuzhnaya Osetiya v retrospektive gruzino-osetinskikh otnoshenii* (Tskhinval: Vladikavkaz Research of the Russian Academy of Sciences and the Tibilov South Ossetian State University, 2007).

in February 1992 rescinded the 1978 Soviet-Georgian constitution, which had granted Abkhazia significant cultural freedoms and political rights within the region (notably the significant over-representation of Abkhaz in political bodies). Instead, the 1921 constitution was restored, which referred to Abkhazia not as an autonomous republic but simply as the Sukhumi region.

The Abkhaz responded in kind, and on 23 July 1992 thirty-five Abkhaz Supreme Soviet deputies voted to restore the republic's 1925 constitution, which declared that Abkhazia was a union republic. A violent dénouement was not long in coming, and on 14 August 1992 the Georgian National Guard under the command of the Georgian minister of defence, Tengiz Kitovani, entered Abkhazia. On 18 August it stormed Sukhumi. The Abkhaz leadership fled to the region around the Russian base of Gudauta, from whence they launched a counterattack that (between late 1992 and into 1993) repulsed the Georgian forces and provoked a massive wave of Georgian refugees. It was in this war that Shamil Basaev led a force of Caucasian volunteers that fought with the Abkhaz (who share the same language group with the Adyghe), with Russian support. A ceasefire was agreed and Russian forces were branded as peacekeepers under the aegis of the CIS. When Abkhazia declared independence on 26 November 1993, the move was roundly condemned by Russia.[42] At the same time, Georgia on occasion played the 'Chechen card'. The Chechen rebels were recognised by Gamsakhurdia and the Georgian parliament, and his successor, Eduard Shevardnadze, up to 2003 allowed the insurgents to recuperate and regroup in the Pankisi Gorge. Georgian sponsorship of insurgent activity across the North Caucasus threatened to open up a new front in Russia's tenuous hold on the region.[43]

The debate continued up to 2008 about whether Russian peacekeeping forces were a force for regional stability or an instrument for Russian neo-imperial dominance in Abkhazia, and a way of exerting influence on Georgia. In numerous publications Stephen Blank has asserted that Russia has been pursuing a neo-imperialist strategy.[44] The basic argument is that the deployment of Russian peacekeepers, the retention of Russian bases, and pressure on Georgia to remain within the CIS and to accept the joint defence of the CIS's external borders were all part of Russia's attempt to keep Georgia and the whole region within

---

[42] K.S. Gadzhiev, *Geopolitika kavkaza* (Moscow: Mezhdunarodnye otnosheniya, 2001), p. 303.

[43] A. Smirnov, 'Georgia threatens to play the rebel card in the North Caucasus', *Chechnya Weekly*, 22 May (2008).

[44] For example, S. Blank, 'Russia's real drive to the south', *Orbis* 29 (1995), 369–86.

its sphere of influence. Part of this narrative is that Russia exacerbated regional conflicts to weaken the new states and to provide an excuse for its continued military presence. A second view would moderate this somewhat, to argue that Russian policy was far more contradictory, with different voices at work in Moscow. Russia's purpose from this perspective could be seen as part of a genuine attempt to ensure that these conflicts did not spiral once again into war. This could be termed the hegemonic argument, in contrast to the neo-imperialist line. There is, of course, a third perspective, and that is the problem of Georgia defining itself as a nation and as a civic state. These problems were exacerbated rather than resolved by the so-called 'Rose Revolution' of November 2003 that brought Saakashvili to power through an intra-elite coup.[45]

Russia's response to Georgia's attack was not the first time that military adventurism by a post-Soviet state had prompted a vigorous reaction. The massive assault by Moldova on the right-bank city of Bendery on 19–20 June 1992, causing 270 deaths and 400 wounded, provoked immediate action, including the intervention of the 14th Army under General Alexander Lebed. This was less about Russia's 'neo-imperial' ambitions than a matter of credibility and a residual sense that Russia – as the dominant power in the region – had a responsibility to ensure that conflicts remained constrained, not least to protect the lives of Russians in the region. Russia certainly had some sort of obligations to the separatists in the Trans-Dniester. It also sought to ensure that Moldova remained a friendly power, and indeed an independent state, but the Yeltsin leadership did not share the views of some of the more extreme Russian nationalists about using Trans-Dniester to subordinate Moldova.[46]

It is into this volatile national and regional situation that Western powers have entered, where ignorance of local realities has often been matched only by misplaced ambition. Following the Rose Revolution America forcefully supported Georgian aspirations to join NATO, and thus advocated granting Georgia a Membership Action Plan (MAP) at the Bucharest summit in April 2008. The US-sponsored Train and Equip programme was designed to bring Georgian forces up to NATO standards. To reciprocate, Georgia sent a large contingent of forces to Iraq – the largest contributor in relation to its population – as well as some 200 military personnel to serve in the NATO-led International

---

[45] See J.A. George, 'Minority political inclusion in Mikhail Saakashvili's Georgia', *Europe-Asia Studies* 60 (September 2008), 1151–75.
[46] D. Sagramoso, *Russian imperialism revisited* (London: Routledge, 2010).

Security Assistance Force in Afghanistan.[47] The 2,000 Georgian troops trained for counter-insurgency operations in Iraq could obviously deploy their skills in other theatres of operation. At the time when conflict began in South Ossetia in August 2008 they were indeed in Iraq, but were swiftly airlifted back to Georgia with American help.

This was a war in which conspiracy theories took the place of mythic narratives, let alone positivistic appreciations of what really happened. A similar process was firmly at work in the Balkan wars of the 1990s. In the case of the Caucasus, two main conspiracy theories, with endless subplots and details, have shaped accounts. The first argues that Russia had long planned a war against Georgia; a version that is linked with two main subplots. These are: (a) Russia started the military action on 7 August 2008 by pouring troops through the Roki tunnel into South Ossetia on 7 August, and the Georgian forces were forced to respond; and (b) even if Georgia had started major military action, Saakashvili had been provoked. Among Russians, Pavel Felgenhauer is the main exponent of this version.

The second version focuses on whether the United States had given the Georgian regime the go-ahead to attack South Ossetia, probably accompanied by an attempt to re-occupy Abkhazia. The intrigue is intensified by former secretary of state Condoleeza Rice's three visits to Tbilisi in the months before the conflict. The last took place just days before the war began, on 30 July 2008. While few would suggest that the Americans gave the Georgians a green light to start major hostilities, the red light was perhaps a dim pink. The advantages of a swift blitzkrieg to re-incorporate the breakaway territories into Georgia would allow Georgia to join NATO and the republic would become the base for American power, dominating the greater Caspian and Black Sea region. The insertion of foreign troops and installations into Georgia under the NATO flag would represent a shift in global power of epochal significance.[48]

The five-day war

According to Blank, the Georgian war demonstrated the success of the Russian military reform since 2003, allowing the Kremlin rapidly to airlift a division of paratroopers from deep in the interior to the scene of combat on its borders. The war also vividly demonstrated that Russia had the most powerful military forces in the CIS, and was not afraid

---

[47] A. Gegeshidze, 'Post-war Georgia: resetting Euro-Atlantic aspirations?', *Caucasus Analytical Digest* 5 (2009), 7.

[48] For a review, see R. Allison, 'Russia resurgent: Moscow's campaign to "coerce Georgia to peace"', *International Affairs* 84 (2008), 1145–71.

to use them when required to defend its interests. Indeed, in Blank's view, the war revealed that 'the very structure of the regime inclines it toward military adventurism, as previously shown by the two Chechen wars and the Pristina (Kosovo) operation of 1999 and confirmed by this war'.[49] There is no evidence for this, and the logic of events suggests that up to 2008 Russia's policy was reactive. It was only *after* the Russo-Georgian war, accompanied by what was perceived by Russia to be an unfair propaganda blitz against its defensive reaction, that elements of neo-revisionism have become more salient.

Although Russian defence spending reached some US$40 billion in 2008 (twenty-five times less than that of the United States), experience suggested that up to half of all allocations were stolen.[50] Like the USSR, Russia linked internal and external threats and sought to respond across the whole spectrum of potential challenges. Although its forces, according to Blank, were poorly prepared for counter-insurgency operations, Moscow was preparing its forces for 'joint operations and long-range power-projection missions to East or Central Asia'.[51] Essentially, Blank argued, Russia was 'creating two armies: one for rapid power-projection missions to the CIS; and another for defence of the homeland and internal security'.[52]

The conduct of the war reflected Russia's domestic politics, with a formal system complemented by informal relations on the ground. Russia fought the war in the way that it had taken Berlin in 1945 and Grozny in 1994: a frontal assault that relied on overwhelming numbers and spared neither its own soldiers nor civilians. Official Russian statistics speak of 64 military personnel killed and 323 injured, and Russia was forced to renege on its promise not to use conscripts in battlefield conditions since there were not enough *kontraktniki*. Russia deployed two battalions of the 19th Motor Rifle Division of the 58th Army. The head of this group was wounded as he led the assault. Russia demonstrated that it was able rapidly to deploy forces from the interior, with the airlifting of airborne troops from the 76th (Pskov), the 98th (Ivanovo), the 31st Air Assault Brigade (Ulyanovsk) and special battalions from Chechnya (Zapad and Vostok, the latter led by Sulim Yamadaev).[53] Despite having recently completed the 'Kavkaz – 2008' military exercises, it was clear that the

[49] S. Blank, 'The US-Russian military agenda: the past as prologue', in A. Cohen (ed.), *Russia and Eurasia: a realistic policy agenda for the Obama administration*, Heritage Special Report, 27 March (2009), p. 13.

[50] Ibid., p. 14, quoting Alexander Golts with figures for 2006.

[51] Ibid., p. 15–16.   [52] Ibid.

[53] S. Secrieru, *Illusion of power: Russia after the South Caucasus battle*, CEPS Working Document No. 311, February (2009), p. 1.

58th Army was not up to the task on its own and hence needed to call on reinforcements. As Roger McDermott notes, in this respect, 'to fully equip, transport, and coordinate the deployment and integration of these [76th Pskov Airborne] forces into combat operations alongside 58th Army units represented a notable demonstration of long-range air-lift capability encompassing more than 100 sorties'.[54] In addition, it featured improved command and staff arrangements. These were aspects that Russia's armed forces in the 1990s had often found challenging.[55] Hence, there was surprising coherence alongside improvisation.

Although the war demonstrated major improvements since the first Chechen war, the conflict revealed gaping inadequacies in Russia's military performance, demonstrating that despite endless talk about military reform, relatively little had been achieved and much of the extra resources had been wasted.[56] Three key problems were revealed: 'poor interoperability between the Air Force and ground units, communications problems during combat, and low-resolution reconnaissance systems'.[57] Although Russia had in conventional terms won the war, much of the early fighting had been conducted by South Ossetian (and Abkhaz) irregulars, and the conduct of operations revealed major flaws in Russia's war-making capacity. There was a lack of air cover and an almost total absence of effective communication equipment. The command structure was inadequate, still overwhelmingly concentrated in the General Staff in Moscow (which at the time of the conflict was in the middle of a move to the old Warsaw Pact building, forcing communications to be routed through the Kremlin). Against a stronger protagonist Russia would probably have endured a humiliating defeat to rank alongside Tsushima Bay in 1905. The victory was at best pyrrhic, and demonstrated that Russia was unable to fight a modern war. Its tactics, equipment, training, inter-service coordination and communications were all found wanting. In response, Russia launched a radical modernisation programme for its armed forces in 2009.

Consequences of the war

According to the *Washington Post*, the Russo-Georgian war marked an epochal break, in which 'historians will view 8 August 2008 as a

---

[54] R.N. McDermott, 'Russia's conventional armed forces after the Georgia war', *Parameters: US Army War College Quarterly* 39 (2009), 66–7.

[55] Ibid.

[56] See Z. Barany, *Democratic breakdown and the Russian military* (Princeton University Press, 2007).

[57] McDermott, 'Russia's conventional armed forces after the Georgia war', p. 68.

pivotal moment, no less significant than 9 November 1989, the day that the Berlin Wall fell'.[58] The article went on to note that the attack by Russia on sovereign Georgia was 'an official return to history – actually a return almost to the rivalry of the great powers in the style of the nineteenth century, where everything is at hand: both unbridled nationalism and battles for natural resources'.[59] The return of history took a very specific form, in which history itself was applied asymmetrically, as part of the broader asymmetric end to the Cold War. Thomas Graham, a special assistant to the US president and senior director for Russia on the National Security Council from 2004 to 2007, has argued that the former Soviet space is the most difficult issue in Russo-American relations and 'no issue did more to poison the overall relationship',[60] with the Orange Revolution ending final hopes that the two countries could forge a strategic partnership. He notes that for America the salience of the former Soviet space for its national identity was of recent origin and perhaps ephemeral, but it became the primary testing ground for America's ability to fulfil its historical mission to promote democracy and the free market.[61]

The consequences of the war for Georgia were catastrophic. A new wave of refugees joined those already displaced by the Abkhaz war in the early 1990s. The 'stable instability' in its relations with the two breakaway regions at least left open the possibility of reunification, as had already been achieved with Ajaria in 2004, but the new dispensation drastically narrowed the possibility of voluntary reunion. The creation of a confederated Georgia was by no means excluded, but it would take a significant change in the composition and attitudes of the Georgian elite for this to happen. A new approach to its own minorities and its relations with Russia would be the absolute minimum even to place this on the agenda.

The prospects for Georgian membership of NATO were postponed indefinitely. Although Paris and Berlin forced the United States to back down from its more extravagant aspirations to accelerate the membership ambitions of Ukraine and Georgia, and ultimately denied them a MAP in 2010, the promise to review the decision aroused expectations

[58] R. Kagan, 'Putin makes his move', *Washington Post*, 11 August (2008). Available at www.washingtonpost.com/wp-dyn/content/article/2008/08/10/AR2008081001871. html

[59] Ibid.

[60] T. Graham, 'US-Russian relations: the challenge of starting over', reprinted in *Ekspert*, March (2009). Available at www.expert.ru/printissues/expert/2009/09/ vozmozhnost_nachat_snachala

[61] Ibid.

that were only finally dashed after the war and the restoration of normal relations with Russia by the Obama administration. The decision to terminate contacts within the framework of the NATO-Russia Council after the war was described by Germany's ambassador to NATO as 'stupid', and in March 2009 normal work was restored. As the German foreign minister, Frank-Walter Steinmeier, put it in an article in *Der Spiegel*, the case for accession to NATO must be based on a three-fold criteria of 'goods': 'the good for the candidate country, good for NATO, and good for pan-European security'.[62] Georgia and Ukraine clearly fail on all three counts. Although Georgia has an Individual Partnership Action Plan, this is unlikely to be upgraded into a full MAP in the near future.[63]

The Russo-Georgian war coincided with the beginning of a deterioration in Russia's economic position, as a consequence of the global financial crisis and a corresponding fall in energy prices that also reflected structural problems – above all, Russia's reliance on commodity exports and lack of competitiveness. The war exacerbated the immediate slide in the fall in stock market values, already damaged by the continuing struggle for control of TNK-BP and Putin's criticism in July 2008 of the Mechel metal-mining company, which within days knocked US$5 billion off its share value. Capital outflow during the military campaign from 8 to 11 August 2008 totalled US$7 billion and peaked in October at US$50 billion. Equally, Russia's foreign reserves, which had peaked at US$597.5 billion in July 2008, dropped precipitously between 8 and 14 August by US$16.4 billion and by the end of 2009 had fallen by a third.[64]

Perhaps worse than all of this, the war distracted Medvedev from his domestic agenda of reform, a fact that he lamented in his meeting with the participants of the Valdai International Discussion Club on 12 September 2008.[65] The new Foreign Policy Concept, adopted just a month before the war, had stressed that the priority was the 'creation of a favourable external environment for the country's modernisation [...], the development of good-neighbourly relations with countries on [Russia's] borders [and] the prevention of conflicts in adjacent regions'.[66]

---

[62] F-W. Steinmeier, 'We face new threats and challenges', *Der Spiegel*, 2 April (2009). Available at www.spiegel.de/international/europe/0.1518.619969.00.html

[63] A. Lobjakas, 'NATO lacks the stomach for South Caucasus fight', *Caucasus Analytical Digest* 5 (2009), 2–4.

[64] Secrieru, *Illusion of power*, pp. 9–11.

[65] D. Medvedev, 'Stenograficheskii otchet o vstreche s uchastnikami mezhdunarodnogo kluba "Valdai"', Moscow, 12 September (2008). Available at www.kremlin.ru/text/appears/2008/09/206408.shtml

[66] *Kontseptsiya vneshnei politiki Rossiiskoi Federatsii*, 12 July (2008). Available at www.kremlin.ru/text/docs/2008/07/204108.shtml

Above all, it stressed 'the formation of an objective perception of Russia as a democratic state with a socially oriented economy and an independent foreign policy'.[67] It also sought to generate a picture of world public opinion about Russia's stance 'on the main international problems, foreign policy initiatives and actions, [and] domestic social-economic developments'.[68] Instead, the conflict provoked an information war of rare intensity in which Russia's image initially took a battering.

The creation of two unrecognised territories created a Cyprus-like situation in the Caucasus. The Turkish invasion of Cyprus in 1974, in response to militant Greek attempts at *Enosis* (unification with Greece), created a *de facto* state in the northern third of the island. The Turkish Republic of Northern Cyprus (TRNC) declared independence in 1983, but was recognised only by Turkey. The latter also maintained a large garrison in the TRNC, many of whom had become permanent settlers. Nearly half a century of negotiations had made little headway in Cyprus, and it would take an act of outstanding political imagination to resolve the situation in the South Caucasus peacefully. Russia, like Turkey, might for years be the only regional power to recognise the breakaway regions. The counter-view would suggest that 'the hasty recognition of Abkhazia and South Ossetia may in the long run be seen as a strategic blunder in its effects on federal centre-periphery relations'.[69] According to this view, the North Caucasus is the epicentre of that struggle, given that attempts to gain independence there have historically been protracted and violent.[70]

This argument is accompanied by the view that the tension between the two arms of the 'tandem', Putin and Medvedev, encouraged a rivalry in which both sought to assert their predominance, leading to arbitrary and ill-thought-out decisions. In particular, by insisting on the recognition of the two entities on 26 August 2008 Medvedev was able to assert his dominance of the policy agenda. Putin had had numerous opportunities to recognise the Caucasian republics if he had so wished, but it was the particular circumstances of the August war that prompted the action. Putin was enraged by what he perceived to be the bad faith and irresponsibility of the West, pouring petrol on what was obviously a highly inflammable situation, while the newcomer, Medvedev, had to prove his credentials. The hasty recognition was prompted by Russia's pervasive sense that victories on the field of battle are snatched away by the great powers at the conference table. This was certainly the Russian sentiment over the way that the provisions of the Treaty of San Stefano

[67] Ibid.   [68] Ibid.
[69] Secrieru, *Illusion of power*, p. 7.   [70] Ibid.

in February 1878 were modified by the Congress of Berlin a few months later, at the insistence of Benjamin Disraeli, and these events were much discussed at the time of the Russo-Georgian conflict.

Soon after the Russo-Georgian war, Medvedev issued a five-point statement, ending with the assertion that, for Russia, post-Soviet Eurasia was a region of 'privileged interests'.[71] It was not entirely clear what this meant, and it was the subject of considerable controversy in 2009 and 2010. Konstantin Kosachëv, the chair of the Duma foreign relations committee, insisted that Russia did not want to 'return' Georgia, Poland or the Baltic republics to 'our sphere of influence', but argued that Russia was concerned about 'specific issues', notably the deployment of weapons, the fate of Russian-speaking populations and the danger of renewed aggression.[72] He argued that 'this is not a question of influence but an essential response to foreign actions that concern our interests'.[73] In other words, Russia could not but respond to Western attempts to fill the leadership vacuum that had emerged in the region following the disintegration of the USSR in 1991. Now Russia's renewed attention to the region reflected a hegemonic rather than a neo-imperial strategy, or so Kosachëv argued.

But both the EU and the United States were pursuing hegemonic strategies in what had once been the USSR (and, before 1917, in the Russian empire). The cold peace between East and West has produced a 'clash of integration processes', with the enlarged EU exerting an ever-deeper influence on the region.[74] The EU's ENP, launched in May 2004, was its first sustained attempt to find an organisational form for this.[75] It was, moreover, an example of a 'structural foreign policy, seeking to change the external environment rather than reacting to events'.[76] From 2009 this was transformed, at the urging of some of the more critical EU members (notably Poland and Sweden), by the Eastern Partnership (EaP). It was clear that the programme represented a new line of division across Eurasia as the 'spheres of interest' of Russia and

---

[71] 'Interv'yu Dmitriya Medvedeva telekanalam "Rossiya", Pervomu, NTV', Sochi, 31 August (2008). Available atwww.kremlin.ru/text/appears/2008/08/205991.shtml

[72] K. Kosachëv, 'Rezhimy prikhodyat i ukhodyat: Mif, budto Rossiya oderzhima zhelaniem vernut' Gruziyu v sferu svoego vliyaniya', *Rossiiskaya gazeta*, 3 March (2009).

[73] Ibid.

[74] T. Casier, 'The clash of integration processes? The shadow effect of the enlarged EU on its Eastern neighbours', in K. Malfliet, Lien Verpoest and Evgeny Vinokurov (eds.), *The CIS, the EU and Russia* (Basingstoke, UK: Palgrave Macmillan, 2007), p. 78.

[75] See T. Casier, 'The new neighbours of the European Union: the compelling logic of enlargement?', in J. DeBardeleben (ed.), *The boundaries of EU enlargement: finding a place for neighbours* (Basingstoke, UK: Palgrave Macmillan, 2008), pp. 19–32.

[76] Casier, 'The clash of integration processes?', pp. 73–94.

the EU not only overlapped, but also increasingly became arenas of geo-political contestation. While Russia put pressure on Armenia, Belarus and Moldova to keep their distance from the EaP, the EU placed no less pressure on Belarus and other countries not to recognise the independence of Abkhazia and South Ossetia.

The war demonstrated that Russia was the regional hegemon, however weak its armed forces might be in comparison to the armies of the West. In response, countries like Azerbaijan and Kyrgyzstan modified their policies, the former indicating a readiness to increase its sales of gas to Russia, and the latter initially hinting that it would reassess the American presence at its Manas base. In short, the Russian victory provided an incentive structure to encourage pro-Russian bandwagoning behaviour in post-Soviet Eurasia, although at the same time it reinforced balancing behaviour. Even though the CSTO is a bandwagoning organisation, this does not mean it is simply a tool of Moscow policy. This was clearly in evidence at its summit on 5 September 2008, when the final declaration condemned Georgia's attempt to use military force to solve its separatist problems and the ensuing humanitarian problems, but insisted on the full implementation of the principles enumerated in the Medvedev-Sarkozy plan, including international negotiations on long-term security guarantees.[77] There was no mention of 'genocide', or endorsement of Russia's recognition of the two new states. A similar approach had been taken by the SCO summit a few days earlier (27–8 August 2008), which demonstrated the PRC's ability to act as a countervailing force to Russia's integrative efforts.[78] Even Belarus feared jeopardising its moves towards rapprochement with the EU by recognising the two regions. Nevertheless, Moscow's demonstration that it was willing to use hard power when it felt that its interests were directly threatened acted as a potentially disciplinary mechanism and tempered some of the more extreme Russophobic temptations among its neighbours.

The 'balancer' camp, notably Georgia, was weakened, and Ukraine remained locked in endemic political paralysis. This was reflected in the declining influence of organisations such as GUAM, created in October 1997 and consisting of Georgia, Ukraine, Azerbaijan and Moldova. This did not mean, however, the conclusive strengthening

---

[77] 'Deklaratsiya Moskovskoi Sessii Soveta Kollektivnoi Bezopasnosti ODKB', Moscow, 5 September (2008). Available at www.kremlin.ru/events/articles/2008/08/205859/205904.shtml

[78] 'Dushanbinskaya Deklaratsiya Glav Gosudarstv Chlenov ShOS', Dushanbe, 27–8 August (2008). Available at www.kremlin.ru/events/articles/2008/09/206197/206216.shtml

of the 'bandwagoning' organisations such as the CSTO and EurAsEc. Some would even go so far as to argue that the war signalled the beginning of a new cycle of imperial 'gathering of the lands'. It is unlikely, however, that 1991 was just a temporary disaggregation of Russian-Soviet territory. The demonstration of will and resolution reinforced Russia's appeal to create a multipolar international system in which it would be recognised as an autonomous power, something for which it has fought for three hundred years.

Conclusion: dualism, cold peace and war in the Caucasus

Chechenisation is not just a problem for the Caucasus but for all of Russia, revealing the scale not just of venal corruption, which Medvedev has condemned on numerous occasions, but also the systemic features of meta-corruption, when fundamental political relationships become the subject of secret deals and informal understandings. The brittle balance between the two arms of the dual state was threatened by the emergence of an authoritarian Chechen state in which the arbitrary power of the Kadyrov regime barely paid lip-service to the constitutional state, and achieved effective autonomy without secession. At the same time, geopolitical challenges in the Caucasus placed further pressures on Russia's tense internal balance, reinforcing the more hard-line factions.

Russia remained outside the European integration process, while its own attempts to lead a Eurasian integration system remained at best partial – in part because of the more powerful attractive properties of the EU. Although the official Russian position had long maintained that EU and CIS integration processes could develop in parallel, it became increasingly clear that they were becoming incompatible. Russia's conduct in the 2008 war was partly an attempt to overcome the asymmetry of the end of the Cold War. By demonstrating that Russia would respond to threats, it released over a decade of pent-up frustration against its portrayal as the aggressor and the misfit in the international system. The war revealed the dangers inherent in the unstable balance achieved by the cold peace. The first European interstate conflict of the post-war era confirmed that the post-Cold War system entailed a higher danger of regional wars than the entrenched confrontation of the Cold War itself. This had already been seen in the Balkans in the 1990s, and now the centre of confrontation shifted to the Caucasus. Under these conditions, geopolitical pluralism gave way to geopolitical contestation.

5   The Russo-Georgian war: identity, intervention and norm adaptation

Beat Kernen and Matthew Sussex

The war between Russia and Georgia in August 2008 had many hallmarks of a typical limited interstate war. It was fought between two independent sovereign states over a territorial dispute that had long been a sticking point. Before the creation of the USSR, Ossetia – and Abkhazia in particular – had been contested, and both Georgia and Russia had a mutual history of enmity over territory. There has been significant debate over who was responsible for the war, and also significant debate about how the West responded (or should have responded). But whilst the broad parameters of the conflict have already been documented in this volume, the war did reveal some interesting developments concerning how states go about pursuing their strategic goals in the former Soviet space. In particular, it revealed much about how war in the contemporary international system might be legitimated.

We argue that three developments are especially instructive. The first was that both Russia and Georgia claimed historical dominion over the Abkhaz and Ossetian spaces by pointing to notions of diaspora and kinship (in the case of Russia), and territorial right to govern (in the case of Georgia). This is not new in itself, but it serves as a useful reminder that the manipulation of identity is common in the development of rationales for war. The second development was the invocation by Russia and Georgia of two different interpretations of sovereignty, which produced diametrically opposing rationales for intervention. Third, Russia turned to a relatively surprising source – human security – to legitimate its claims.

In this chapter we demonstrate that the intractability of the conflict over South Ossetia and Abkhazia further entrenched the Caucasus as a site of contestation between Russia and the West. Yet it also marked a subtle shift in Russian strategy. By endorsing a notion of sovereignty that discouraged extra-regional interference, and by referring explicitly to new developments in the UN's human rights policy toolkit, Russia pursued what we term an *adaptationalist* agenda:

the deliberate manipulation of normative concerns for instrumental purposes. The result was that Russia came to endorse a hybrid model of norm-entrepreneurship that had both old and new elements. On the one hand, Russia articulated an adapted view of sovereignty based on diaspora populations that had some grounding in international legal precedent. This revolved around claims of legitimate intervention to protect its citizens. On the other hand, Russia adapted rationales for humanitarian intervention to fit its strategic agenda. Georgia, meanwhile, attempted to internationalise the conflict by appealing to a more traditional Westphalian/Vattelian model, calling for NATO to respond to Russian aggression. But, as we demonstrate below, for Georgia the simple assertion that a Russian 'invasion' was a violation of international law was made more complex by Kosovo's declaration of independence earlier in 2008.

The geostrategic importance of the Caucasus

The South Caucasus – here defined as consisting of Armenia, Azerbaijan and Georgia – occupies a crucial geostrategic position as the intersection of East–West trade routes, a theatre for great power rivalry, and the source of regional and local instability and conflict. The region became even more important after the collapse of the USSR and the launching of the 'war on terror' under the leadership of the United States. Since then, the South Caucasus has been the subject of interest for at least seven external actors. Russia considers the region its legitimate sphere of influence and part of its 'near abroad'. The United States has involved regional actors in its war on terrorism and eyes the area's resources. Turkey pursues the strengthening of its ethnic relations and economic interests. Iran has stepped in for security and energy needs. The EU has moved closer to the Caucasus since its expansion to twenty-seven members, and has provided its mediating offices to resolve regional conflicts. NATO, through its expansions and PfP initiative, focuses on the geostrategic significance of the region. And the CIS is attempting to stave off regional and external influence. Russia, because of its historic connection with the area and its stormy and volatile relationships with its members – especially Georgia – clearly has the most to lose, not only in the South Caucasus but also in its own North Caucasus. This is due to the ethno-cultural links between both regions and the danger of spillover from one area to the other.

The Russo-Georgian war of 2008 did not mean the formal abandonment of Vladimir Putin's 'new realism' (integrating Russia into the international community on its own terms, made forcefully in his

February 2007 Munich speech).[1] But it certainly cemented the move toward a more assertive foreign policy in the face of Russian disillusionment with Western actions such as NATO enlargement.[2] We can clearly observe this in Russia's foreign policy towards Georgia, whereby Russia viewed Georgia's (and Ukraine's) application for NATO membership 'as a flagrant overstepping of the "red line"'.[3] Besides, Georgia's publicly confessed goal of eventually joining Western military and politico-economic alliances, Russia's increased presence, and the vacillating support of Georgia by the United States and other Western nations explain why the region has become the object of 'renewed competition between the United States and Russia', as well as between the EU and Russia.[4] Some have even gone as far as to suggest that Abkhazia and South Ossetia symbolise the 'new Cold War frontline'.[5] Unlike the old Cold War, however, Russian foreign policy under Putin (and arguably under Medvedev as well) reflected much more of a return to Russian tradition: rhetorically emphasising Russian identity, as well as concerns about stability and security along its borders, rather than global ideological competition.[6]

Given Abkhazia's and South Ossetia's *de facto* independence for almost two decades, Russia basically faced three options before its decision to recognise the independence of these two regions in 2008, although only two of them were really viable. The first was to support complete and *de jure* independence of Abkhazia and South Ossetia as new nation-states. The second was to opt for integration (assimilation) of the regions into Russia. A third option, to encourage the reintegration of the areas into Georgia, in some form of federation or confederation, was out of the question in the face of Abkhazian-Georgian

---

[1] International Crisis Group, 'Georgia and Russia: clashing over Abkhazia', *Europe Report* 193, 5 June (2008), 12–13 and fn. 147. Available at www.crisisgroup. org/en/regions/europe/caucasus/georgia/193-georgia-and-russia-clashing-over-abkhazia.aspx

[2] Sakwa, '"New Cold War" or "twenty years' crisis"?' On the notion of a new cold war, see also E. Lucas, *The new Cold War* (New York: Palgrave MacMillan, 2008), and M. MacKinnon, *The new Cold War: revolutions, rigged elections and pipeline politics in the former Soviet Union* (New York: Carroll and Graf Publishers, 2007).

[3] V. Aviutsky, 'The South Ossetia conflict', *Défense nationale et sécurité collective* (October 2008), 41.

[4] Centre for Strategic and International Studies (CSIS), 'Overview', Russia/Eurasia Program, Caucasus Initiative (2009). Available at www.csis.org/ruseura/caucasus

[5] 'Georgia: how a tiny breakaway province could become the new Cold War frontline: while Georgia hopes to join NATO, its rebel Abkhazia area is being wooed by Russia', *The Guardian*, 17 April (2008).

[6] L.T. Caldwell, 'Russian concepts of national security', in R. Legvold (ed.), *Russian foreign policy in the twenty-first century and the shadow of the past* (New York: Columbia University Press, 2007), pp. 326–30.

and South Ossetian-Georgian animosities since the brutal wars of the 1990s, as well as the pro-Russian (or independence-minded) attitude among Abkhaz and South Ossetians. Russia was reluctant to adopt the first option because of the clear dangers involved, including a costly war with Georgia; unwillingness by the international community to extend its recognition and involvement on the side of Georgia; and the risk of setting a dangerous precedent for Russia's own restive regions, especially Chechnya. The second option, on the other hand, whilst desirable for most South Ossetians, did not meet the expectations of all Abkhaz who either desired full independence, or were pro-Russia for pragmatic rather than sentimental reasons. Had the war not occurred, it is likely that Russia would have continued a policy of 'Russification' in Abkhazia and South Ossetia that would have fallen short of outright independence. While this option also would have guaranteed the continuation of the 'frozen conflicts', the outcome of 2008 put the situation in Georgia on ice, given the unwillingness of either side to compromise or concede defeat.

Georgia clearly shares many similarities with other parts of the South Caucasus, just as the South Caucasus is a reflection of the ever-present territories and nationalities questions in the former USSR. If we label Azerbaijan and Armenia as the 'stable' and consistent poles on either side of the political spectrum – the former pursuing and capable of conducting a relatively 'balanced' foreign policy (despite the 'frozen conflict' in Nagorno-Karabakh) – and the latter either forced or willing to follow a policy of 'dependency' on Russia, then Georgia clearly falls in the middle. It is caught between its desire to pursue an independent policy and its vulnerability to Russian pressure. The reason is simply that Georgia is threatened by territorial disintegration in Abkhazia, South Ossetia and (until recently) in Adzhara until Russia fully guarantees the integrity of the territory it claims.

Russia's problems with Georgia began almost immediately after the collapse of the USSR, when it not only faced a virtual civil war in Georgia, but it also faced the dilemma of either supporting the Georgian government in its quest to maintain its territorial integrity, or undermining it and fostering disintegration into 'parts that might be more amenable than the republic as a whole to an expansion of Russian influence'.[7] Whilst the declaration of independence by both Abkhazia and South Ossetia in 1990 was triggered by the nationalistic policies pursued by Georgia's first post-Soviet president, Zviad

---

[7] M. Goldman (ed.), *Global Studies: Russia, the Eurasian Republics, and Central/Eastern Europe*, 10th edn (Dubuque, IA: McGraw-Hill/Dushkin, 2005), p. 60.

Gamsakhurdia,[8] Russia's sword of Damocles could be witnessed in all three areas of conflict in the early 1990s. Separatism in Abkhazia compelled Georgia under Eduard Shevardnadze to join the CIS. The introduction of Russian, Georgian and South Ossetian peacekeeping forces, and the renouncement of force by both Russia and Georgia in the region, stabilised the insurgency in predominantly Muslim South Ossetia under the Sochi Agreement. And the independence movement by the Russian-supported and self-proclaimed 'President of Adzhara', Aslan Abashidze, was dissolved only when Georgia's new president, Saakashvili, forced Abashidze to seek exile in Russia, and reinstated Georgian control over the south-west corner of the country. In doing so, however, he was unable to get rid of the Russian base in Butumi.[9] Despite Saakashvili's success in Adzhara (a region with which Russia, unlike Abkhazia and South Ossetia, has no ethno-cultural links), the unresolved and interrelated problems between Russia and Georgia have remained virtually intact. They find their basic roots in the policies and attitudes of both states, as well as those of Abkhazia and South Ossetia, the two minor players.

Prior to the 2008 war Russia, for its part, had continued to support Abkhaz and South Ossetian separatists militarily, economically and politically. It also hindered the normalisation of economic and trade relations between Moscow and Tbilisi with visa restrictions on Georgian business. This was intensified by the closing of gas pipelines between Russia and Georgia and Russia's opposition to the BTC pipeline until it opened in 2005. Ultimately, it prevented Georgia from taking full control over its territory by continuing Russia's military presence in the form of CIS (Russian) peacekeeping and regular forces in Abkhazia and South Ossetia.[10]

---

[8] Donaldson and Nogee, *The foreign policy of Russia*, pp. 198–200.

[9] See 'Abashidze resigns; Saakashvili's next target – Abkhazia', *Pravda.ru*, 22 June (2007), available at http://english.pravda.ru/world. Russia is obliged to vacate its military bases in Georgia under the provisions of the Istanbul Agreement (the 'Adapted CFE Treaty'). However, these contain no deadlines. Furthermore, in 2007 Russia suspended its participation in the CFE Treaty altogether, citing 'extraordinary circumstances'; see R. Synovitz, 'Russia suspends participation in key arms treaty', Radio Free Europe/Radio Liberty (RFE/RL), 14 July (2007).

[10] P. Normark, 'Time is ripe for Russian policy change towards Georgia', European Rim Policy and Investment Council, *Perihelion Articles*, 16 February (2003), available at www.erpic.org/perihelion/articles2003/february.georgia. Paradoxically, existing and planned oil pipelines designed to bypass Russia, the BTC and the Nabucco pipelines, may have fallen victim to the conflict in Georgia to the benefit of Russia. Nabucco may never materialise and BTC may face capacity cuts because of Azerbaijan's concern over the conflict in Georgia and its decision to pump more oil through the Baku-Novorossiysk pipeline to Russia. See A. Bonner, 'Georgian losses and Russia's Gain', *Middle East Policy* 15 (Winter: 2008), 90.

Russia's foreign policy towards Georgia in the 1990s thus reflected foremost its domestic political aspirations that, especially during the Yeltsin period, translated into inconsistency and unpredictability. It resulted from both the conflict between the executive (publicly confessing support for Georgia's territorial integrity despite some ambivalence on Yeltsin's part) and the nationalistic legislature (including speaker Ruslan Khasbulatov) that supported the secessionist provinces.[11] There were even disagreements within these two branches due to a 'struggle between neo-imperialist and isolationist political factions'.[12] Despite these inconsistencies, a tripartite agreement – the Sochi Agreement – was signed in 1993, and a Russian-led (and CIS- and UN-sponsored) peacekeeping operation began in 1994 to uphold the ceasefire.[13] At the very least, Russia under both Yeltsin and Putin achieved its primary goal of stability in Abkhazia and, until the Russo-Georgian war of 2008, in South Ossetia. As precarious as this stability may appear, Russia thereby averted instability in the North Caucasus.

Seen from this perspective, Russian foreign policy under both Yeltsin and Putin reflected classic geostrategic objectives, linked to the domestically rooted fear of spillover, as well as to the external fact that the breakaway regions welcomed the Russian presence on their territory as a guarantee of their security. In the words of Gerasim Khugaev, the South Ossetian leader: '[W]e are much more worried by Georgian imperialism than Russian imperialism. It is closer to us, and we feel its pressure all the time.'[14] Thus, Russia could legitimately argue that it was not seeking new territory, but preventing a renewed escalation of the conflict that simultaneously ensured its own security.[15] President Medvedev's insistence on solving the Russo-Georgian conflict 'by ourselves', without the need for external mediation efforts, mirrored Moscow's ultimate goal of preventing Georgian membership in NATO.[16] However, the danger to Russia's North Caucasus from instability in the South Caucasus cannot be exaggerated since the North Caucasus is indeed 'a hot region

---

[11] Donaldson and Nogee, *The foreign policy of Russia*, p. 200.

[12] D. Danilov, 'Russia's role', in *A question of sovereignty: the Georgia-Abkhazia peace process, Accord* 7 (September 1999). Available at www.c-r.org/our-work/accord/georgia-abkhazia/russias-role.php

[13] For a history of Russia's foreign policy towards Georgia in the early 1990s, see E.M. Kozhokin, 'Georgia-Abkhazia', in J.A. Azrael and E.A. Payin (eds.), *US and Russian policymaking with respect to the use of force*, Conference Report (RAND Centre for Russian and Eurasian Studies: RAND Corporation, September 1995).

[14] Cited in M. Dobbs, '"We are all Georgians"?', p. B01.

[15] S. Markedonov, 'The paradoxes of Russia's Georgia policy', *Russia in Global Affairs* 2 (April–June 2007).

[16] 'Russia: Moscow warns Georgia, Ukraine; brushes off Abkhaz mediation offer', Radio Free Europe/Radio Liberty (RFE/RL), 7 June (2008). Available at www.rferl.org/featuresarticleprint/2008/06

which can explode as a result of [even] a small change in temperature in the South Caucasus'.[17] Furthermore, the West, whilst pursuing its own geostrategic and economic interests in the South Caucasus, is reluctant to get directly involved in this hot spot bordering on Russia. This is demonstrated by the failure of NATO to extend a membership invitation to Georgia at its April 2008 Bucharest meeting, and its subsequent vacillation over extending a MAP to Georgia in 2010.[18]

Whilst Russia may pursue a foreign policy towards Georgia that is rational or 'responsible' from Moscow's perspective,[19] there are also intrinsically subjective factors rooted in the personalities involved in Russo-Georgian relations, especially when comparing this relationship with Russia's foreign policy towards Azerbaijan. Following Yeltsin's hard-line rhetoric and actions towards both countries, Putin nurtured a friendly relationship with both Heydar Aliyev (a fellow KGB graduate) and his son, Ilham Aliyev. The result was cordial Russo-Azeri relations that allowed Azerbaijan to pursue a balanced foreign policy by accommodating Russia's interests (to the extent that they did not undermine Azerbaijan's own security), and friendly relations with the West and Georgia. Azerbaijan needs stability in Georgia for its economic development, especially in the energy sector, and it requires Western direct investment for its oil exploration. By contrast, Shevardnadze never succeeded in shedding his image as one of the architects of the USSR's collapse in post-Soviet political circles, and Saakashvili irritated the Russians by his overt reorientation of Georgia's foreign policy towards the United States and NATO.[20]

Russia, Georgia and the manipulation of identity in Abkhazia and South Ossetia

One of the key facets of Russia's public position on South Ossetia and Abkhazia has been the politics of identity. Building on Milton Esman's

---

[17] 'Georgian pundit views policy in South Ossetia, relations with Russia, Turkey', BBC Monitoring, Trans Caucasus, transcribed 24 July (2007) from *24 Saati*, 23 July (2007).

[18] For EU and US objectives, see S. Markedonov, 'The paradoxes of Russia's Georgia policy'; see also J. Nichol, 'Russia-Georgia conflict in South Ossetia: context and implications for US interests', *CRS Report for Congress* (Washington, DC: Congressional Research Service, 24 October 2008); and O. Kurtbag, 'EU's response to the Georgia crisis: an active peace broker or a confused and divided actor?' *Journal of Central Asian and Caucasian Studies* 3 (2008), 58–74.

[19] R.G. Suny, 'Living in the hood: Russia, empire, and old and new neighbours', in R. Legvold (ed.), *Russian foreign policy in the twenty-first century and the shadow of the past* (New York: Columbia University Press, 2007), pp. 33–76.

[20] A. Peterson and T. Ziyadov, 'Azerbaijan and Georgia: playing Russian roulette with Moscow' (Washington, DC: Central Asia-Caucasus Institute, October 2007).

work in the 1980s, Yossi Shain and Aharon Barth generated a useful typology to assess the roles adopted by diasporic populations. Writing in *International Organisation*, they argued that diasporas could be active, exerting significant influence over the foreign policies of their homeland. A diaspora may be able to do so in a variety of ways: through lobby groups; by developing political parties to act as proxies; by developing economic clout; or via a combination of these factors. As a result, a diaspora can be a source of inspiration for the kin-state, especially when the kin-state is involved in violent conflict. During this time a diaspora can be decisive in the homeland state's desire to continue fighting or to sue for peace.[21] Conversely, a diaspora can be passive, acting more as an agent of a state's foreign policy, in which claims to common kinship and identity are manipulated in the pursuit of more instrumental ends. Under this scenario, the home state can use identity politics to stir up the sentiment that a diasporic population is in need of urgent help, or to publicly represent its kin regardless of whether the diasporic population desires it or not. While this can sometimes be authentic, Shain and Barth point out that such claims 'may also be aimed at reinforcing ties between an empowered kin abroad and a needy homeland, or at gaining leverage over internal or external affairs of weak neighbour'.[22] In this context Igor Zvelev has made a similar point, stressing the significance of ethnic Russian populations as factors legitimating post-communist foreign policy in Russia.[23]

The latter description is appropriate for understanding how Moscow has used the question of kinship for the 25 million or so ethnic Russians in what used to be called the 'near abroad'.[24] Whether this is construed as a strong link to the Russian Federation, as Vladimir Shlapentokh has suggested, or as a looser tag like the term 'Russian settler community', it is indisputable that Russia has sought to leverage domestic sentiment in favour of Russian-speaking minorities, as well as to use the issue in its dealings with its neighbours.[25] This predates the Soviet era, and

---

[21] See Y. Shain and A. Barth, 'Diasporas and international relations theory', *International Organisation* 57 (2003), 449–79; and M. Esman, 'Diasporas and international relations', in G. Sheffer (ed.), *Modern diasporas in international politics* (New York: St Martin's Press, 1986), pp. 333–49.

[22] Shain and Barth, 'Diasporas and international relations theory'.

[23] I. Zvelev, *Russia and its new diasporas* (Washington, DC: US Institute of Peace Press, 2000).

[24] On the degree to which ethnic Russians identify with their notional homeland, see E. Poppe and L. Hagendorn, 'Types of identification among Russians in the "near abroad"', *Europe-Asia Studies* 53 (2001), 57–71.

[25] V. Shlapentokh, *The new Russian diaspora: Russian minorities in the former Soviet republics* (New York: M.E. Sharpe, 1994).

reinforces the particularistic (and yet multi-ethnic) pan-Slavic identity of a 'Greater Russia' that united people from a variety of groups, tribes and clans.

This has also had ramifications for identity construction, in both Russia and Georgia, with respect to how each nation views the other. Here, perceptions of the Russo-Georgian relationship are paradoxical. From one perspective, close cultural, social and political links have existed between the two countries for more than two hundred years. This earned Georgia the nickname – among its neighbours and ethnic minorities – of a 'Little Empire' in alliance with the 'Great [Russian] Empire'. But viewed from another perspective, one can argue that the relationship has been marred by mutual accusations, distrust and hostilities since the late Soviet period, and even before the USSR existed. Most importantly, Georgia under Saakashvili translated the ethnic conflicts in Georgia into Georgian-Russian conflicts. His own narrative focused on 'fleeing the Russian Empire', and instead sought integration with the West. Whilst earlier leaders such as Eduard Shevardnardze had attempted to steer more closely to the middle ground, anti-Russian sentiment became the *sine qua non* of Georgian foreign policy under Saakashvili's leadership.[26]

Even so, identity politics on their own are insufficient for Georgia to achieve its aspirations. As one commentator has put it, notwithstanding its desired shift in orientation, the circumstances for Georgia remain such that the

reality is that many answers to its problems are to be found in Moscow. Without a supportive Russian policy, it will be extremely difficult for Georgia to regain control over Abkhazia and South Ossetia. Russia still has strong economic leverage and Russia will also control energy resources flowing to and through Georgia for many years to come.[27]

Whilst Georgian attitudes towards Russia reflect relations between a large, dominant power and an adjacent small and feeble state,[28] Georgian nationalism has a long-standing tradition rooted in the mid-nineteenth century. This construction viewed Russia (in its tsarist form) as the 'natural' enemy. Conversely, the West, however defined, was seen as its logical ally. Its politicised and present version, however, is more accurately traced to Georgia's brief independence in the immediate

---

[26] Sergei Markedonov, 'The paradoxes of Russia's Georgia policy'.

[27] Normark, 'Time is ripe for Russian policy change towards Georgia'.

[28] A. Rondelli, *Russia and Georgia: relations are still tense* (Luleå, Sweden: CA&CC Press AB Publishing House, 2006). Available at www.ca-c.org/c-g/2006/journal_english

post-tsarist Soviet period of 1918–21.[29] If Russia was seen as the enemy, it also meant that Georgia perceived its internal opponents as 'accomplices of Russia'. This is a view that has obviously been strengthened by Russia's (and the USSR's) support for ethnic minorities. Furthermore, whereas Georgian nationalism may simply be 'exclusionist', rather than non-assimilationist and non-imperialist, Georgia also views those territories and peoples that have been part of the Georgian nation-state as eternally belonging to Georgia.[30] Within the multi-ethnic state dominated by Georgians, the Georgians view themselves as 'host people' who have a historical right to a unified and independent nation in which 'guests' (the minorities) are expected to know their place and to accept the dominant group.[31]

In this context, Saakashvili's provocation of Russia in South Ossetia was certainly the result of serious strategic miscalculations, including the unexpected proximity of Russian forces, misplaced anticipation of a speedy victory, and unrealistic expectations of external military assistance. But his decision also reflected a highly nationalistic and personalised notion of the Georgian nation. This bordered, according to some, on the pathological.[32] Nonetheless, these perceptions explain the high degree of consensus on what Georgian territorial integrity implies among Georgia's political and social establishment and society at large, including the Georgian Orthodox Church.[33] Most importantly, Georgians generally came to associate the Soviet period with the source of imperialism that had illegitimately suppressed their independence since 1921.

In stark contrast, Abkhaz legitimise their claim to independence by reference to the Soviet era when Abkhazia gained the status of the

[29] G. Nodia, 'The conflict in Abkhazia: national projects and political circumstances', in B. Coppieters, G. Nodia and Y. Anchabadze (eds.), *The Georgians and Abkhazians: the search for a peace settlement* (Brussels: Vrije University, 1998).

[30] Ibid.

[31] O. Vasileva, *Georgia as a model of postcommunist transformation* (Moscow: s.n., 1993), p. 45, as quoted by E. Ozhiganov, 'The Republic of Georgia: conflict in Abkhazia and South Ossetia', in A. Arbatov, A. Chayes, A.H. Chayes and L. Olson (eds.), *Managing conflict in the former Soviet Union: Russian and American perspectives* (Cambridge, MA: MIT Press, 1997), p. 343, fn. 5.

[32] For the unfolding of the South Ossetian conflict, see V. Aviutsky, 'The South Ossetian conflict', 44–6; on Saakashvili's miscalculations and personality, see G. Toal, 'Russia's Kosovo: a critical geopolitics of the August war over South Ossetia', *Défense nationale et sécurité collective* (October 2008), available at www.colorado.edu/ geography/class_homepages/geog_4712_f08/ToalSouthOssetia.pdf; and A. Bonner, 'Georgian losses and Russia's gain', 81, 86.

[33] 'Head of Georgian Church warns Russia against recognising breakaway regions', BBC Monitoring, Trans Caucasus, transcribed 17 February (2008) from *Rustavi-2 TV* (Georgia), 17 February (2008).

Abkhaz Soviet Socialist Republic in 1921, and they view the change to an autonomous region within the Georgian Soviet Socialist Republic (GSSR) in 1931 as a 'demotion'. Despite – or perhaps because of – this setback imposed by Stalin (a Georgian!), in Abkhaz eyes Georgia acquired the image of the enemy, and Russia that of protector against 'Georgian imperialism'.[34] And although Abkhaz recognise that Russia pursues its own geostrategic and economic objectives that mandate Russia's support for, and presence in, Abkhazia (and South Ossetia),[35] and any relationship with Russia may be more practical than emotional, two consistent themes in Abkhazia's independence campaign are that there must be no return to Georgia, and that Russian peacekeepers must stay. Moreover, memories of the brutal war between Georgia and Abkhazia of 1992–3 (which Abkhazia won) reinforced the Abkhaz perception that any political settlement short of quasi –if not *de jure* – independence would be highly unpalatable.[36]

A similar but even more intense situation evolved in South Ossetia following the conflict of August 2008. In contrast to Abkhazia, South Ossetia never enjoyed the status of a Soviet socialist republic (SSR) or even of an autonomous Soviet socialist republic (ASSR), but gained that of 'only' an autonomous oblast (AO), or district, within the GSSR in April 1922. This followed the brutal repression by Georgia of South Ossetian peasants, and foiled attempts at integration with Soviet Russia after Georgia's declaration of independence in 1918. The creation of the GSSR thus left a legacy of distrust of direct rule from Tbilisi that never disappeared from South Ossetian-Georgian relations.[37]

Most importantly, Georgia revoked South Ossetia's autonomous status in December 1990. This fateful step triggered a series of unsuccessful Georgian military incursions into the region, and the subsequent declaration of independence by South Ossetia in 1992, followed by the ceasefire brokered by Russia. Whilst the South Ossetians have traditionally sought closer ties with their linguistically and ethnically related brethren in North Ossetia, the Russo-Georgian war of 2008, coupled with Russia's recognition of the republic's independence, provided the South Ossetians with an equally strong urge for complete independence as the Abkhaz. Paradoxically, the war of 2008 also

---

[34] Nodia, 'The conflict in Abkhazia'.
[35] For Russia's principal objectives in the South Caucasus, see Danilov, 'Russia's role'.
[36] V. Erofeyev, 'A promising pariah on the Black Sea: Abkhazia', *The International Herald Tribune*, 29 June (2006); see also 'Abkhaz leader rules out being part of Georgia', BBC Monitoring, Former Soviet Union, transcribed 30 April (2008) from Channel One TV (Russia), 30 April (2008).
[37] Toal, 'Russia's Kosovo', p. 4.

offered Russia an opportunity to find a long-term solution that, whilst not meeting with broad international acceptance, might be preferable to assimilation or outright annexation of South Ossetia and Abkhazia. This is especially the case given Russia's own volatility in the North Caucasus, and uncertainties about long-term allegiances among Abkhaz and even South Ossetians.

Not surprisingly, Abkhazia's and South Ossetia's stance appears to be the most steadfast and immutable among the four players involved in the conflict. Not only has the Abkhaz goal of *de jure* independence officially been reached by gaining recognition from Moscow, its nationalism, derived from the actual or perceived threat of ethno-cultural oblivion, has translated into a politically firm position.[38] Unlike South Ossetia, Abkhazia has always seen independence as an end in itself, rather than as a step toward integration with Russia, although it has considered establishing 'associate relations' with Russia.[39] The most interesting and novel legal situation created by independence is that two new nation-states have emerged with populations that are predominantly Russian citizens.

The politics of identity, therefore, were significant for all groups involved in the 2008 war between Russia and Georgia. The structure of nationalist discourse, in addition, has been influential in identity construction across the former USSR. As Vera Tolz argued in 1998, confusion between civic nations and ethnic nations was producing not only different narratives on how post-Soviet identity would be shaped in the 'near abroad', but the resonance of ethnic nationhood also offered opportunities for the Russian Federation to use the nationalities question for foreign policy purposes.[40] Indeed, it was Russia that used the question of identity most skilfully. In a policy dating back to 2002, when it had altered its citizenship laws to allow for the mass distribution of passports to people in the former USSR, Russia was able to consistently invoke the pretext that it was defending its citizens. A typical example of this occurred at the May 2009 Victory Day parade in Moscow, where President Medvedev first referred obliquely to Russia's defeat of fascism as a warning to those who might seek 'military adventurism'.

---

[38] Nodia, 'The conflict in Abkhazia'.

[39] 'CIS unrecognised states to coordinate policy in Georgia's Abkhazia', BBC Monitoring, Trans Caucasus, transcribed 1 November (2007) by B. Kernen, Regnum News Agency, 1 November (2007); on South Ossetia's position, see 'Georgia's South Ossetia possibly recognised in 2008 – separatist leader', BBC Monitoring, Trans Caucasus, transcribed 20 February (2008) from *Regnum News Agency* (Russia) 20 February (2008).

[40] V. Tolz, 'Forging the nation: national identity and nation-building in postcommunist Russia', *Europe-Asia Studies* 50 (1998), 993–1022.

Somewhat more overtly, after commending the troops who had fought the Georgians, he added that 'any aggression against our citizens will be decisively rebuffed'.[41]

Competing interpretations of sovereignty

In addition to making use of identity politics, both Russia and Georgia adopted what seemed to be different notions of sovereignty in attempts to legitimate their positions in relation to South Ossetia and Abkhazia. In turn, this provided different ways to legitimate intervention. On the Georgian side, Saakashvili called Russian military action a direct invasion of Georgia, whereas the Russian side also invoked sovereignty and international law. Putin, who was later to threaten – during mediation meetings sponsored by the EU – to hang Saakashvili 'by the balls', backed a statement by Sergei Lavrov that Russia had acted 'on the basis of international law to protect the lives' of Russians who had been attacked by the Georgian military.[42]

As one of the leading scholars on the topic, Stephen Krasner identified several different conceptions of sovereignty in his landmark work *Sovereignty: Organised Hypocrisy*. The first type he examined was the most commonly used: the notion of Westphalian (also referred to as Vattelian) sovereignty.[43] This represents the classic principle of non-intervention – in other words, the right of states and statespeople to conduct their internal affairs free from external interference. On this basis, ethnic Russians (or even non-ethnic Russians accorded Russian citizenship) who lived outside the Russian Federation would have no claim to formal ties to Russia. This is because the dominant statist paradigm – the Westphalian model – sees a state's legal reach stopping at its physical boundaries. Yet in terms of international legal sovereignty, it is instructive that there are numerous treaties and agreements that states make with others in order to protect their citizens abroad. The point here is that states and their leaders are required to protect their people, even though their definition of who qualifies as a citizen may vary. In fact, *all* states practice such behaviour to some degree. For instance, one would be hard pressed to find a consulate, embassy or high commission

---

[41] M. Scott and D. Solvyov, 'Medvedev says Russia will rebuff aggression', 9 May (2009). Available at http://uk.reuters.com/article/2009/05/09/us-russia-parade-idUKTRE5480NM20090509

[42] 'Press conference with Sergei Lavrov', Russian Federation mission to the United Nations, September (2008). Available at www.mid.ru/rus_fp_e_17.html.

[43] S. Krasner, *Sovereignty: organised hypocrisy* (Princeton University Press, 1999), chapter 1.

that does not include the protection of its citizens abroad as a primary task in its mission statement. As an institutionalised phenomenon in international law this rarely results in major problems, given that the majority of instances pertain to foreign individuals who violate the laws of their host state. Under such circumstances, the home government can do little more than have its representatives meet the individual, make them aware of their rights, work with non-governmental organisations (NGO)s to ensure they have fair treatment, and potentially seek to have them extradited if a prisoner-exchange agreement has been negotiated between the two states in question.

However, states can also employ military assets to protect their citizens. This is a more recently accepted practice in international politics, and shows that norms relating to the providing of security to civilians have come quite a long way in a fairly short timeframe. Here, the evacuation of a nation's citizens from a country suffering civil war, disaster or state failure – often using military planes, ships or ground troops to do so – has become a routine occurrence. Article 5 of the Russian Federation Law on the Procedure for Entry and Exit provides a typical example of this. It states that when 'an emergency situation occurs in the territory of a foreign state, the Russian Federation shall guarantee the implementation of diplomatic, economic and other measures provided for by international law, to ensure the security of citizens of the Russian Federation residing in the territory of this foreign state'.[44] A similar rationale was behind mass evacuations of foreigners from Thailand after the tsunami of 26 December 2004. Likewise, the Israeli bombing campaign in Lebanon in 2006 prompted what resembled a multi-nation naval exercise in the harbour at Beirut, as the United States, the UK and other nations sent warships to evacuate their citizens. Earlier the *Mayaguez* incident in the mid-1970s had prompted vigorous debate about the use of military force to protect a state's nationals abroad.[45] This issue has arisen more recently in the context of protecting cruise liners and commercial vessels from Somali pirates.[46]

[44] 'Federal Law of the Russian Federation on the Procedure of Exit from the Russian Federation and Entry into the Russian Federation', adopted 15 August (1996). Available at www.imldb.iom.int/viewDocument.do?id=%7B927CB59B-EC52–4DA5-B353–2463C835A8E3%7D

[45] Some identified it as a core responsibility of states, and others argued that it was in fact illegal to do so. The merchant vessel *Mayaguez* was seized in Cambodian-claimed territorial waters by Khmer Rouge gunboats in May 1975, prompting a much-criticised US attempt to rescue it. See, for instance, M. Akehurst 'The use of force to protect nationals abroad', *International Relations* 5 (1977), 3–23.

[46] This is also tied to arguments that the international community had a 'duty to prevent' various emergencies. See L. Feinstein and A-M. Slaughter, 'A duty to prevent', *Foreign Affairs* 83 (2004), 136–46.

As part of its move toward a hybrid approach to norm-entrepreneurship that sought to legitimate its participation in armed conflict in South Ossetia and Abkhazia, Russia explicitly identified its lawful right to protect its own citizens overseas. This extended to using armed force on the territory of another sovereign state without that state's consent. In doing so, it came to endorse a model of sovereignty that blurred the line between international legal sovereignty and interdependence sovereignty (concerned with the free movement of capital and migration). This had several effects. First, and most obvious, it allowed Moscow to claim that it was simply exercising sovereign rights by taking up arms against aggression that was directed against people who held Russian citizenship and had Russian passports. Second, it reinforced to the West that Russia regarded the conflict as a local struggle and did not require external assistance. Thus, ironically, in appealing to internationalist norms Russia deliberately sought not to internationalise the conflict. Third, it sent a powerful message to Tbilisi – not to mention Ukraine, Moldova and the Baltic states – that Moscow was prepared to back up its interpretation of citizenship with force if its interests were threatened.

For its part, Georgia, which had been developing closer ties with the Bush Jnr administration in the US, articulated a much more traditional conception of Westphalian sovereignty, in which territorial integrity was the main criterion underpinning its claims to legitimately govern South Ossetia and Abkhazia. This represented an attempt to internationalise the conflict by appealing to the international community to respond to an external act of aggression. Indeed, it had made a failed attempt to do so previously by inviting NATO, the EU, the UN and others to replace Russian-dominated peacekeeping forces. But Abkhazia and South Ossetia had unequivocally supported the Russian presence, and mutually pledged collective defence against Georgian aggression.[47] Moreover, the pro-Russian mood in Abkhazia itself increased, especially among the opposition movement that was critical of President Bagapsh for pursuing a 'multi-vector foreign policy' that could have led to the involvement of NATO and brought an end to Abkhazia's aspirations for independence.[48]

Georgia's position therefore shifted from an insistence on a unitary state (a stance that had triggered the Abkhaz and South Ossetian

---

[47] 'CIS unrecognised states to coordinate policy in Georgia's Abkhazia'.

[48] J. Popjanevski, 'Parliamentary elections in Abkhazia: opposition on the rise?', *Central Asia-Caucasus Analyst*, 2 July 2007); see also L. Fuller, 'Analysis: domestic pressure on Abkhaz President intensifies', Radio Free Europe/Radio Liberty (RFE/RL), 6 June (2008).

independence movement in the first place) to conceding 'broad auton-omy' within a Georgian federation.[49] It sought to create an economically developed, democratic and European country that entertained 'good relations' with Russia. As a result, it was anticipated that this would engender support from Abkhaz and South Ossetian citizens.[50] Prior to the war in 2008 a prominent Georgian political commentator had outlined a similar picture, expressing the hope that a 'united, demo-cratic and prosperous Georgia' would find support amongst Abkhaz and South Ossetians and induce them to abandon their corrupt leader-ships.[51] Yet at the same time, Georgia faced strong internal divisions, mainly over the separatist situation and a worsening economy. These pitted Saakashvili against his opponents, a situation that weakened Georgia's position in its dealings with the breakaway regions.[52]

In forcefully articulating a version of sovereignty that included diasporic populations, Russia's position on Abkhazia's and South Ossetia's political status and, correspondingly, the issues of Georgia's territorial boundaries had solidified even before the 2008 war. However, the debate in Moscow turned away from an insistence on the reincor-poration of South Ossetia and Abkhazia into the Russian Federation, and instead came to endorse self-determination. In March 2008 the Duma, dominated by the pro-Putin United Russia, had passed a dec-laration 'On the policy of the RF vis-à-vis Abkhazia, South Ossetia, and Trans-Dniester'. This proposed that Putin and Medvedev should seek to formalise the sovereignty of South Ossetia and Abkhazia by recognis-ing their independence. In the event, it took until 26 August for this to occur. But already in April 2008 Russia had extended mutual assistance packages to the provinces in order to beef up its military presence there, in a decision that fell outside agreements with the UN and OSCE. It had also decided to lift the CIS embargo against Abkhazia, threatened to 'adjust its line toward Abkhazia and South Ossetia', and noted that it would address the issue of the regions' statehood 'incrementally'.[53]

---

[49] Erofeyev, 'A promising pariah on the Black Sea'.
[50] 'Georgian President tells Russia to forget "caricature" images of past', BBC Monitoring, Trans Caucasus, transcribed 6 May (2006) from *Rustani-2 TV* (Georgia) 6 May (2006).
[51] V. Rukhadze, 'Abkhazia and South Ossetia – Russia's never-ending game', Abkhazia Institute for Social and Economic Research, 8 July (2007). Available at www.abk-hazia.com/research-blogs/politics/535-abkhazia-and-south-ossetia-russias-never-ending-game
[52] See, for example, F. Weir, 'Mass protests in Georgia aim to unseat Saakashvili', *Christian Science Monitor* 8 April (2009).
[53] 'Russia attacks "provocative" Georgia after ministerial talks', BBC Monitoring, Former Soviet Union, transcribed 30 August (2007) from Russian Ministry of Foreign Affairs website, 30 August (2007).

Earlier, Russia had appeared to be wavering because its political establishment was divided between support for outright independence of
Abkhazia and South Ossetia, keeping the status quo of the 'frozen conflicts' or endorsing a Georgian federal or confederal system. Although
Russia's preferred option, as viewed from its own logical perspective,
was the continuation of the status quo, it was nonetheless already shifting its position in favour of independence prior to August.[54]

One of the reasons for this was the declaration of independence by
Kosovo. Its recognition (albeit far from unanimous in the West) by the
United States provided Russia with a clear precedent on the question
of the political status of Abkhazia and South Ossetia.[55] Whilst the West
(and Georgia) argued that Kosovo was different, the fact remains that
Kosovo could not be compelled to rejoin Serbia, just as Abkhazia and
South Ossetia could not be compelled to rejoin Georgia.[56] Abkhazia
and South Ossetia were clearly encouraged by Kosovo's declaration of
independence, and viewed at it as a way to achieve their own statehood
and recognition by the international community.[57] This is especially
the case given that Tbilisi had lost any perception of credibility and
trustworthiness amongst the Abkhaz and South Ossetians.

Meanwhile, Georgia faced a dilemma in the wake of Kosovo's independence: namely, how to deal with its independence in the face of
its recognition by Georgia's principal ally, the United States. Georgia
not only refused to extend recognition to Kosovo, but also viewed the
latter's independence as violating international law, while citing the
forced exodus of Georgians from Abkhazia as the main difference to
the situation in Kosovo.[58] If, however, Kosovo's independence was a
violation of international law, it follows logically that the recognition of

[54] Ibid.
[55] C.J. Chivers, 'Russia warns it may back breakaway republics in Georgia', *New York Times*, 16 February (2008); and 'Deputy speaker says West provoking Russia into recognising breakaway republics', BBC Monitoring, Former Soviet Union, tran-scribed 20 February (2008) from ITAR-TASS, 20 February (2008). On Georgia's dilemma, see G. Lomsadze, 'Georgia: treading carefully on the matter of Kosovo independence', *Eurasianet*, 21 February (2008), available at www.eurasianet.org/departments/insight/articles/eav022108a.shtml
[56] A. Lieven, 'Balkan unrest remains a recipe for disaster', *Financial Times*, 14 January (2008); Georgia's prime minister, Lado Gurgendidze, has argued that Kosovo is a *sui generis* case not applicable to Georgia. See T. Barber, 'Georgia fears impact of Kosovo crisis', *Financial Times*, 7 December (2007).
[57] 'Georgia: South Ossetian call for recognition; cites "Kosovo precedent"', Radio Free Europe/Radio Liberty (RFE/RL), 6 March (2008); 'Abkhazia appeals to world organisations over independence', BBC Monitoring, Former Soviet Union, tran-scribed 7 March (2008) from ITAR-TASS, 7 March (2008).
[58] 'Abkhazia, South Ossetia want independence', *Kavkaz Center News Agency*, 18 February (2008). Available at www.kavkaz.org.uk

that independence was also illegitimate. Georgia was therefore clearly at odds with Washington, and paradoxically put itself in the same camp as Russia on the question of Kosovo's sovereignty. Moscow, by contrast, did initially shy away from diplomatically recognising Georgia's breakaway regions, but responded to Kosovo's independence by 'adjusting its line' on what it came to argue was a valid claim on the part of the Abkhaz and South Ossetians.

Human security and the R2P

The second part of Russia's attempt to hybridise norms at the time of the war with Georgia explicitly linked the question of sovereignty to international standards on human rights. This took the form of an announcement by Lavrov – to a fairly incredulous international media contingent – that Russia was pursuing its legitimate 'responsibility to protect' what Lavrov called 'the life and dignity of Russian citizens, especially when they find themselves in armed conflict'.[59] At a roundtable conducted by the Council on Foreign Relations, following a frosty meeting with then-US secretary of state Condoleeza Rice after the five-day war had ended, Lavrov referred even more explicitly to the R2P. Defending Russia's decision to engage in hostilities in Georgia, he challenged the international community to stand up for the principles it had supported. As Lavrov noted:

If all this talk about responsibility to protect is going to remain just talk, if all this talk about human security is going to be used only to initiate some pathetic debate in the UN and elsewhere, then we believe this is wrong. So we exercised the human security maxim, we exercised the responsibility to protect, and did so in strict compliance with Article 51 of the charter.[60]

The R2P is a relatively new development in the international human rights regime. Its purpose is to expand the options open to the UN in response to genocide and other extreme humanitarian crises. Its origins can be traced back throughout the human security movement to the *Agenda for Peace* commissioned by former UN secretary-general Boutros Boutros-Ghali. But its first major use in a formal setting was the 2004 report of the UN High Level Panel on Threats, Challenges and Change, entitled *A More Secure World*. According to the report, '[T]here is a growing acceptance that while sovereign Governments

---

[59] See www.un.int/russia/new/MainRoot/docs/off_news/090808/newen2.htm.
[60] 'A conversation with Sergei Lavrov' (New York: Council on Foreign Relations, 28 September 2008). Available at www.cfr.org/un/conversation-sergey-lavrov/p17384

have the primary responsibility to protect their own citizens [...] when they are unable or unwilling to do so, that responsibility should be taken up by the wider international community.'[61] The UN General Assembly (UNGA) distilled the recommendations of the report that were in favour of firm criteria for intervention or the use of force, and instead deferred to the UN Security Council (UNSC) to make that judgment. The UNSC ultimately endorsed R2P in Resolution 1674 as a concept to be further developed, just six months after the UNGA had done so.[62] Upon taking over from Kofi Anan, UN Secretary-General Ban Ki-Moon keenly embraced the task of getting R2P 'from word to deed' during a speech on UN Day in September 2007.[63] It was subsequently enlarged into a strategy in December 2008 with the development of three pillars: the protection responsibilities of the state; the provision of international assistance; and meeting humanitarian emergencies with decisive and timely responses.[64]

Just as Russia had earlier adapted its view of sovereignty to justify intervention in South Ossetia and Abhazia, Russia's deliberate reference to the R2P to legitimate its five-day war with Georgia in 2008 represents an adaptationalist approach to international human rights norms. In fact, Russia had previously made dozens of representations to the UN, OSCE and other bodies regarding its concerns about the mistreatment of ethnic Russians by Tbilisi. But it was not just Georgia that was targeted. Russia had frequently objected to the repressive language laws adopted in Estonia that linked command of the Estonian language to citizenship, and left almost 400,000 ethnic Russians effectively stateless. Similar laws were enacted in Latvia, where more than 600,000 ethnic Russians live.

But, as demonstrated above, there were also strategic dimensions to Russia's posture. While Russia continued to respect Estonian sovereignty, despite countless examples of state-sponsored discrimination, it was in Abkhazia and South Ossetia that it was prepared to use military force. During the wars in Chechnya the Kremlin had regularly chastised Georgia for being unable (or unwilling) to clean up safe havens for

---

[61] United Nations, *A more secure world: our shared responsibility*, Report of the High-Level Panel on Threats, Challenges and Change (New York: UN Department of Public Information, 2004), available at www.un.org/secureworld/report2.pdf. On the High-Level Panel, see D. Malone, 'The High-Level Panel and the Security Council, *Security Dialogue* 36 (2005), 370–2.

[62] United Nations Security Council, Resolution 1674, 28 April (2006).

[63] See www.un.org/News/Press/docs/2007/sgsm11203.doc.htm

[64] United Nations General Assembly, 63rd Session, *Implementing the responsibility to protect*. Report of the Secretary General, 12 January (2009).

terrorists. After 9/11, European and US perceptions of the campaign in Chechnya underwent an overnight shift from suspecting Russia of mass atrocities, to endorsing it as an ally against radical Islamism. Both presidents Putin and then Medvedev exploited the new benevolent climate in international opinion by justifying Russian intervention in the lawless Pankisi Gorge, on the grounds of legitimate pre-emptive action to disband terror-training cells.[65]

Yet by the time of the Russo-Georgian war, the 'strategic partnership' between Russia and the United States had turned into a 'cold peace' that was even more frosty than the state of affairs that had characterised Russo-US relations prior to 9/11. Hence for many Western commentators the five-day war was based entirely on the broader geopolitics of the Caucasus, in which issues like energy security and NATO expansion affected vital Russian interests. The move to use force in Ossetia was therefore reminiscent of an imperialist foreign policy, as a resurgent Russia emerged from the economic and social malaise that had characterised its stalled transition to democracy under the problematic leadership of Boris Yeltsin.

However, it would be mistaken to view the Russo-Georgian war as purely a symbol of great power contestation, as – for instance – it was frequently characterised by both presidential candidates in debates leading up to the US election in November 2008.[66] Rather, the conflict had its roots in the end of the last Cold War instead of representing the opening salvo of the next one. In fact, it was the product of the *absence* of great power rivalry during the bipolar era, and the ramifications of a power vacuum in the former Soviet space left in the wake of the USSR's collapse. Economic, social and political conditions left the Caucasus ripe for conflict as new nationalisms, identities and ideas flourished without a firm Soviet sphere of influence to keep them in check.

There is some credence to Moscow's claim that human rights were a factor in its desire to champion Abkhazian and Ossetian separatism. But these were only a contributing factor linked to Russia's broader national interests, which since the collapse of the USSR have been dictated by the need to provide a safe and secure environment in the near abroad. This is reflected in every major policy manifesto Russia has issued, from its first articulation in 1993 to its 1998 Security Blueprint, and the 2008 Foreign Policy Concept.[67]

---

[65] V. Gurev, 'The Georgian theme', *International Affairs* (Moscow) 52 (2005), 96–101.

[66] In fact, Russia was the lead question put to the candidates in the 26 September debate.

[67] See 'Kontseptsiya vneshnei politiki Rosiiskoi Federatsii', *Diplomaticheski Vestnik* (special issue), January (1993); 'Konseptsiya natsional'noi bezopasnosti', *Rossiiskaya*

Thus, as Roy Allison has pointed out, this was not suggestive of 'an extraordinary volte-face' in Russia's characterisation of humanitarianism as a Western political instrument,[68] and even if the R2P criteria are discarded, Russia's 'insistence on its right to defend by force its citizens outside its borders is open to manipulation'.[69] This is especially so since claims about the legality of intervention in disputed territories are frequently contested, making the 'right intention' to intervene a multifaceted interpretive question. Given the rapidity with which the International Crisis Group, and other organisations affiliated with the International Commission on Intervention and State Sovereignty (ICISS), produced press releases denying that Russia's actions in Georgia were consistent with the responsibility to protect,[70] it is evident that leading R2P advocates were acutely sensitive to such a suggestion.

Russia's adaptationalist use of the R2P to justify its intervention in Georgia is by no means the first time Moscow (or any state for that matter) has utilised normative goals to advance its interests. On the fascinating question of how norms are interpreted and shaped to fit interests, the R2P practically invites manipulation by states wishing to do so. Moreover, there is little that international society can do to prevent adaptationalist agendas from being utilised by great powers. A core component of the R2P concerns the need for a reasonable prospect of success, noting that 'the consequences of action should not be worse than the consequences of inaction. Military action must not risk triggering a greater conflagration.'[71] There was no question of NATO marching into Ossetia to protect Georgians from harm, and the West was unwilling to fully commit to the dubious credentials of Mikhail Saakashvili. Equally, there was no prospect that the UNSC would censure Moscow, given the Chinese and Russian veto.

---

gazeta, 26 December (1997), 4–5; and the full text of the 2008 Foreign Policy Concept is available at www.maximsnews.com/news20080731russiaforeignpolicy-concept10807311601.htm

[68] Allison, 'Russia resurgent', 1152.

[69] Ibid., 1154.

[70] The Global Centre for the Responsibility to Protect rushed out a formal critique on 18 August, less than ten days after Lavrov's interview with the BBC. It quickly made its way worldwide into newspapers such as the *Los Angeles Times* and the *Australian*, and appeared in full in the October edition of *New Perspectives Quarterly*. For the text of the rebuttal, see www.globalr2p.org/pdf/related/GeorgiaRussia.pdf; and see also G. Evans, 'Russia in Georgia: not a case of the responsibility to protect', *New Perspectives Quarterly* 25 (2008), 53–5.

[71] G. Evans and M. Sahnoun, 'The responsibility to protect', *Foreign Affairs* 81 (2001), 103.

Implications: adaptational normative strategies and the legitimation of war

A number of implications can be drawn from the war between Russia and Georgia in 2008. As this chapter has demonstrated thus far, these revolve around the way that war is legitimated by actors in their pursuit of broader objectives. More specifically, the events of August 2008 generate three lessons. They pertain to our understanding of Russian strategic policy; remind us that actors can manipulate identity and choose multiple interpretations of sovereignty; and provide a lesson about the malleability of supposedly robust new principles of global human rights aimed at preventing genocide.

To begin with, it is possible to identify the Russo-Georgian war as the point at which Russia put the West on notice that its frequent emphasis on regional security concerns was more than just empty rhetoric. The public declaration by Medvedev at the Munich Security Conference in 2008 of a sphere of 'privileged interest' on the territory of the former USSR was a reiteration of past Russian policy statements that had made exactly the same point on numerous occasions. Medvedev's comments followed logically on from Putin's notion of 'sovereign democracy', which eschewed Western polyarchal notions of freedoms, political pluralism and civil liberties. Instead, Putin and Medvedev both exhibited a preference for an illiberal but specifically 'Russian' democracy. This in turn dovetailed with an earlier pronouncement – made by Yevgeni Primakov during Yeltsin's time as president – that Russia sought to enable the emergence of a multipolar world order.

The five-day war was therefore not a radical break from past Russian policy. On the contrary, Russian policy has been remarkably consistent on the question of the near abroad, on the need for spheres of influence, and on the rejection of encroachment by Western economic and military-security organisations in the former Soviet space. However, the war did mark the point at which Russia was prepared to back up with deeds its earlier attempts to create new norms. In this context, Russian foreign policy was essentially reactive during the 1990s, when – due largely to its weakness – it was expected to acquiesce to Western principles relating to human rights, market reform and sovereignty. But under Putin, and then Medvedev, Russia's consolidation of national power gave it the ability to articulate a new normative vision of its own that was distinct from the democratic individualism propagated by the West.

An important component of this new narrative was the manipulation of identity. On the Georgian issue, as a microcosm of its broader attempts to exercise hegemony over the former USSR, Russia deliberately focused on the issue of ethnic citizenship, even though many might question how 'Russian' the population of Abkhazia and South Ossetia were, aside from common language, their complex Soviet-era and Tsarist histories, and the desire to free themselves from Georgia. In contrast to the government in Tbilisi, which fell back on tried-and-true visions of total independence for the Georgian people and the unity of its territory, successive Russian governments played divide-and-rule by promising security, prosperity and citizenship to separatist regions.

This, however, was not useful without a reinterpretation of what statehood meant in the former USSR. Russia's first step in a hybrid approach to norm-entrepreneurship was to utilise a view of sovereignty that – ironically – fitted uncomfortably with the focus on non-intervention that it previously (and subsequently) championed as a permanent member of the UNSC. By appealing to well-established practices in international law, in which states routinely exercise the right to protect their own citizens, sometimes even with military force, Russia sent a dual message. That message was that it was endorsing a 'progressive' view of sovereignty (as befitted its special status in its region), but at the same time would not tolerate outside interference in its pursuit of what it saw as its sovereign responsibilities. The decision to alter its position to support for South Ossetian and Abkhazian independence, rather than reintegration, did not undermine this position: on the contrary, it strengthened it by forestalling criticisms that it was acting as an imperial power in the region.

In contrast, Georgia found itself strenuously articulating a pro-Western vision of its future, envisaging a confederal structure with significant autonomy and economic opportunities for the populations of Abkhazia and Ossetia. But it ran up against Western allies that were reluctant to test Russian resolve on the issue of the South Caucasus, at the same time as it was caught in the uncomfortable position of refusing to recognise the independence of Kosovo, while simultaneously denying independence for its separatist regions. As Krasner has pointed out, weak states tend to emphasise Westphalian/Vattelian conceptions of sovereignty in order to protect their territorial integrity.[72] This was true of Georgia as well, but weak states also tend to come off worse when larger states take them to task. The Saakashvili government emerged from the five-day war with an international reputation in tatters, which was not assisted by Saakashvili's statements, some of which became increasingly foolish. Certainly, his subsequent rhetoric continued to play up the threat to Georgia. In an address to his top

---

[72] S. Krasner, 'Think again: sovereignty', *Foreign Policy* 121 (2001), 21.

military commanders in August 2010 he claimed that Russia wished to 'overthrow Georgian democracy and occupy our entire territory'.[73] To prevent this, he argued, the military must prepare to 'liberate our territories and achieve full de-occupation'.[74] Announcing plans to create a civil defence force that would see every Georgian village protected by a small team of trained fighters, Saakashvili also used the language of human rights by suggesting that 'if the enemy force decides to advance from the ethnically cleansed territories, each and every square metre of the Georgian land should burn beneath them'.[75]

The final part of Russia's adaptational norm promotion strategy that was highlighted by the war with Georgia was to play the West at its own human rights game by adapting norms to fit interests. In doing so, it stood ready with accusations of double standards if the West refused to recognise that Russian concerns about its diaspora were as legitimate as concerns for the safety of Albanian Kosovars, or for Chechens. Because Russia deliberately adopted new principles of human security that had been championed in the West, invoking the R2P in the process, it was able to wedge the EU and transatlantic NATO members between their norms and their interests.

However, Russian behaviour on this point raises an interesting flaw in the global human rights regime that should have been apparent the moment R2P was endorsed at the UN. The risk is that increased use of adaptational strategies could see the R2P come to resemble other struggling regimes with weak compliance mechanisms, such as the moribund Non-Proliferation Treaty. The potential for the use of R2P as a Trojan horse will arguably be tempting for states seeking to promote action on human rights in order to serve more pragmatic interests. Already the PRC, which was so hostile to the R2P that it did not bother to send a representative to the ICISS roundtable when it met in Beijing, has come to tacitly endorse R2P as an instrument to preserve territorial integrity. Its argument has been that the PRC has a responsibility to protect its citizens from terrorism and 'splittism', by which it means potential separatist groups such as the Uighurs in Xinxiang province. Indeed, the fact that many of the world's most powerful second-tier actors remain outside the International Criminal Court (ICC), but within the human rights regime through their endorsement of R2P, means that the door is ajar for adaptationalism by others in future.

---

[73] D. McLaughlin, 'Georgian president claims Russia set on ousting him', *Irish Times*, 7 August (2010). Available at www.irishtimes.com/newspaper/world/2010/0807/1224276378730.html
[74] Ibid.   [75] Ibid.

Conclusions: is an enduring peace possible in Abkhazia and South Ossetia?

Finding a comprehensive and permanent peace settlement will require two prerequisites: Georgia, Russia, Abkhazia and South Ossetia must accept each other and negotiate with one another as equal players. This would, at least symbolically, give the breakaway regions the status of nation-states, and the Georgian government has gone on record to express its opposition to such an eventuality. At the same time, though, we cannot expect Abkhazia and South Ossetia to accept less than that status. Second, a comprehensive peace plan would require the participation of the international community, including NATO, the United States, the EU and the UN, to satisfy at least Georgia's demands. As previously outlined, Russia has gone to some lengths to prevent this kind of 'internationalisation' of the conflict, and instead insists on searching for a solution among the players directly involved. And any peace plan negotiated under the auspices of the UN and the Security Council would run the risk of either Russia or the United States asserting their right of veto.

The UN- and CIS-sponsored (but almost exclusively Russian-dominated) peacekeeping force in Abkhazia and the Russian force left in South Ossetia under the EU-endorsed Sarkozy Plan each represent a double-sided coin. On the one hand, they have been successful in keeping the conflicts frozen. On the other hand, they are at the heart of Abkhaz-Georgian and South Ossetian-Georgian tensions because of Russia's dual role of peacekeeper and mediator. Georgia views them as 'an impediment to effective Russian mediation' because it wants a peacekeeping force that helps restore its territorial integrity, whereas Abkhazia and South Ossetia see the Russians as a 'prerequisite for effective [Russian] mediation that ensures Abkhazia's [and South Ossetia's] independence and peace in the region'.[76]

Given these seemingly irreconcilable positions and perceptions among Russian, Georgian, Abkhaz and South Ossetian policymakers and publics, it is not surprising that a solution has proved elusive. Three interrelated factors may prove to be major impediments to the implementation of any mutual compromises. First, the position of all actors in the region may have hardened to the point of no return. Second, outside (Western or international) forces may be unacceptable to one or more of the regional players, or lack the political will or capability to implement any significant involvement, thus mandating a continued

---

[76] Danilov, 'Russia's role'.

Russian presence to avoid a dangerous vacuum. Third, any concessions by Russia and Georgia must take into account the reactions by the leaderships and peoples of the breakaway regions that could undermine or derail any Russo-Georgian deal.

For the time being, the most realistic and feasible option might be what has been called the 'Azerbaijanization' of Russo-Georgian relations.[77] In essence, it would de-emphasise the most contentious issues (the political status of Abkhazia and South Ossetia and Georgia's relations with these secessionist regions), and focus instead on issues of mutual concern. These include Russo-Georgian border security, anti-terrorism capabilities and economic cooperation, as well as humanitarian relief efforts.[78] After these 'non-confrontational' issues had been resolved, the rough outlines of a final settlement of the conflict in Georgia could emerge. This might encompass, as a basic feature, formal independence for Abkhazia and South Ossetia, thereby acknowledging their irreconcilable differences with Georgia. In return, Abkhazia and South Ossetia might allow some Georgian refugees with prior long-term residence to settle back in Abkhazia and South Ossetia and guarantee their political and socio-economic rights. Second, a mutual and internationally guaranteed 'no-use-of-force' or non-aggression agreement by all players in the region might be implemented, to be supervised by a multinational and UN-sponsored monitoring force, and with firm attendant sanctions against transgressors. Finally, a common market among Georgia, Abkhazia and South Ossetia might gradually be expanded to Russia and other regional players.

The situation in South Ossetia and Abkhazia reflects policy failures by successive Georgian governments under Gamsakhurdia and Saakashvili. Whilst Russia is not innocent in its covert and overt support of Abkhazia and South Ossetia and its exploitation of Georgia's weaknesses, the ultimate desire for independence and closer ties with Russia is rooted in these regions themselves. In many ways, Georgia today is paying the price for policies it has pursued since the collapse of the USSR. These include its refusal to (re)join the CIS; a nationalistic fervour that was bound to meet with strong resistance from Georgia's minorities; a vocal anti-Russian foreign policy coupled to active steps to integrate Georgia into Western military and politico-economic organisations; and (most provocative in Russia's eyes) open military

---

[77] Markedonov, 'The paradoxes of Russia's Georgia policy'.

[78] Ibid.; see also S. Markedonov, 'Abkhazia in geopolitical game in the Caucasus', *RIA Novosti*, 13 August (2007), available at www.gab-ibn.com/IMG/pdf/Ge3-_Abkhazia_In_Geopolitical_Game_In_The_Caucasus.pdf

collaboration with the US. In sum, Georgia may have ignored fundamental geostrategic realities, and Russia has reminded it and the West of those realities. Even so, the West's response to Russia's newfound assertiveness, reflected in its transition from norm consumer to norm entrepreneur, will determine much about the future politics of the region. While NATO temporised over the provision of new MAPs in 2009 and 2010, repeated statements by the United States in support of Georgian sovereignty, including by Secretary of State Hillary Clinton, indicated that the West intends to remain invested in the security politics of the South Caucasus. Given that Russia was prepared to go to war in 2008, backing up its words with actions, one would have to assume that the South Caucasus will remain a hub of contestation between great powers.

6   Why not more conflict in the former USSR? Russia and Central Asia as a zone of relative peace

Neil Robinson

In many ways the 2008 conflict between the Russian Federation and Georgia was a surprise. It would be too much to say that the former USSR was peaceful before that event, but there had been no *new* outbreaks of *major* violence since the collapse of Soviet power. The major conflicts of the post-Soviet period – the fighting in Chechnya, the ongoing disputes over Nagorno-Karabakh, Trans-Dniester, Abkhazia and Ossetia, and the civil war in Tajikistan (which ended in 1997) – all started during, or were provoked by, the collapse of the USSR.[1] Most of these conflicts have never really ended, but they have 'frozen' due to stalemate or Russian force.[2] Consequently, whilst they are not free of violence, the violence they have suffered has been generally low in intensity and extensity. Where there has been new conflict it has been short-lived and localised. Clashes between state forces, rebel and other armed groups in various parts of the former USSR since 1991, such as the fighting in Moscow following the closure of parliament in 1993, or in Central Asia with the Islamic Movement of Uzbekistan (IMU) after 1999,[3] were either small-scale or contained, and did not spread despite

[1] See the list of violent post-Soviet conflicts in Hughes and Sasse (eds.), *Ethnicity and territory in the former Soviet Union*, xiii. Only the conflicts in Tajikistan and Chechnya post-date the end of the USSR, but each was intimately related to the USSR's demise. The end of the USSR prompted the conflict in Tajikistan and the protagonists formed up for the fight in the last months of 1991 by creating militias, ready for the outbreak of war in 1992. See J. Heathershaw, *Post-conflict Tajikistan: the politics of peacebuilding and the emergence of legitimate order* (London: Routledge, 2009), pp. 19–30. The origins of the conflict in Chechnya also lay in the USSR's dying days despite the fact that the major bouts of fighting there took place between 1994 and 1996, and 1999 to (at least) the mid-2000s. See R. Sakwa, 'Introduction: why Chechnya?', in R. Sakwa (ed.), *Chechnya: from past to future* (London: Anthem Press, 2005), pp. 1–20; and Hughes, *Chechnya*.
[2] For an overview of the frozen conflicts see D. Lynch, *Engaging Eurasia's separatist states: unresolved conflicts and de facto states* (Washington, DC: United States Institute of Peace Press, 2004).
[3] V.V. Naumkin, *Militant Islam in Central Asia: the case of the Islamic Movement of Uzbekistan* (Berkeley, CA: Berkeley Program in Soviet and Post-Soviet Studies, 2003). Available at http://repositories.cdlib.org/iseees/bps/2003_06-naum

some apocalyptic warnings.[4] Violence against civilians in the form of human rights violations has in at least one case – Andijan in Uzbekistan in 2005 – led to large-scale loss of life, but, again, the violence was contained and short-lived as mass and open fighting and repression.[5] There has been violence during political succession struggles, as during the 2005 'Tulip Revolution' in Kyrgyzstan. However, again, the extensity of conflict associated with these events is low so that in the post-Soviet space overall the scale of new conflicts, the Russo-Georgian war aside, has been relatively low.

This zone of comparative stability across the former USSR is the topic of this chapter. It discusses why there has been no widespread violence – in the form of civil war or interstate conflict in the region – since 1991. It then examines whether this absence of conflict can be expected to continue in the near future. In particular, it will focus on Central Asia and Russia, although mention will be made of other cases too, and to the relationship between domestic politics and civil war and interstate conflict. Russia and Central Asia are areas where more conflict has been expected than has occurred, and where gauging the prospects and sources of future conflict is important because of their geopolitical and economic significance. They are also broadly comparable to other parts of the former USSR, so that understanding them – and the potential for conflict within them – may give us some clue to the reasons for conflict in other post-Soviet areas in the past, and the prospects for future conflict there.

Here the focus on domestic politics should not be taken to mean that international politics and exogenous factors are not important. Rather, I argue that thus far conflict has been dampened down in the region because of the ways in which domestic political developments have weakened social mobilisation and co-opted domestic elites. The area's relative peace is, however, highly contingent. It is in many ways unexpected and, especially when we consider the wider region into which Central Asia fits, unusual. Thus, post-Soviet Central Asia is a zone of relative stability within wider Central Asia (roughly post-Soviet

---

[4] A. Rashid, *Jihad: the rise of militant Islam in Central Asia* (New Haven, CT: Yale University Press, 2002), chapters 7 and 8. For a recent assessment of the prospects of Islamicist violence that doubts the strength of insurrectionist forces inside Central Asia, see M. Olcott, 'Velika li ugroza dzhikhada v Tsentral'noi Azii?', *Pro et Contra* 13 (2009), 39–52.

[5] On Andijan see Human Rights Watch, '"Bullets were falling like rain": the Andijan massacre, May 13, 2005' (2005), available at http://hrw.org/reports/2005/uzbekistan0605, OSCE/ODIHR *Preliminary findings on the events in Andijan, Uzbekistan, 13 May 2005* (Warsaw: Office for Democratic Institutions and Human Rights, 2005). Available at www1.osce.org/documents/odihr/2005/06/15233_en.pdf

Central Asia plus Afghanistan and Pakistan) and the larger Middle East (roughly the above plus Iran, Iraq, the Arab states and Israel. These have been labelled the 'world's most unstable region' and a 'threat to global security'.[6]

In order to appreciate the contingency of the region's relative peace the chapter starts by examining expectations about the prospects for conflict in the area. The belief that there should be conflict in Central Asia has been widespread since 1991. As a quick look at the titles of many of the books on the region's wider politics shows, many contain the word 'conflict', or the words 'blood' and 'oil', in their titles.[7] Zbigniew Brzezinski once described the region (roughly around the Indian Ocean) as an 'arc of crisis'.[8] The idea that there should have been more conflict in the region comes from the analytical frameworks used to assess the prospects for peace. These have often been based on two assumptions that have sometimes operated singularly, and sometimes together: that peace needs to be based on the construction of democracy; and that peace will only come about through the construction of states in the region that have capacity to develop the societies they manage. This chapter unpacks these assumptions and argues that they do not necessarily apply to the region *as yet*. Instead, it argues that the avoidance of democracy and related state building has helped to preserve the relative peace of the area. Instead of trying to develop democracy and/or to build up state capacity, political leaders in the region have concentrated on regime building and the management of elites. In Central Asia this has sometimes happened with the connivance – deliberate and accidental – of outside powers, most notably Russia and the PRC. Yet political leaders in the area have been relatively successful at regime building. I make a simple argument as to why state building is more dangerous than regime building: state building threatens elites, and regime building can be used to buy them off.

A general preference for regime building over state building does not mean that violence and conflict are permanently off the agenda in Central Asia. Indeed, the ability to build regimes at the expense of state building

---

[6] A. Rashid, *Descent into chaos: the world's most unstable region and the threat to global security* (London: Penguin, 2009).

[7] See, for example, G.K. Bertsch et al. (eds.), *Crossroads and conflict: security and foreign policy in the Caucasus and Central Asia* (New York: Routledge, 2000), or Ebel and Menon (eds.), *Energy and conflict in Central Asia and the Caucasus*. For journalistic accounts see L. Kleveman, *The new great game: blood and oil in Central Asia* (London: Atlantic Books, 2003), or R. Johnson, *Oil, Islam and conflict: Central Asia since 1945* (London: Reaktion Books, 2007).

[8] See S. Akiner, *Central Asia: a new arc of crisis?* (London: Royal United Services Institute, 1993).

has taken place in fairly unusual circumstances. These have provided rulers with the resources to suborn rivals and forestall conflict, but they may not be able to do this over the longer term. Issues of state building might still have to be faced, and the dangers of conflict dealt with more forcefully and directly. This is potentially the case both locally and in respect to involvement by the broader international community. In other words, predictions of violence in the area have not been true in the past, but they may yet come back to haunt the region and its inhabitants.

'Apocalypse soon': expectations of conflict in the post-Soviet space[9]

The post-Soviet space, and especially Central Asia, has many of the features that we associate with conflict both between, and especially within, states. The expectation that there will be conflict within the area has been fairly constant since 1991. As already noted, the reasons for this are due to the analytical frameworks through which the region is viewed. These expect that conflict will be produced in the absence of democracy, and/or of states with some capacity to develop their societies. Such assumptions about democracy and conflict, and states and conflict, are based on expectations about war derived from the literature on comparative politics and international relations. Below I examine these assumptions, and then evaluate their actual utility.

The assumption that non-democracy leads to conflict is a product of the large body of scholarship surrounding the idea of democratic peace (the notion that democracies do not fight one another). This has had two spin-off effects. First, the idea that democracies do not go to war with one another has been adapted to distinguish between full democracy (or what Robert Dahl called *polyarchy*), and fledgling democracies. Whilst the former are peaceful in their relations with one another, the latter are not. Indeed, one line of argument suggests that new democracies might be more war prone than stable authoritarian states.[10] This is because elites whose positions are insecure in a transitional polity, or who fear that they will lose traditional prerogatives in the process of change, might provoke conflict to protect their interests. This is

---

[9] With apologies to Francis Ford Coppola and C. Benard: 'Central Asia: "apocalypse soon" or eccentric survival?', in A.M. Rabasa et al., *The Muslim world after 9/11* (Santa Monica, CA: Rand Corporation, 2004), 321–66.

[10] E. Mansfield and J. Snyder, 'Democratisation and the danger of war', International Security 20 (1995), 5–38; J. Snyder, *From voting to violence: democratisation and nationalist conflict* (New York: W.W. Norton, 2000); P. Collier, *Wars, guns and votes: democracy in dangerous places* (London: The Bodley Head, 2009).

arguably easier to achieve in a transitional polity where questions of identity and interest may be in flux, and where institutional practices are still novel. These can make it easier to mobilise for conflict and to leverage domestic problems into support for military action. Second, there is the idea that unfinished democratisation and the political chaos that comes from failing to consolidate a particular form of political regime creates the basis for intra-state conflict. This is because an unfinished democracy allows for collective action (unlike dictatorship), but does not create channels to make such collective action effective (unlike full democracy). The result is frustration and this leads to violence by political losers. When rulers respond in kind, a cycle of violence ensues. Unfinished democracies – variously labelled semi-democracies or anocracies – are thus more prone to political violence generally[11] and civil war specifically.[12] Legitimacy is also in shorter supply in an anocracy so that the recourse to violence is not constrained by social attitudes.

The assumption that states with the capacity to manage and transform their societies are required to avoid conflict is related to the perceived need to consolidate democracy at a normative level. Democracy is frequently regarded as providing state capacity since it creates autonomy and legitimates power. By providing state autonomy democracy frees rulers from having to satisfy powerful social interests so that they can manage society more easily, and hence avoid conflict. This helps provide additional legitimacy, but democracy's own legitimacy drawn from the ballot box and political participation also generates some state capacity through the creation of infrastructural state power.[13] This form of power sees the state intersect with society and able to draw on social resources and compliance to generate capacity. Democracy and state capacity are thus related, at least in theory.[14] The failure to develop one is often taken as a proxy for the failure to develop the other.

This has been especially common in Russia. The failures of state development in the 1990s were frequently ascribed to the same factors

---

[11] T. Ellingsen and N.P. Gleditsch, 'Democracy and armed conflict in the third world', in K. Volden and D. Smith (eds.), *Causes of conflict in third world countries* (Oslo: International Peace Research Institute, 1997), pp. 69–81.

[12] J. Fearon and D. Laitin, 'Ethnicity, insurgency, and civil war', *American Political Science Review* 97 (2003), 75–90; H. Hegre et al., 'Toward a democratic civil peace? Democracy, political change, and civil war, 1816–1992', *American Political Science Review* 95 (2001), 33–48.

[13] M. Mann, 'The autonomous power of the state: its origins, mechanisms and results', *Archives Européennes de Sociologie* 25 (1983), 187–213.

[14] For an example of this connection in a study of the wider post-Soviet region see T.W. Simons, *Eurasia's new frontiers: young states, old societies, open futures* (Ithaca, NY: Cornell University Press, 2008).

as the failures of democracy. The failures of democratic transformation and of state development were also each ascribed to the other.[15] The ultimate danger perceived in this is that it places states within the region at risk of failing. Failed states are synonymous with conflict (and the export of conflict). This is because in a failed state the monopoly over violence that is core to the state's definition disappears, and is contested by would-be violence-monopolists.

If we work from these assumptions, Central Asia and (to a lesser extent) Russia were always going to be prey to conflict in the post-communist era because of the weakness of their putative democracies and the fragility of their states. There was more active campaigning for independence – at least in the form of sovereignty – in Russia than in Central Asia, but independence exposed the structural weakness of statehood in both areas. Central Asia was 'profoundly' unprepared, as Pauline Luong Jones put it, since the new countries there 'lacked viable economies as well as state structures and ideologies capable of linking indigenous leaders to their societies'.[16] Likewise Russia – or so it was argued – lacked a cohesive national identity that could rally its population behind a project of renewal.[17] State-building tasks were therefore huge and involved not just reordering of economies and systems of public administration, but also questions of identity. The bigger the task of state building, the greater the danger, especially because weak democracy creates the prospect of violence arising from the inability of emerging political systems to contain protest.

This danger was predominantly described in ethnic, clan (and other forms of tribal and familial affinity) and regional terms in Central Asia, although the distinctions between these different categories are often obscure due to their overlap.[18] The very act of state building, in

---

[15] See, *inter alia*, R. Bova, 'Democratisation and the crisis of the Russian state', in G. Smith (ed.), *State-building in Russia: the Yeltsin legacy and the challenge of the future* (Armonk, NY: M.E. Sharpe, 1999), 17–40; V. Sperling, 'Introduction: the domestic and international obstacles to state-building in Russia', in V. Sperling (ed.), *Building the Russian state: institutional crisis and the quest for democratic governance* (Boulder, CO: Westview, 2000), 1–23.

[16] P. Luong Jones, 'Introduction: politics in the periphery: competing views of Central Asian states and societies', in P. Luong Jones (ed.), *The transformation of Central Asia: states and societies from Soviet rule to independence* (Ithaca, NY: Cornell University Press, 2004), p. 11.

[17] D. Blum, 'Conclusion: is disintegration inevitable and why should we care?', in D. Blum (ed.), *Russia's future: consolidation or disintegration?* (Boulder, CO: Westview, 1994), 147–8.

[18] Indeed, clans have been described as a form of sub-ethnic group. See K. Collins, 'Clans, pacts and politics in Central Asia', *Journal of Democracy* 13 (2002), 137–52. For other assessments see E. Schatz, *Modern clan politics and beyond: the power of*

particular the ideational dimensions involved in creating some form of citizenship around which state and reform mobilisation could be based, would, it was believed, provoke ethnic hostilities. These ethnic hostilities had been largely hidden under Soviet rule until perestroika had reactivated them as actual or potential sources of political and social mobilisation.

Ethnic identities had thus been a source of violence as the USSR collapsed. This was notable in Nagorno-Karabakh, but also in Central Asia where clashes over land rights between Kyrgyz and Uzbeks around the city of Osh in the Fergana valley – where Kyrgyzstan, Tajikistan and Uzbekistan intersect – have occurred frequently, most recently in 2010.[19] Post-Soviet state building, it was believed, would reinforce emergent ethnic identities and set them against one another even more as the process of creating state citizenship would inevitably marginalise some ethnic identities. Indeed, it was posited that the very fact of independence created a surge of ethnic tension because independence shifted relations of domination that had existed in the Soviet period down a level: Russian ethnic domination was automatically replaced by the domination of titular nationalities (that is, the nationality around which Soviet republics had been formed) so that new hierarchies of domination and resistance were created.[20]

What was true of ethnic domination was also true of regional and clan patterns of domination. Ethnicity, however, was seen as especially dangerous because all of the Central Asian states had highly mixed ethnic populations, and because there was a 'disjuncture between state and national boundaries' due to the arbitrary establishment of republican borders.[21] The republics of Central Asia from which the new states were formed were largely artificial creations of the Soviet colonial power in the late 1920s and early 1930s. This solidified notions of ethnicity that had often been loose and malleable. It also frequently turned them against each other (rather than against Moscow), as different ethnic groups worked to distinguish themselves from one another,

---

'blood' in Kazakhstan (Seattle: University of Washington Press, 2004); D. Gulette, 'Theories on Central Asian factionalism: the debate in political science and its wider implications', *Central Asian Survey* 26 (2007), 373–87.

[19] On the Osh conflict see V. Tishkov, *Ethnicity, nationalism and conflict in and after the Soviet Union: the mind aflame* (London: Sage, 1997), chapter 7.

[20] I. Bremmer, 'Post-Soviet nationalities theory: past, present, and future', in I. Bremmer and R. Taras (eds.), *New states, new politics: building the post-Soviet nations* (Cambridge University Press, 1997), p. 19.

[21] R. Menon and H. Spruyt, 'Possibilities for conflict and conflict resolution in post-Soviet Central Asia', in B. Rubin and J. Snyder (eds.), *Post-Soviet political order: conflict and state building* (London: Routledge, 1998), p. 112.

and ensured their dominance in the republic where they were the titular nationality. Moreover, borders made no concessions to ethnic affinities or economic rationality. The new republics, and hence their successor states, were left with far larger minority groups than might have been the case and were weakened economically by the arbitrary division of what had previously been common economic spaces.[22]

Consequently, there were multiple points of potential conflict within former USSR and Central Asia in particular. In Central Asia these problems seemed particularly entrenched because the regimes there were defined as 'nationalising' due to the absence of any prior historical national identity that could be drawn on to consolidate stateness.[23] In short, because they had farther to go to define themselves as states the potential for conflict in their unfinished democracies looked that much greater. There were fears that mobilisation of ethnicity would be a strategy adopted by elites trying to compensate for weak democratic and systemic legitimacy, or trying to force their way into (or out of) the political system by playing the nationalist card.[24] The multi-ethnic nature of the region, and the large potential for conflict envisaged as a result, made the prospect of this mobilisation more dangerous and likely. Conflicts over state building in one nation might spill over and draw in outside powers tempted to shore up their regimes by protecting their fellow ethnics across a historically poorly defined border. In the words of one analyst, there was a danger that the region would move from being a 'melting pot' to a 'cauldron'.[25] There was also a large Russian diaspora across the former USSR, and fears that it would be mobilised. On top of this it was sometimes asserted that Russia would have difficulty adjusting to its new status as a post-imperial power. This might lead it to adopt a more aggressive foreign policy as it sought to compensate for its loss of status and as leaders gravitated towards nationalist issues.[26]

---

[22] A good brief description can be found in O. Roy, *The new Central Asia: the creation of nations* (London: I.B. Tauris, 2000), pp. 61–78.

[23] A. Bohr, 'The Central Asian states as nationalising regimes', in G. Smith (ed.), *Nation-building in the post-Soviet borderlands: the politics of national identities* (Cambridge University Press, 1998), pp. 139–66.

[24] Tishkov, *Ethnicity, nationalism and conflict*, chapter 11.

[25] S. Akiner, 'Melting pot, salad bowl – cauldron? Manipulation and mobilisation of ethnic and religious identities in Central Asia', *Ethnic and Racial Studies* 20 (1997), 362–98.

[26] See A. Motyl, 'After empire: competing discourses and inter-state conflict in post-imperial Eastern Europe', in B. Rubin and J. Snyder (eds.), *Post-Soviet political order: conflict and state building* (London: Routledge, 1998), pp. 14–33; and W. Zimmerman, *The Russian people and foreign policy: Russian elite and mass perspectives, 1993–2000* (Princeton University Press, 2002).

All told, then, Central Asia and Russia seemed to be a perfect breeding ground for violence as weak democracies (at best) and as nationalising states searched for a rallying identity. The area incorporated problems like Russia's failure to consolidate its democracy; the mobilisation of nationalist forces from both right and left in opposition to reform; the large vote for ultra-nationalist parties like Vladimir Zhirinovsky's Liberal Democratic Party of Russia in elections in 1993 and 1995; the Tajik civil war; and the Russian invasion of Chechnya at the end of 1994. All these seemed to confirm that the semi-democracies of the region were promoting conflict, or at least barely containing it. This brought into play the second assumption that has underlain expectations about conflict in the region: the state assumption. If democracies could not stabilise and contain conflict, and if the new polities of the area could not create political systems that could manage reform, then there was the danger that they would fail to generate the state capacity needed to manage society.

There were two possible outcomes from this. One was that anocracy would endure. This might not mean conflict and violence, but it would mean that conflict and violence could not ever be ruled out: enduring liberal peace would not be built. As Gail Lapidus put it, 'the potential for future conflict remains high' because of a 'striking failure to create strong and efficacious states where the rule of law and the protection of minorities are not only enshrined in institutions and law but also assimilated in the dominant political culture and patterns of behaviour'.[27] Another outcome was the prospect that in the absence of strong states being built state failure would occur. State failure by its very definition involves intra-state conflict and potentially leads to the exportation of this conflict to neighbours and/or a diminution of their economic capacity, which in turn can impact their existence as states.[28] Its civil war meant that Tajikistan failed as a state before it was even really independent, and there has been repeated speculation since about the prospects of Russia and other Central Asian states failing (or, in Tajikistan's case, failing for a second time).

This speculation grew partly as interest in the role of failed states in international politics expanded after 9/11, and partly as there was a failure to develop states in the region through democracy promotion

---

[27] G.W. Lapidus, 'Ethnicity and state-building: accommodating ethnic differences in post-Soviet Eurasia', in M. Beissinger and C. Young (eds.), *Beyond state crisis? Postcolonial Africa and post-Soviet Eurasia in comparative perspective* (Washington, DC: Woodrow Wilson Center Press, 2002), p. 353.

[28] P. Collier, *The bottom billion: why the poorest countries are failing and what can be done about i*t (Oxford University Press, 2007), chapter 4.

and economic reform. Increased attention to the problems created by failed states after 9/11 led to various measures of state failure constructed to spot the next failed state. These included the Fund for Peace's 'Failed States Index'; the World Bank's 'fragile states' or 'Low Income Countries under Stress' studies; George Mason University's Political Instability Taskforce 'state failure' project; and the Brookings Institution's 'Index of State Weakness in the Developing World'. Each of these has listed one or more of the Central Asian states on their 'at danger' lists, or as very weak states, and these states frequently score low on political and economic measures.[29] All the Central Asian states are listed in Paul Collier's 'bottom billion' list of borderline and already failed states.[30] More specifically, there have been a number of studies that have analysed developments in Russia and Central Asia as leading them to, or raising the prospect of, state failure. The economic crisis of 1998 in Russia, for example, was described as creating the conditions in which state failure might occur.[31]

Prophecies of failure are even more common for Central Asia. A core assumption of the failed state concept is that weak states can be pushed over the edge and into failure by any kind of crisis – political or economic, or natural disaster – or an event that elsewhere would be innocuous. Such precipitating events can be domestic or international in origin. All post-Soviet states have been described as weak from both domestic and international perspectives.[32] The problem is magnified for post-Soviet Central Asia due to its border with Afghanistan and the possibility of the conflicts there spilling over. This creates an obvious source of potential state failure, especially since cross-border incursions played a role in the Tajik civil war, and Afghanistan was a base for the IMU, from which it launched incursions into the region before

[29] The 'Failed states index' is available through the Fund for Peace's web pages at www.fundforpeace.org. The World Bank research on fragile states is available at http://web.worldbank.org/WBSITE/EXTERNAL/PROJECTS/STRATEGIES/EXTLICUS/0,,contentMDK:20247661~menuPK:4168000~pagePK:64171540~piPK:64171528~theSitePK:511778,00.html. The Political Instability Taskforce datasets on failed states and related research can be found at http://globalpolicy.gmu.edu/pitf. For the Brookings Institution index see S.E. Rice and S. Patrick, *Index of state weakness in the developing world* (Washington, DC: Brookings Institution, 2008).

[30] Collier, *Wars, guns and votes*, pp. 239–40.

[31] D. Hoffman, 'Russia is sinking into the void of a "failed state"', *International Herald Tribune*, 27 February (1999), p. 1; and G. Herd, 'Russia: systemic transformation or Federal collapse?', *Journal of Peace Research* 36 (1999), 259–69. For a general discussion of some of the issues around a Russian breakdown, see Hale and Taagepera, 'Russia: consolidation or collapse?', 1101–25.

[32] A.P. Tsygankov, 'Modern at last? Variety of weak states in the post-Soviet world', *Communist and Post-Communist Studies* 40 (2007), 423–39.

the defeat of the Taliban.[33] However, since more or less any event can lead a weak state to failure, the prospect of failure can be constantly invoked. Political succession, economic problems, environmental issues and events such as the killings in Andijan (when Uzbek interior ministry troops fired into a crowd of demonstrators on 13 May 2005) can all be talked of as precursors to state failure. These prophecies are most commonly invoked for Tajikistan, Uzbekistan and Kyrgyzstan, where the combination of poverty (particularly for Kyrgyzstan and Tajikistan) and high levels of political repression (particularly in Uzbekistan, but intermittently for the other two) means that they score particularly poorly on measures of state weakness.[34]

The false premises of expectations

Expectations of conflict have thus outstripped the level of conflict in the post-Soviet space. What is holding the region back from falling into the conflict traps to which being poor (in all senses of the word) democracies and weak states would seem to doom them? Here I posit two reasons. First, the ideas underpinning the regime and state assumptions about conflict are faulty, or at least not as watertight as they might seem. Consequently we can question their application to the area. Second, there are some crucial differences between Central Asia and Russia, and other weak democracies and states, which have kept the former relatively conflict free.

To begin with, there has not been a straightforward translation of regime type and state weakness into conflict in Central Asia. The relationship between regime, state and conflict therefore needs to be

---

[33] B. Rubin, 'Central Asia wars and ethnic conflicts – rebuilding failed states', Human Development Report Office Occasional Paper (New York: United Nations Development Program, 2004).

[34] See, *inter alia,* International Crisis Group, 'Kyrgyzstan: a faltering state', *Asia Report* 109, 16 December (2005), available at www.crisisgroup.org/en/regions/asia/central-asia/kyrgyzstan/109-kyrgyzstan-a-faltering-state.aspx; International Crisis Group, 'Kyrgyzstan on the edge', *Asia Briefing* 55, 9 November (2006), available at www.crisisgroup.org/en/regions/asia/central-asia/kyrgyzstan/B055%20Kyrgyzstan%20on%20the%20Edge.aspx; International Crisis Group, 'Uzbekistan: stagnation and uncertainty', *Asia Briefing* 67, 22 August (2007), available at www.crisisgroup.org/en/regions/asia/central-asia/uzbekistan/B062-uzbekistan-stagnation-and-uncertainty.aspx; International Crisis Group, 'Tajikistan: on the road to failure', *Asia Report* 162, 12 February (2009), available at www.crisisgroup.org/en/regions/asia/central-asia/tajikistan/162-tajikistan-on-the-road-to-failure.aspx; J. Engvall, *Kyrgyzstan: the anatomy of a failed state* (Uppsala: Central Asia-Caucasus Institute, Silk Road Studies Program, 2006); and R.M. Auty, 'Transition to mid-income democracies or to failed states?', in R.M. Auty and I. de Soysa (eds.), *Energy, wealth and governance in the Caucasus and Central Asia* (London: Routledge, 2006), pp. 3–16.

qualified. Anocracy is arguably no more associated with civil war than any other form of regime.[35] This raises the issue of reverse causality: it is not regime form that determines political violence in the case of anocracies, but political violence that creates them, and this may lead to civil war. A semi-democracy is thus no more likely to collapse into violence than any other regime. This puts a new face on the prospects of avoiding conflict in Russia and Central Asia since political violence (repression excepted), as opposed to violence driven by economic motives (crime), has been low. The collapse of the USSR was, as many studies have noted, remarkably free of violence in comparison to the collapse of other empires and in comparison to the collapse of Yugoslavia.[36] Outside of the Chechen and Tajik cases, violence at the moment that the USSR collapsed did not generally beget violence, nor was it the source of weak democracies. The other conflicts that had already broken out in Georgia and between Azerbaijan and Armenia before the USSR's collapse either froze with the collapse of the USSR, or at least began to wind down.

It would be hard to say that this freeze weakened democracy in the region, and until the Russo-Georgian conflict it had not led to war. It is instructive to note that since 2008 a frozen peace has again been the dominant condition in South Ossetia and Abkhazia, as leaders in Moscow and Tbilisi both respected the Russian-enforced status quo throughout 2009 and 2010. Yet it is hard to take seriously the argument that Georgia, Moldova, Azerbaijan and Armenia would have had a smoother transition to democracy if they had settled their border disputes; or that Tajikistan would have been destined for democracy if it had not had a civil war. By the same token, Russia's erratic democratisation would have been erratic with or without Chechnya. Democratic weakness in the region had multiple sources, but these do not seem to have been responsible for generating conflict. Indeed, one could argue the opposite has often been the case: that democracy has been weakened in part so that conflict can be contained and avoided.

The reason for this is not altruism on the part of rulers. They have simply been trying to consolidate their power and head off threats, and their repression of violence is no different in this regard to the suppression of pluralism. Leaders have thus learnt from the past and contained conflict. All the leaders of the region learnt from Uzbekistan's Fergana

---

[35] J.R. Vreeland, 'The effect of political regime on civil war: unpacking anocracy', *Journal of Conflict Resolution* 52 (2008), 401–25.

[36] For example, A. Lieven, 'Empire's aftermath: a comparative perspective', in S.N. Cummings (ed.), *Power and change in Central Asia* (London: Routledge, 2002), pp. 24–41.

valley conflicts during perestroika and from the war in Tajikistan that conflicts might be latent in the region, and in Kyrgyzstan that conflict can even threaten retention of power. The settlement of the Tajik conflict has led to the construction of a non-democratic regime rather than the democratic settlement called for by international agencies charged with securing peace. This has been achieved via an 'illiberal' deal that has actually worked to contain conflict.[37]

Just as the construction of non-democratic regimes has not bred conflict, the case of Russia and Central Asia demonstrates that there are similar problems with the idea that state weakness is a precursor to war. The dividing line between a weak state and a failed one is conceptually unclear. The extent of conceptual confusion can be seen in the different terms and definitions of weak and failed states: for some analysts a state that does not deliver public goods is a failed state, whereas for others it is merely weak. For some, there is a difference between a failed state, where there is conflict over political order, and a collapsed state (where that order has evaporated). For still others, this is not the case since both conflicts over political order and state failure entail political violence and contests over the right to monopolise that violence.[38]

This is exacerbated by structural reading of how the international system affects weak states, which focuses on how it creates or constrains conditions that enable weak states to survive. The argument here is that the bipolar competition of the Cold War years generated resources and substituted for state building in some parts of the world so that conflict was relatively contained. Where there was still conflict it had state-like attributes – warring factions had a state project and a mobilising ideology, thanks to their sponsorship by the capitalist West or the socialist East. Conflicts and wars were therefore not as common as might have been expected, and even when they were civil wars they were forms of state-to-state conflict by proxy. The end of Cold War bipolarity, and the failure of a new world order to build an effective and legitimate state system, not to mention a rigorous system of intervention, has meant that conflicts are more intractable because their nature has changed. With the end of the Cold War the costs of violence in weak states declined to the outside world so there was less international pressure to control and contain it.[39] At the same time the security rents that weak states got from

---

[37] Heathershaw, *Post-conflict Tajikistan*, especially pp. 172–9.

[38] See N. Robinson, 'State-building and international politics: the emergence of a "new" problem and agenda', in A. Hehir and N. Robinson (eds.), *State-building: theory and practice* (London: Routledge, 2007), pp. 1–28.

[39] R.H. Bates, *Prosperity and violence: the political economy of development* (New York: W.W. Norton, 2001), pp. 97–100.

their sponsors disappeared, as did other financial aid that had flowed to them.[40] With less outside constraint, compounded by revenue squeezes, the result was conflict as groups competed for scarce resources.

Consequently, the form of this conflict was framed as 'new wars', or as 'resource wars', where struggles centred on controlling resources that were easy to appropriate, and where conflict was more intractable because combatants did not want to surrender seized resources, or were desperate to seize their share.[41] This pattern theoretically applies wherever there are weak states.[42] Yet the proof of this structural reading of the security dilemmas facing weak states consists of analogies. Initially, the analogies drawn were to the former Yugoslavia and its wars. Increasingly, however, the analogy drawn has been between Central Asia and Africa. Central Asia (and sometimes the post-Soviet space more generally) and Africa are said to share certain characteristics that make them prone to state failure.[43] These have already been referred to above: they are the same features of Central Asia that help to weaken them as democracies and states. Arbitrary borders create complex ethnic mixes, post-colonial economic deformations, absence of a pre-colonial state history, and varying forms of tribalism and sub-ethnic clan affinities. Since these led to conflict in Africa – in Somalia, the Great Lakes region, Liberia and Sierra Leone – they were expected to have an analogous impact in the post-Soviet region.

These analogies are, however, just that. They are not watertight explanations, and the grounds on which they are made are not that secure. It is debatable whether there is any more conflict now than in the recent past. The Cold War may have been a 'long peace', as John Lewis Gaddis put it, in North America and Europe, but not elsewhere.[44] Arguably – it

---

[40] M. Ayoob, 'State-making, state-breaking and state failure: explaining the roots of third world insecurity', in L. Van de Goor et al. (eds.), *Between development and destruction: an enquiry into the causes of conflict in post-colonial states* (Basingstoke: Macmillan, 1996), pp. 67–86; and N. van de Walle, 'The economic correlates of state failure: taxes, foreign aid, and policies', in R. Rotberg (ed.), *When states fail: causes and consequences* (Princeton University Press, 2004), p. 108.

[41] M. Duffield, *Global governance and the new wars: the merging of development and security* (London: Zed Books, 2001); M. Kaldor, *New and old wars.*

[42] For such a global perspective see P.G. Cerny, *Rethinking world politics: a theory of transnational neopluralism* (Oxford University Press, 2010), chapter 11.

[43] See M.R. Beissinger and C. Young (eds.), *Beyond state crisis? Post-colonial Africa and post-Soviet Eurasia in comparative perspective* (Washington, DC: Woodrow Wilson Center Press, 2002).

[44] J. Lewis Gaddis, *The long peace: inquiries into the history of the Cold War* (Oxford University Press, 1989). On the European bias in some of Gaddis's work that is mirrored in the idea that the end of the Cold War created conflict in the third world, see T. Judt, *Reappraisals: reflections on the forgotten twentieth century* (London: Penguin, 2009), pp. 368–83.

depends in part on what counts as war – there is now actually *less* conflict than there was during the Cold War.[45] Indeed, it is possible to argue that the problem is not the post-Cold war international system but the process of getting to that system. The end of the old Soviet order caused by the collapse of some of the states that formed it has died down as the new order took shape. The war in Tajikistan would be a case in point, just as the wars in former Yugoslavia were. These conflicts were not caused by post-Cold War multipolarity but by the events that led to the collapse of bipolarity. Moreover, once the shift from one form of international balance of power was completed, these wars also ended.

The distinction between state building and regime building

There are thus good grounds to doubt the strength of the link between changes internationally and the outbreak of war. Likewise we should doubt whether there is an automatic progression from weak democracy and weak statehood to conflict. The development of weak democracy (at best) is not a cause of conflict in the former USSR, but has so far constrained it. Likewise the weakness of post-Soviet states is not – or at least is not yet – a source of instability. Rather, it is a result of regime-building strategies that have controlled conflict. The post-Soviet space has for the most part departed from widely accepted norms about states, regimes and conflict. It has done this because of the success of many post-Soviet leaders in substituting regime building for state building. This is based on Soviet legacies, patrimonial political economy and a particular security environment. To understand this we must first understand that there are differences between state and regime building and how they can be traded off against each other.

State and regime building are related processes. However, whilst building a state implies the construction of a regime, constructing a regime does not always lead to the development of a strong state, or indeed to the development of any great state capacity at all. This is because state building and regime building have different criteria for success and failure, and need not be complementary. A regime may be consolidated when elites achieve a set of political rules that they cannot change without incurring a disproportionate cost to themselves. State formation is consolidated when officials have the ability and resources to perform state functions of maintaining order and security. The essential difference between state and regime, therefore, is that state

---

[45] Collier, *War, guns and votes*, pp. 4–5.

formation is not *just* a matter of elite competition. Conversely, in the short-term regime formation may be just that: a struggle during which elites may or may not respond to, or they may ignore, state-building pressures. States as functional (albeit unconscious) structures have some interest that is autonomous of elites: in particular, they have an interest in international competition and domestic order. This makes them, in Skocpol's classic formulation, an 'autonomous structure'. In other words, they have 'a structure with a logic and interests' that is 'not necessarily equivalent to, or fused with, the interests of the dominant class in society, or the full set of member groups in the polity'.[46]

The degree to which states are autonomous 'can come and go', as Skocpol later put it, since the structural potential for autonomous action – as well as stimulus for it – can vary over time, and from state sector to state sector.[47] Pressure to develop the state can come from one, few, or all of a state's composite officials and institutions, or be brought to bear on them from society. But no matter where the pressure comes from, state formation involves more complex tasks of social and economic management than regime formation. Keeping order generally requires organisation and resources additional to those needed to keep order among competing elites, and gathering these resources may strain elite agreements about the economic basis of a regime. Second, state formation has an international dimension to it that is structural. Traditional security concerns – real and perceived – are still an issue in many parts of the post-communist world, and states still need to develop as military and extractive structures to cope with security demands. This creates pressures for state development. Where these pressures are absent is equally telling, since there is a possibility that a regime might develop without having to pay much attention to state development. This would mean that state and regime might be stable, despite state weakness and inability to deal with transformation tasks.

State building over time thus influences regime stability, but in the short-run regime formation primarily involves elites and is determined by their interaction, the pressures upon them and the environment in which they interact. Regime building may overlap with state building, as an elite may try to prop up its preferred regime by delivering greater state capacity and public goods.

---

[46] T. Skocpol, *States and social revolutions: a comparative analysis of France, Russia and China* (Cambridge University Press, 1979), p. 27.

[47] T. Skocpol, 'Bringing the state back in: strategies of analysis in current research', in P. Evans et al. (eds.), *Bringing the state back in* (Cambridge University Press, 1984), p. 14.

Alternately, regime building might substitute for state building as elites capture rather than develop the state. Both strategies can be successful. But over the longer term, the better developed a state the more likely there is to be government stability (and hence regime stability), since continuity of government is less likely to call into question the basis on which power is accessed and used. How long this lasts depends on the pressures that a country has to deal with. Where pressures are great, supplanting regime building for state building will be dangerous, especially if the state has low capacity to begin with. A regime in a state with high capacity has more resources to deploy, better chances of extracting extra resources to deal with problems, and potentially broader reserves of political loyalty to fall back on, because it is able to deliver a wider range of public goods through the state. Moreover, there is less chance of political fragmentation if the delivery of these goods is not directly from the regime, but is filtered through a state with capacity. Where states deliver public goods they can be rationed in times of crisis or shortage; where delivery of goods is personalised through connection to the regime there is more chance of political contestation because power within a regime depends on ability to deliver resources. Thus they become objects of struggle between regime groups or unevenly distributed so that regime legitimacy declines.

The consolidation of state formation in post-communism is potentially a far more difficult thing to achieve than the consolidation of a regime, because managing the classic state functions of social order and national security involves questions of borders, citizenship and the establishment of new forms of economic exchange and rules to govern them. A regime may be consolidated before a state develops and fulfils the classic functions of a state easily. If this occurs, the question before a regime is whether it can contain and ameliorate problems of reconstruction, and maintain social order and national security to survive ruling through a weak state. If a regime cannot manage these pressures some other way (e.g., by gaining aid or security guarantees from other states) then it will come under pressure to evolve further and to develop the state. Where this pressure exists – and is not responded to – the long-term viability of a regime will be open to question.

Regime building at the expense of state building is thus a short-term solution to problems of consolidating and maintaining political order. Substituting regime building for state building has two main dimensions. First, there are state-building issues involving questions of identity, citizenship and borders. These are obviously important to new states, and may be particularly important for controlling the extent and intensity of potential ethnic unrest. Favouring regime building over state building has meant either that state-building projects have been weakened, or at least that they are weak at crucial moments in time when they might be more disruptive and conflict-prone. Second, there is the issue of elite stability in the face of reforms to build up the capacity of the state as an administrative and economic actor. Reform and the development of state capacity mean the alteration of existing power relations, and the redistribution of power amongst elites to uncertain (and hence undesirable) ends. This is especially the case where political power is a prerequisite for economic affluence.[48]

Where regime building is favoured over state building, balancing power and ensuring that economic capacity is maintained will be as important as passing power from elites and social groups to state institutions. Developing the state to promote economic growth, for instance, will change the balance of economic fortune and power. The forms of conflict that are potentially involved here may be less extensive and bloody than communal violence, since they may be more focused as coups, or conflicts over election results. However, they are potentially structurally violent in that they may damage the economic fortunes of a nation, and often lead to wider conflict.[49]

Avoiding conflict in Russia and Central Asia: state-building and regime-building practices

State building as a process of identity formation involves the development of citizenship through language and education policies, and the creation of new political and economic borders. It was responsible for the breakdown of peace at the end of the USSR. It was subsequently responsible for the perpetuation of conflicts in the Caucasus. Such conflicts have brought protest, if not sustained violence, to the Crimea. Sometimes conflict was actively provoked by a state-building effort – as in Georgia under Zviad Gamsakhurdia, who attempted to develop a notion of Georgian statehood and citizenship as part of the independence struggle with the USSR, or more recently under Mikhail Saakashvili, who returned to the politics of state building after the interregnum under Eduard Shevardnadze when state-building efforts were

---

[48] For the theory behind this see B. Geddes, *Politician's dilemma: building state capacity in Latin America* (Berkeley: University of California Press, 1994), pp. 1–42.

[49] On structural violence see J. Galtung, 'Violence, peace, and peace research', *Journal of Peace Research* 6 (1969), 167–91. On the economic affects of coups and their potential to lead to further conflict see Collier, *Wars, guns and votes*, pp. 142, 152–4.

sidetracked.[50] Sometimes the mere threat of a state-building project was enough to create a pre-emptive backlash, as in Moldova. In this case, the population of Trans-Dniester feared some form of 'Romanianisation', either through the reintegration of Moldova with Romania, or via the development of an independent Moldovan state.[51]

In both the Caucasus and Moldova this violent reaction to state building was facilitated by the Soviet federal structure, particularly the existence of autonomous republics and regions – Trans-Dniester, Abkhazia, South Ossetia and Adjara – within larger Soviet republics that were in the process of emerging as new states. The existence of these sub-republican federal units gave elites objecting to state-building projects a framework through which to mobilise and create alternative crypto-states of their own, especially since they could appeal to the still existing Soviet centre for protection of their federal rights.[52] Appealing to Moscow enabled them to protest emerging national citizenship by appeal to the greater Soviet identity of which they were still a part and which protected their local identity.

Crucially, however, this was not as evident in Russia and Central Asia, where conflict through Soviet federal structures was not universal. This was because state-building projects were not equally recognised or given an ethnic character at key moments of crisis. In Russia itself, any idea that a particularistic national identity might be emerging as the USSR collapsed was ameliorated by the poor electoral showing of Russian nationalists, who were largely tied intellectually to the declining Communist Party of the USSR.[53] Second, the rhetoric of Russian opposition was also not nationalist since it often downplayed the issue of succession. This is best demonstrated by Boris Yeltsin's famous call for the autonomous republics and regions to 'take as much sovereignty as you can swallow', and assiduous courting of autonomous areas as allies.[54]

[50] J. Wheatley, 'Managing ethnic diversity in Georgia: one step forward, two steps back', *Central Asian Survey* 28 (2009), 119–34; and J.A. George, 'The dangers of reform: state building and national minorities in Georgia', *Central Asian Survey* 28 (2009), 135–54.

[51] On the manipulation of language and cultural issues in Moldova see S. Roper, 'Regionalism in Moldova: the case of Trans-Dniester and Gaugazia', *Regional & Federal Studies* 11 (2001), 101–22.

[52] On the importance of Soviet federal arrangements see J.A. George, 'Expecting ethnic conflict: the Soviet legacy and ethnic politics in the Caucasus and Central Asia', in A.E. Wooden and C.H. Stefes (eds.), *The politics of transition in Central Asia and the Caucasus: enduring legacies and emerging challenges* (London: Routledge, 2009), pp. 75–102.

[53] K. O'Connor, *Intellectuals and apparatchiks: Russian nationalism and the Gorbachev revolution* (Lanham, MD: Lexington Books, 2006).

[54] T.J. Colton, *Yeltsin: a life* (New York: Basic Books, 2008), pp. 186–7.

With the exception of Chechnya (and there are several ways in which Chechnya can be seen as exceptional) the breakup of the USSR did not provoke ethno-nationalist collapse in Russia since no state-building project was in place as the collapse took place. It only emerged after it, and then weakly. The stress in official Russian discourses on citizenship is placed on non-ethnic Russian (*rossiiskii*) citizenship rather than ethnic Russianness (*russkii*). Compromises over centre-federal relations and the development of an asymmetric federalism under Yeltsin, allowing for the political ambitions and power of regional elites, was a crucial factor in the weakening of Russian economic reform, which was at the heart of Yeltsin's efforts to build up state power relative to elite groups.[55] Regime stability – keeping Yeltsin in power, protecting the power of economic groups from the Communist Party of the Russian Federation (KPRF), and maintaining the balance of power between centre and federal units – thus outweighed state building in Russia. Although there was often a push for secession in Russia's autonomous republics,[56] the weakness of the federal centre and its willingness to compromise its policies meant that local leaders could mediate between centre and republic to moderate demands from below and transform them into resource flows from the centre.[57]

Similar patterns can be seen in Central Asia, where threats of ethnic conflict were diffused in potential flashpoints by policies of accommodation and power devolution.[58] In Central Asia there was no mass movement to secession and political leadership in the republics worked to control nationalism. In this, they were very mindful of the potential for conflict in the area. In Uzbekistan, for example, the main secessionist movement, *Birlik*, was pushed aside and the government's repressions were legitimised by fears of violence in the Fergana valley.[59] The

[55] On asymmetric federalism and the management of secession in Russia generally, see M. Crosston, *Shadow separatism: implications for democratic consolidation* (Aldershot, UK: Ashgate, 2004); J. Hughes, 'Managing secession potential in the Russian Federation', *Regional & Federal Studies* 11 (2001), 36–68. On economic reform as state building in Russia, and its compromise see N. Robinson, *Russia: a state of uncertainty* (London: Routledge, 2002), pp. 102–31.

[56] E. Giuliano, 'Secessionism from the bottom up: democratisation, nationalism and local accountability in the Russian transition', *World Politics* 58 (2006), 276–310.

[57] D. Treisman, 'Fiscal redistribution in a fragile federation: Moscow and the regions in 1994', *British Journal of Political Science* 28 (1998), 185–200; and D. Treisman, 'Deciphering Russia's federal finance: fiscal appeasement in 1995 and 1996', *Europe-Asia Studies* 50 (1998), 893–906.

[58] G. Sasse, *The Crimea question: identity, transition, and conflict* (Cambridge, MA: Harvard University Press, 2007).

[59] L. Markowitz, 'How master frames mislead: the division and eclipse of nationalist movements in Uzbekistan and Tajikistan', *Ethnic and Racial Studies* 32 (2009), 716–38.

relative absence of nationalist rhetoric – and for many Central Asian elites the absence of a desire for secession – made it harder for post-Soviet leaders in Central Asia to drape themselves fully in national-ist garb immediately after the Soviet collapse. Some development of a national identity was inevitable, not least because *de facto* sovereignty had to be addressed, and that meant the practical management of bor-ders and ethnic minorities. But nationalism was muted and reactions to it less extreme than had been the case where it had been used a vehicle for political advancement in the last days of perestroika. This was partly because of the out-migration of Russian and other Slavs. Part of it was also because, as in Russia, distinctions continued to be drawn between ethnicity and citizenship.[60]

Although there have been language laws and other policies to pro-mote titular ethnic groups, ethnicity has not dominated state-building projects in the same way that it did in Georgia, for example. The very multi-ethnic composition of all of the Central Asian states has played a part in this continued Soviet-style separation of ethnicity and citi-zenship: if ethnicity became the basis of citizenship, leaders across the region would run the risk of claims to citizenship rights being made across borders, and raise the danger of low-key localised ethnic dis-putes becoming interstate conflicts. Central Asian leaders have been more concerned to guard their sovereignty in deciding how to structure their political and economic systems to their own advantage. There has also been co-optation of regional elites to head off opposition. This was less institutionalised than in Russia, but it was still an important means of heading off potential threats, especially in the early years of inde-pendence.[61] Later, as power was consolidated in Central Asian regimes, the balance between coercion and consensus sometimes changed.[62] However, by that time the moment of crisis that had allowed conflict to develop in the Caucasus and Moldova had passed, and the costs of revolt would have been much higher against what were, in contrast, much stronger Central Asian regimes.

State-building projects have not, therefore, been strongly exclusionary at the most dangerous time for Russia and the new states of Central Asia. Whilst this lessened the risk of communal violence it might have increased

---

[60] See Roy, *The new Central Asia*, pp. 175–7; E. Schatz, 'Framing strategies and non-conflict in multi-ethnic Kazakhstan', *Nationalism and Ethnic Politics* 6 (2000), 71–94.

[61] S.N. Cummings, *Kazakhstan: centre-periphery relations* (London: Royal Institute of International Affairs, 2000).

[62] For an overview across three states see N.J. Melvin, 'Patterns of centre-regional rela-tions in Central Asia: the cases of Kazakhstan, the Kyrgyz Republic and Uzbekistan', *Regional & Federal Studies* 11 (2001), 165–93.

the risk of political degeneration since it meant that regimes had one less tool at their disposal to bind together their populations. Moreover, they ran the risk of nationalism being used to mobilise against them. Russia is a case in point, as nationalist and communist forces re-emerged as a threat after 1991 and linked up with disaffected members of the political elite in parliament in 1993. This alliance, plus Yeltsin's actions against his parliament, combined to create the violent events of October 1993. Countering the risk of mobilisation meant insuring that elites' incentives to defect from ruling coalitions were minimised. As partial democracies or proto-authoritarian regimes at the time of Soviet collapse, and with popular mobilisation generally low, other elite groups and members were the chief danger to new rulers. They formed the 'selectorate', the group with the political resources to remove incumbents, and had to be mollified if leaders were to survive politically.[63]

Ensuring the support of their selectorates meant raising the risks attendant on opposition. In the main this meant co-option, so that elite groups had too much to lose by threatening to break with incumbents or supporting oppositional activity. How far a new leadership had to go to raise the risks of opposition and how far it had to co-opt elites to support it varied from state to state.[64] Conflict was most marked where there was no dominant elite view.[65] Presidentialism gave all leaders some powers and incentives to consolidate regimes, but they were not able to do so uniformly. In Uzbekistan and Turkmenistan, and to a lesser extent in Kazakhstan, regimes were constructed consensually thanks to elite continuity. This was particularly the case in terms of continuity of rulers, but also for continuity of a ruling party (as local Communist Party organisations were transformed into new ruling parties), with a relatively high degree of continuity of economic and social power.[66]

---

[63] On selectorates see B. Bueno de Mesquita et al., *The logic of political survival* (Cambridge, MA: MIT Press, 2003).

[64] On the variables affecting consensus and division see A. Grzymala-Busse and P. Luong Jones, 'Reconceptualising the state: lessons from post-communism', *Politics & Society* 30 (2002), 529–44; V. Gel'man, 'Iz ognya da v polymya? Dinamika postsovetskikh rezhimov v sravnitel'noi perspektive', *Polis* (2007), 81–108.

[65] M. McFaul, 'The fourth wave of democracy and dictatorship: noncooperative transitions in the postcommunist world', in M. McFaul and K. Stoner-Weiss (eds.), *After the collapse of communism: comparative lessons of transition* (Cambridge University Press, 2004), pp. 58–95.

[66] Essays on early moves to consolidate power in Kazakhstan and Uzbekistan can be found in T.J. Colton and R.C. Tucker (eds.), *Patterns in post-Soviet leadership* (Boulder, CO: Westview, 1995). Broader overviews can be found in G. Gleason, *The Central Asian states: discovering independence* (Boulder, CO: Westview, 1997); S.N. Cummings (ed.), *Power and change in Central Asia* (London: Routledge, 2002); P. Luong Jones,

In Tajikistan there was immediate contestation over the regime caused by the collapse of the state and the huge fiscal gap created by the end of Soviet revenue transfers. This led to the privatisation of coercion to capture what scarce resources were left along regional lines and civil war between armed factions.[67] The settlement of the civil war gradually led Tajikistan back to the Central Asian norm: the stabilisation of the regime around President Imomali Rahmonov ended the contestation over power. Political struggles were internalised within the regime as in other parts of Central Asia, and substituted regime powers for state capacity.[68] In Kyrgyzstan, the presidency of Askar Akaev began as Central Asia's great democratic and reformist hope. But the needs of political survival and struggles over the distribution of resources amongst elites soon saw compromise and personalistic politics replace efforts at building up a reformist and impersonal state that could carry through economic reform in the country.[69]

Regimes therefore emerged in most of Central Asia that dominated and deflected state-building projects. In Russia, as in Kyrgyzstan, the process took place over a longer time since there was no consensus over the successor regime. The difference between the Russian, Tajik and Kyrgyz cases and the more stable cases of regime consolidation in the other Central Asian states is explained in part by their different initial political conditions, but also by their economic structures and sizes. The leaders of Kazakhstan, Uzbekistan and Turkmenistan were aided in their regime consolidation and had less incentive to reform because of the wealth of their natural resources base, and/or because of the economic structures of their countries. This meant they had resources to distribute. They also had greater control over economic sectors such as energy and the cotton economy in Uzbekistan, and spread resources around more easily across their generally small economies. Cumulatively

Institutional change and political continuity in post-Soviet Central Asia: power, perceptions, and pacts (Cambridge University Press, 2002); M. Olcott, *Central Asia's second chance* (Washington, DC: Carnegie Endowment for International Peace, 2005); and D. Lewis, *The temptations of tyranny in Central Asia* (London: Hurst, 2008).

[67] L. Markowitz, *The micro-foundations of rebellion and repression: rents, patronage, and law-enforcement in Tajikistan and Uzbekistan* (Seattle, WA: The National Council for Eurasian and East European Research, 2008).

[68] See Gleason, *The Central Asian states*; M. Atkin, 'Tajikistan: a president and his rivals', in S.N. Cummings (ed.), *Power and change in Central Asia* (London: Routledge, 2002), pp. 97–114; Lewis, *The temptations of tyranny*, pp. 161–81; and Heathershaw, *Post-conflict Tajikistan.*

[69] See Markowitz, *The micro-foundations of rebellion and repression*; and R.A. Spector, *The transformation of Askar Akaev, president of Kyrgzstan* (Berkeley, CA: Berkeley Program in Soviet and Post-Soviet Studies, 2004). Available at http://repositories. cdlib.org/iseees/bps/2004 02-spec

these made their economies regime-supporting, so few incentives to reform existed.[70] Initial redistribution of property was more manageable, not a struggle as in Russia, and regimes adapted their institutional structures over time to protect the patrimonial systems that emerged as a result.[71] This did not isolate them from economic downturn in the 1990s, but the regimes were strong enough to be able to maintain an unequal division of wealth without sparking effective protest.

In Russia and Central Asia, the closed political systems that supported economic structures were a reason that regime building could be used to supplant state building. These circumstances are probably unique in much of the contemporary world. The massive redistribution of property that accompanied the establishment of new regimes in the post-Soviet space was probably more extensive than redistributions elsewhere, even amongst many post-colonial states. It also took place whilst market relations were weak so that it was primarily a political process whose outcome was not derailed by market reactions. This gave great power to those at the apex of the new political systems and bound elites to them much more thoroughly. The political economy of post-communism thus worked for regime building in a way that political economies elsewhere in weak democracies/states might not.

External factors also helped. Economically, the area was aided by subsidies from Russia in the early 1990s, both direct (through transfers and through Russia lifting debt burden from them) and indirect (by former Soviet republics exporting their inflation to Russia). This gave Central Asian states some breathing space in the first years of independence whilst property was being distributed amongst elites, and regimes consolidated. After the initial redistribution of property in the 1990s the stability of regimes in Kazakhstan, Turkmenistan, Tajikistan and Uzbekistan was aided by high energy prices and by the growth of Russia's economy.[72]

External economic support for regimes has been matched by the security rents that post-Soviet regimes have enjoyed. There has not

---

[70] Again, this process was more easily accomplished in Uzbekistan and Turkmenistan than in Kazakhstan and more complete there than in Kyrgyzstan or Russia. See R.M. Auty and I. de Soysa, 'Incentives to reform in the Caucasus and Central Asian political states', in R.M. Auty and I. de Soysa (eds), *Energy, wealth and governance in the Caucasus and Central Asia* (London: Routledge, 2006), pp. 135–51.

[71] For a discussion of this in Kazakhstan see R. Isaacs, 'Between informal and formal politics: neopatrimonialism and party development in post-Soviet Kazakhstan', PhD thesis (Oxford Brookes University, 2009).

[72] See the figures in N. Robinson, 'Patrimonial political economy and the global economy'. Paper delivered to the ISA-ABRI Joint International Meeting, Rio de Janeiro (2009). Available at www.allacademic.com/meta/p381097_index.html

been an analogous withdrawal of great power support from the post-Soviet space as it is claimed has been the case in Africa.[73] Although Russia suffered a loss of power, territory and prestige in the wake of the USSR's collapse it did not withdraw as completely from its former 'colonies' as some other states (such as Portugal) did during de-colonialisation, nor did it curtail relations that supported statehood. Russia has remained involved in the security of post-Soviet space in various ways and to varying degrees, either directly or as a part of some sort of collective security arrangement.

Indeed, one could argue that there has been a surfeit of security arrangements since the collapse of the USSR. Some were organised multilaterally through the CIS, or with other regional powers (such as the SCO, which includes the PRC, Russia and the Central Asian states). Some were bilaterally negotiated between Russia and states in the region, such as the 2006 security treaty with Uzbekistan. On top of this there has been the involvement of the United States, especially post-9/11 and the war in Afghanistan, and NATO (through PfP) in the area.

This 'game' of security, as it has been labelled,[74] in Central Asia has not resolved many of the security issues in the region in that it has not resolved the threat of breakdown in Afghanistan, nor ended the narcotics and other smuggling rackets in the region. However, it has meant that some of the costs that are expected to fall on weak actors when outside powers reduce their commitment to them have not been borne by post-Soviet states. Their statehood has been guaranteed by international agreement and by Russian commitment to the area, regardless of the fact that this may be self-serving and destructive of other aspects of sovereignty.

The gains from these external guarantees of statehood have sometimes been direct and tangible in Central Asia, and sometimes not. Tangible and direct benefits to the regimes of the region include the revenue that Kyrgyzstan accrued through leasing the Manas air force base to the United States, a rental equal to 7–10 per cent of Kyrgyz GDP. The rental also helped secure largesse from Moscow in early 2009, which was subsequently balanced by rent increases levied on the United States. More generally, there has been an influx in military and other aid flowing into Central Asia since 9/11 as the United States

---

[73] van de Walle, 'The economic correlates of state failure', 108–10.
[74] C. Bluth and O. Kassenov, 'The "game" of security in Central Asia', in Y. Kalyuzhnova and D. Lynch (eds.), *The Euro-Asian world: a period of transition* (Basingstoke, UK: Macmillan, 2000), pp. 28–44.

increased its presence in the region.[75] Uzbekistan in particular has been very keen to play off the United States and Russia, and resultant security guarantees have meant that war has not had to make the state in Central Asia.

Although it is difficult to measure Central Asian military spending, on balance it seems to have been comparatively low for most of the area's independent history, rising slightly over the past few years because of the economic growth generated by Russia's boom, and by higher energy prices.[76] In other words, there has not been a need to build up military capacity in the region to deal with security threats. Instead, leaders have been left to use economic resources to support their regimes. This is despite the quite often-parlous state of relations within the regions over borders and cross-border trade, and water resources and their transit. These have not resulted in a build-up of military strength commensurate to deal with them, in large part because such strength could not be used for fear of a punitive response from either Russia or the PRC.

More intangible benefits of Central Asia's security arrangements have been the protection of regimes from threats, which have in turn deadened the development of conflict. The presence of Russian troops in Central Asia, especially in the form of the CSTO rapid reaction force deployed in 2009, probably lessens the risk of internal conflict. Occasionally, this reduction has been explicitly invoked. The Russo-Uzbek security treaty signed after the events in Andijan in 2005 provided for Russian intervention in Uzbekistan to suppress threats to the regime there. More generally, it is the case elsewhere in the world that coups are discouraged by either the presence of foreign troops,[77] or by implicit support of a major military power, such as Russia still is in the region.[78] Russia and the SCO have also worked politically to stabilise the regimes of Central Asia.[79]

---

[75] See the figures in S.W. Babus, 'Democracy-building in Central Asia post-September 11', in D.L. Burghart and T. Sabonis-Helf (eds.), *In the tracks of Tamerlane: Central Asia's path to the twenty-first century* (Washington, DC: National Defence University Center for Technology and National Security Policy, 2004), pp. 115–38.

[76] S. Perlo-Freeman and P. Stålenheim, 'Military expenditure in the South Caucasus and Central Asia', in A.J.K. Bailes et al. (eds.), *Armament and disarmament in the Caucasus and Central Asia* (Stockholm International Peace Research Institute, 2003), pp. 7–20.

[77] R.H.T. O'Kane, 'A probabilistic approach to the causes of coups d'état', *British Journal of Political Science* 11 (1981), 287–308.

[78] Collier, *Wars, guns, and votes*, pp. 86–7.

[79] T. Ambrosio, 'Catching the "Shanghai Spirit": how the Shanghai Cooperation Organisation promotes authoritarian norms in Central Asia', *Europe-Asia Studies* 60 (2008), 1321–44; and T. Ambrosio, *Authoritarian backlash: Russian resistance to democratisation in the former Soviet Union* (Aldershot, UK: Ashgate, 2008).

Conclusions

Prophecies of conflict in the post-Soviet space have so far not been fulfilled. The existence of weak states and weak democracies has not on their own been enough to tip the region, or parts of it, into conflict. This is despite predictions that draw analogies between these phenomena and conflict in other parts of the globe. The post-Soviet cases of Russia and Central Asia show that something extra needs to be added to the mix to push weak states and weak democracies over the edge and into conflict. Moreover, some factors, such as the redistribution of economic resources when it is on the scale of post-Soviet redistribution, might even help to avert it. So far, Russia and Central Asian countries have avoided the abyss in large measure because they have held back on state-building policies. These policies would have alienated parts of their populations, riven elites and made them mobilise against one another, or used nationalism to shore up their domestic position, turning post-Soviet states against each other in the process.

Is the substitution of regime building for state building and the avoidance of conflict sustainable over time? The extent to which post-Soviet countries have been able to avoid harsh choices varies and so too will their ability to maintain this pattern of development and relative peace in the future. Some of the circumstances that may have helped Central Asian nations avoid conflict in the past will probably not be available to them in the future. For example, the redistribution of property will be difficult to achieve again without violence.

Avoiding state building may also be inherently unstable in the long term. The Russian and the Kyrgyz cases show the instability that can come with regimes dominating and supplanting state building. In Russia, the relationship between Yeltsin, regional and economic elites weakened economic reform efforts and was in part responsible for the 1998 economic crisis.[80] In Kyrgyzstan the derailing of reform in the 1990s led to a huge build-up of foreign debt as the country traded on its reputation as the most progressive Central Asian state. This debt placed the economy and presidency of Akaev under great strain and was a factor contributing to the Tulip Revolution of 2005 that overthrew him.

And yet neither the 1998 crisis nor the Tulip Revolution led to prolonged conflict. In Kyrgyzstan the Akaev regime was replaced by that of President Kurmanbek Bakiyev. Like others in the region before him, Bakiyev used electoral manipulation, threats and coercion to stabilise

---

[80] N. Robinson, 'The global economy, reform and crisis in Russia', *Review of International Political Economy* 6 (1999), 531–64.

his regime. Similarly, in Russia the 1998 economic crisis was followed by a fresh effort at regime building under Vladimir Putin that was supposed to create the basis for a renewed round of state building. This was to include cleaning up corruption, the reassertion of federal control over the regions, the subjugation of economic elites to political authorities, and the generation of new forms of growth led by state agencies. Both the Russian and Kyrgyz regimes were fortunate that their crises occurred as international economic and political factors gave their economies a fillip, so that crisis segued into economic growth and state building did not have to be pushed home aggressively.[81]

Once again, then, regime building was more successful than state building. But whilst this remains the case across the post-Soviet space the potential for crisis remains great. Crises, when they occur, might be of a regime (a succession crisis, for example),[82] of the state (a fiscal crisis like that of 1998), or a combination of both (like the Tulip Revolution). There is no reason why a crisis might not be solved, of course, or why fortuitous circumstances might not intervene to save the day. But even saying that points, finally, to the very contingent and fragile nature of factors preventing a slide into conflict in large parts of the post-Soviet space. In short, expectations of conflict within the former USSR have been wrong so far, but that is no reason to be confident that this will endure.

[81] On the Russian case see N. Robinson, 'Russia: limiting the impact of crisis in a post-communist transitional economy', in J. Robertson (ed.), *Power and politics after financial crisis: rethinking foreign opportunism in emerging markets* (Basingstoke, UK: Palgrave Macmillan, 2008), pp. 212–28.

[82] See Olcott, *Central Asia's second chance*, pp. 124–72, on the succession problems in Central Asia.

7 Transnational crime, corruption and conflict in Russia and the former USSR

Leslie Holmes

A November 2008 survey of Russians revealed that almost 60 per cent of respondents considered corruption to be the most important problem President Medvedev needed to address.[1] Given that the survey was conducted at the peak of the global financial crisis (GFC), the significance of corruption to Russians is highlighted well by this survey response.[2] That it is a key issue is endorsed by the fact that, in June 2009, former Soviet leader, Mikhail Gorbachev, identified 'bureaucracy and corruption' as Russia's main problems.[3] Certainly, President Medvedev made the fight against corruption his top priority when he first took office. On 19 May 2008, he signed a decree aimed at breathing new life into the Russian state's efforts to combat the phenomenon.[4] In early November 2008, in his first annual 'state of the nation' address to the Federal Assembly, Medvedev identified corruption as the 'number one enemy for a free, democratic and just society'.[5] And outgoing President Putin stated in mid-February 2008 that corruption had been the most intractable problem he had faced

I wish to thank the Australian Research Council for research awards (ARC Large Grant No. A79930728 and Discovery Grant No. DP0558453) that greatly facilitated the research for this chapter.

[1] VTsIOM, 'Obshchestvennaya povestka dnya: bor'ba s korruptsiey i preodolenie krizisa', *Press-vypusk* 1099, 21 November (2008). Available at: http://wciom.ru/arkhiv/tematicheskii-arkhiv/item/single/11021.html?no_cache=1&cHash=dee60cc421

[2] The result also challenges the contention of a number of Russian analysts who maintain that Russians have now accepted corruption as simply a normal part of everyday life – see, for example, G. Satarov, 'Corruption, Western and Russian', in Y. Senokosov and E. Skidelsky (eds.), 'Corruption in Russia', *Russia on Russia* 4 (Moscow School of Political Studies and Social Market Foundation, 2001), 8; V. Shlapentokh, 'Russia's acquiescence to corruption makes the state machine inept', *Communist and Post-Communist Studies* 36:2 (2003), esp. 152–3.

[3] BBC Monitoring, Former Soviet Union, 29 June (2009), cited in *Johnson's Russia List*, no. 121, 1 July (2009), item 5.

[4] 'Ukaz Prezidenta Rossiyskoy Federatsii ot 19 maya 2008g N 815, "O merax po protivodeystoju korruptsii"', *Rossiyskaya Gazeta*, 22 May (2008).

[5] D. Medvedev, 'Poslanie Federal'nomu Sobraniyu Rossiyskoy Federatsii', available at http://news.kremlin.ru/transcripts/1968

146

as president.[6] Russians apparently see the fight against corruption and bribery as his biggest failure as prime minister too, according to a July 2009 survey by the Levada Center.[7] Much more recently, a poll in August 2010 by the Levada Center revealed that Russians saw the fight against corruption and bribery as Putin's single biggest failing over his decade in high office.[8] Clearly, the issue is a significant one in post-communist Russia.

But so too is organised crime. While such assessments must be treated as no more than informed guesses, *Izvestiya* claimed in 1994 that organised crime controlled some 70–80 per cent of banking and private business in Russia.[9] Even though this was almost certainly a sensationalised exaggeration – and is based on a very broad definition of organised crime – the statement itself reveals how serious an issue the Russian administration perceived the problem of organised crime to be, or at least how seriously it wished to portray it. This point is endorsed by the 1993 statement by President Yeltsin that '[o]rganised crime has become a direct threat to Russia's strategic interests and national security'.[10]

It is not only the Russian authorities that have identified Russian corruption and organised crime to be major threats. While 9/11 shifted the focus of Western governments to terrorism, both the US government and Interpol had in the 1990s identified Russian corruption and organised crime as particularly serious dangers. For example, the (then) heads of the CIA and the FBI, John Deutch and Louis Freeh respectively, warned the US Congress in 1996 that Russian corruption and organised crime were already undermining the Russian system, and could pose a threat to the United States.[11] Later that year, former CIA director James Woolsey claimed that corrupt officials in the Russian Ministry of Defence were colluding with Russian organised crime gangs.[12] Since the West was at the time seriously concerned about the smuggling of

---

[6] See www.kremlin.ru/eng/speeches/2008/02/14/1011_type82915_160266.shtml

[7] Interfax, 'Grazhdane Putinu: zdes' u vas nedorabotki', 27 July (2009). Available at www.interfax.ru/business/txt.asp?id=92162&sw=%CB%E5%E2%E0%E4%E0&bd =23&bm=7&by=2009&ed=30&em=7&ey=2009&secid=0&mp=0&p=1

[8] See L. Kim, 'Putin's biggest failure is fight against Russian corruption, poll shows', 12 August (2010). Available at www.bloomberg.com/news/2010-08-12/putin-s-biggest-failure-is-fight-against-russian-corruption-poll-shows.html

[9] Cited in M. Goldman, *The piratisation of Russia: Russian reform goes awry* (London: Routledge, 2003), p. 177.

[10] G. Talalayev, 'Boris Yeltsin addresses all-Russia conference on problems of the fight against organized crime and corruption: full text of speech', Moscow, ITAR-TASS, 12 February (1993).

[11] Cited in W. Webster (ed.), *Russian organised crime: global organised crime project* (Washington, DC: Center for Strategic and International Studies, 1997), p. 3.

[12] Ibid.

nuclear materials from Russia that could be used by so-called rogue states or terrorist organisations to create WMD, the significance of such an allegation comes sharply into focus. Corruption and organised crime across the former USSR were perceived to be becoming a serious threat to global security. Indeed, another former director of both the FBI and the CIA, William Webster, claimed in 1997, 'Corruption of the official Russian bureaucracy poses, in many ways, the most serious threat to the interests of the United States and other countries.'[13]

Unfortunately, it is far from clear that the worst of this threat has passed. According to a 2007 statement by the deputy head of the Russian Interior Ministry's Department for the Struggle Against Organised Crime and Terrorism, the trend for Russian organised crime to become transnational intensified in the first few years of the new millennium.[14] Ever more cases of cybercrime are surfacing around the world, and Russians – and sometimes other ethnic groups from various parts of the former USSR – have been implicated in many of them. For example, the major case of computer hacking that permitted criminal access to some 134 million credit cards in the United States, and which appeared to have been finally cracked in August 2009, was said to have involved two co-conspirators based 'in or near Russia' among the three-person team that ran the operation.[15]

In fact, organised crime and corruption are often bedfellows. As intimated above, both sometimes interact with terrorism to exacerbate conflicts, and both continue to be a threat way beyond Russia's borders. This chapter examines some of the evidence relating to corruption and organised crime in Russia and other states of the former USSR, as well as some of the limited evidence on their ties to terrorism. Regrettably, the very nature of organised crime and corruption is such that much activity remains hidden, and far more of the evidence cited has to be strongly circumstantial (as distinct from proven) than would be desirable. This said, avoiding any analysis of crime-related topics that are difficult to study empirically simply plays into the hands of criminals. This brief overview of some of the evidence is followed by a particular focus on transnational aspects, both as they relate to countries that were once part of the USSR, and as they affect other parts of the world. It will be argued that globalisation, as well as corruption at the top of the Russian system, have played into the hands of lower-ranking corrupt officials and organised crime gangs, who remain one step ahead

---

[13] Ibid.
[14] Interfax Russia and CIS General Newswire, 20 August (2007).
[15] B. Krebs, 'Three indicted in identity theft case', *Washington Post*, 18 August (2009), p. A11; 'Hacker "stole 130m credit card numbers"', *Independent*, 19 August (2009), 27; *Guardian International*, 19 August (2009), p. 17.

of law enforcement agencies. But while globalisation has contributed to the rise of Russian and former Soviet crime, it will be demonstrated that there are also many factors peculiar to post-communism that contribute to the rise of organised crime and corruption in the region. On the prescriptive level, it will also be argued that making the Russian and other former Soviet systems more authoritarian is not the way to address the crime and corruption problem, contrary to what many Russians apparently believe. In the concluding section, the dynamic nature of corruption and organised crime will be considered, and reasons for very cautious optimism about the future will be advanced.

Corruption in Russia

While it is impossible to provide definitive statistics on the amount of corruption in Russia – or indeed in any country – the various methods that specialists use provide clear evidence that Russia has been, and remains, one of the world's most corrupt countries. It is also one of the most corrupt among relatively developed states. Among the many methods used for assessing the level of corruption are official statistics, popular- and mixed- (citizens, businesspeople, experts) perception surveys, business-perception surveys, popular experiential surveys, and business experiential surveys.[16] Some of the most significant findings of these various methods will be briefly summarised here. Following this, consideration is given to some of the other ways in which corruption can be assessed.

There are several types of official statistics that can be considered when attempting to judge the scale and trend-lines of corruption in any country. These include legal statistics (number of police investigations, number of prosecutions, number of convictions, number and type of sentences), and official figures on the scale of bribery. Unfortunately, there are also numerous reasons why official statistics on corruption in most states must be treated at least carefully, if not with a pinch of salt.[17] However, it can sometimes be useful to consider some of these statistics, in part because it can help analysts understand how mass perceptions

---

[16] Another possible method is tracking surveys, such as public expenditure tracking surveys. These are not explored or explained here, since they do not appear to have been conducted in former Soviet states to date. Russia has only recently finished conducting such a survey – see http://web.worldbank.org/WBSITE/EXTERNAL/TOPICS/EXTPUBLICSECTORANDGOVERNANCE/EXTPUBLICFINANCE/EXTPEAM/0,,contentMDK:20235447~pagePK:210058~piPK:210062~theSitePK:384393,00.html

[17] On the various problems involved in using official statistics on corruption in post-communist states, see L. Holmes, 'Crime, organised crime and corruption in post-communist Europe and the CIS', *Communist and Post-Communist Studies* 42:2 (2009), esp. 266–8 and 278.

are formed. If the authorities are constantly informing citizens that a particular issue is serious, the populace will believe that there is a major problem, whether or not this corresponds to reality or their own experiences. In this context, it is worth noting that the Department of Economic Security in Russia's Ministry of Internal Affairs announced that the size of the average bribe in Russia in 2009 amounted to 27,000 rubles, which represented a threefold increase on the 2008 average, while the number of cases of bribery had increased by almost a third.[18] Despite the fact that President Medvedev immediately challenged these figures,[19] many citizens prefer to believe more sensational statistics.[20]

Despite its various methodological problems, the most frequently cited survey on corruption levels around the world remains Transparency International's (TI) 'Corruption Perceptions Index' (CPI).[21] This is described by TI itself as a 'poll of polls', and is based primarily on surveys of businesspeople. It has been produced annually since 1995, although Russia was first assessed in 1996. The CPI is scaled 0–10. The higher the score, the lower the perceived level of corruption. Russia scored an unimpressive 2.9 in the 1996 survey, and had deteriorated to 2.4 by 1998 and further still to 2.0 in 2000. The situation improved during Putin's first presidency, although the score never rose above 2.8 (2004). It then began to deteriorate once again, slipping to 2.1 in 2008, rose marginally to 2.2 in 2009, and fell back to 2.1 again in 2010.[22]

Within Russia, two of the best-known sources of survey data on corruption are VTsIOM/Levada Center and the INDEM Foundation.[23] A September 2007 survey by the Levada Center in Moscow revealed that almost half (48%) of the 1,600 respondents believed that the level

---

[18] 'Srednyaya velichina vzyatki povysilas' do 27 tysyach rubley', *Kommersant*, 27 July (2009). Available at www.kommersant.ru/doc.aspx?DocsID=1211294&ThemesID=239

[19] 'Korruptsiya popravila prezidenta', *Kommersant*, 28 July (2009). Available at www.kommersant.ru/daily/?date=20090728

[20] For further recent official statistics on corruption, cited by Russia's prosecutor-general, see ITAR-TASS, 23 May 2009, reproduced in *Johnson's Russia List*, no. 97, 26 May (2009), item 10.

[21] For an analysis of the methodological issues involved in using the CPI see F. Galtung, 'Measuring the immeasurable: boundaries and functions of (macro) corruption indices', in C. Sampford et al., *Measuring corruption* (Aldershot, UK: Ashgate, 2006), pp. 101–30.

[22] See Transparency International, 'Corruption perceptions index 2010' (2010). Available at www.transparency.org/policy_research/surveys_indices/cpi/2010/results

[23] Yuri Levada formerly headed VTsIOM (All-Russian Center for the Study of Public Opinion). But he left this agency to start his own in 2003, following what he perceived to be moves by the Russian state to interfere in the work of VTsIOM – see O. Yablokova, 'Levada leaves VTsIOM for VTsIOM', *Moscow Times*, 10 September (2003), p. 6.

of 'stealing and corruption' had not declined under Putin compared with the Yeltsin era, while only a quarter (26%) believed the situation had improved.[24] While the former figure was an improvement on some earlier years of the Putin presidency (it compares with 59% in September 2002 and 54% in December 2006), it nevertheless suggests that approximately half the Russian population believed that Putin had not made any inroads in the fight against corruption during his presidency.[25] Unfortunately, early responses to Medvedev's concerted efforts to address the corruption issue were not encouraging. A December VTsIOM 2008 survey (N = 1,600) revealed that only 1% of respondents believed that the introduction of anti-corruption legislation had been an achievement of the Medvedev presidency.[26]

The surveys cited so far are perceptual ones. But there has been a number of experiential surveys conducted in recent years that provide concrete evidence on Russians' actual experience of corruption, primarily in terms of bribery. Some of these surveys focus on the general public, while others target the business community. For example, the preliminary results of detailed surveys of Russian businesspeople, comparing their views and experiences in 2001 and 2005, were published by INDEM in 2005.[27] These revealed that while the average *number* of bribes paid by businesses had decreased quite significantly (about 20 per cent) over the period, the *value* of the average bribe had soared more than thirteenfold. Even allowing for general inflation, this was a massive increase. According to INDEM, the value of the business corruption market in 2005 was 2.7 times higher than the federal government's total budget revenues.[28]

---

[24] Cited in 'Presidential performance', *Russia Votes* (Centre for the Study of Public Policy, University of Aberdeen/Levada Center, Moscow), www.russiavotes.org/president/presidency_performance.php?PHPSESSID=ec4620a625f8c4d5d8c90fe50dcdf4ff

[25] 'President's performance in office – trends', *Russia Votes*, www.russiavotes.org/president/presidency_performance_trends.php#214

[26] 'Results of public opinion polls, December 2008–February 2009', *The Monitoring of Public Opinion: Economic and Social Changes (VTsIOM)* (January–February 2009), p. 54. Available at http://wciom.com/fileadmin/user_upload/file_monitoring/2009_1%2889%29_11_Contents.pdf

[27] On 14 June 2011 the Ministry of Economic Development of the Russian Federation published the INDEM report 'Condition of the Everyday Corruption in the Russian Federation'. It examined petty bribery from 2001 to 2010 as well as the efficiency of government anti-bribery measures. For details, see the INDEM website: www.indem.ru/en/Projects/EverydayCorru2010.htm

[28] G. Satarov, *Vo skol'ko raz uvelichilas' korruptsiya za 4 goda: rezul'taty novogo issledovanija Fonda INDEM* (Moscow: INDEM, 2005), 1–2 and 12, available at www.anti-corr.ru/projects.htm#2005. For the results of both expert interviews and two mass surveys (one of citizens, the other of businesspeople) on corruption conducted by INDEM

The best-known and most comprehensive analyses of businesspeople's experience of bribery and corruption are contained in the World
Bank's 'Business Environment and Enterprise Performance Surveys'
(BEEPS). These have so far been conducted four times (1999, 2002,
2004–5, 2008–9). According to the World Bank's own comparisons,
corruption appeared to have become more of a problem for Russian
businesses between 2002 and 2005, in that a higher proportion of
firms in the latter year (some 40 per cent) responded that corruption
was a problem in doing business than had indicated this in the earlier
year (about 28 per cent). Conversely, bribes as a share of annual sales
declined over the period.[29]

For those who accept TI's argument that corruption can only occur
within the private sector (B2B, or business-to-business), there is one
final survey worth considering in this brief overview of Russian corruption, primarily because it is of direct relevance to the question of
the transnational ramifications of the phenomenon. This is TI's 'Bribe
Payers Index' (BPI). This index has been published four times since
1999, and is based on the results of surveys that ask senior businesspeople – initially only in the developing world, but nowadays in developed,
transition and developing states – to indicate which countries' firms are
most likely to offer them bribes. The BPI lists only some 20–30 states –
it varies from one index to the next – since it primarily considers countries that are major investors in other countries. Russia was not assessed
for the 1999 BPI. But in each of the three subsequent BPIs, Russian
companies emerged as those either most likely or among those most
likely to offer bribes to potential overseas business partners.[30] This is
one more piece of evidence to suggest that corruption is very much part
of the post-communist Russian way of operating.

While comparison of the above data reveals certain anomalies, it
also indicates general agreement that the corruption situation in Russia
is dire. But survey data must always be treated with caution, and are
only one source of information on corruption in Russia. Another is

in 1999–2001, see G. Satarov, *Diagnostika rossiyskoy korruptsii: sotsiologicheskiy analiz*
(Moscow: INDEM, 2002).

[29] World Bank, 'Russia: BEEPS at-a-glance' (2009), pp. 3–4. Available at http://
siteresources.worldbank.org/INTECAREGTOPANTCOR/Resources/
BAAGREV20060208Russia.pdf

[30] The respective positions were twenty-first out of twenty-one in 2002, twenty-eighth
out of thirty in 2006 and twenty-second out of twenty-two in 2008 – 'Bribe payers index 2002', available at www.transparency.org/policy_research/surveys_indices/
bpi/bpi_2002; 'Bribe payers index 2006', available at www.transparency.org/policy_
research/surveys_indices/bpi/bpi_2006; J. Riaño and R. Hodess, 'Bribe payers index
2008' (Berlin: Transparency International, 2008), p. 5.

corporate behaviour. Thus, the (basically) Swedish transnational corporation IKEA has frequently complained to the Russian authorities about the corruption it faces on a day-to-day basis in trying to conduct business in Russia. While this has been reported in the media for about a decade,[31] the situation appears to have worsened dramatically in 2009, with IKEA making it clear that it was not prepared to continue to invest in Russia under the existing conditions of 'administrative processes'. This was widely interpreted to refer to the continuing explicit and implicit demands for bribes from Russian officials, which IKEA wants the authorities to stop.[32]

Corruption elsewhere in the former USSR

While Russian corruption levels are high, the situation is even more dire in many of the other CIS states. Although Ukraine's scores are similar to those of Russia over time (though marginally better in the 2008 CPI, at 2.8), they have occasionally been even worse than those of its neighbour. In 2000, for instance, Ukraine's score dropped to 1.5. A highly detailed report on corruption in Ukraine produced for the United States Agency for International Development in February 2006 concluded that an improvement in the corruption situation was one of many anticipated outcomes of the November–December 2004 Orange Revolution, although there was not yet much to report.[33] But, based partly on World Bank research findings, it endorsed the notion that Ukraine's level of corruption had deteriorated between 1996 and 2004, and that it had considerably more corruption than other states with similar levels of income.[34] Conversely, Estonia invariably emerges as the least corrupt of all the former Soviet states in the CPIs, as well as in other surveys.

Another former Soviet country that has fared poorly in the past is Georgia. According to the second 'International Crime Victims Survey' (ICVS), almost 21% of respondents were asked for, or expected to pay, a bribe to officers of the state in 1991–2.[35] By the time of the next ICVS

---

[31] See, for example, *The Economist*, 1 April 2000; *Newsweek*, 23 October (2006).

[32] B. Horowitz, 'IKEA and the graft factor', *Moscow Times*, 23 July (2009); *New York Times*, 24 June 2009; *Business Week*, 13 July 2009, p. 33.

[33] Ukraine's record since the Orange Revolution has been mixed, according to the CPI. Its 2006 score of 2.8 represented a clear improvement; but it then began to slide again, and by 2008 was back down at 2.5.

[34] B. Spector et al., *Corruption assessment: Ukraine – final report*, 10 February 2006 (Washington, DC: Management Systems International/USAID, 2006), esp. pp. 9–10.

[35] A. Siemaszko, 'Central and Eastern European victimisation rates: to compare or not to compare?', in A. Alvazzi del Frate et al. (eds.), *Understanding crime: experiences of crime and crime control* (Rome: UNICRI, 1993), p. 92.

(surveys conducted 1995–7), the situation in Georgia had deteriorated, with almost 30% of respondents indicating that they had directly experienced corruption (bribery) in the previous twelve months. This was even worse than the next most corrupt former Soviet state analysed – Kyrgyzstan – in which a little over 21% of respondents had been directly asked or were expected to pay a bribe to a state official in the previous year. At the other end of the spectrum, 'only' 3.8% of respondents in Estonia had had direct experience of corruption during the same period.[36]

By the time of the fourth ICVS (surveys conducted 2000–1), the corruption situation appears to have been worst in Azerbaijan, Belarus and Lithuania among former Soviet states surveyed. In the capitals of the first two of these countries, 21% of respondents indicated that they had either been explicitly asked for, or had inferred they were expected to offer, at least one bribe to an officer of the state. The figure was even higher – 23% – in Vilnius.[37]

But in recent years, the corruption situation in Georgia appears to have improved – at least as reflected in the perception-based CPIs – and the highest levels of corruption appear to have been in the Central Asian states. Most of these have only been assessed in the CPIs since the mid-2000s. But the CPI results suggest that Kyrgyzstan, Turkmenistan and Uzbekistan shared the inglorious title of 'most corrupt post-communist state' in 2008, each scoring 1.8 in the index.[38] According to at least one recent analysis, the corruption (and organised crime) situation has changed (but not improved) in Kyrgyzstan since the so-called Tulip Revolution of 2005.[39] Diagnostic surveys conducted by the World Bank

---

[36] U. Zvekic, *Criminal victimisation in countries in transition* (Rome: UNICRI, 1998), pp. 20, 47–9.

[37] A. Alvazzi del Frate and J. van Kesteren, *Criminal victimisation in urban Europe: key findings of the 2000 International Crime Victim Surveys* (Turin: UNICRI, 2004), pp. 25–8. Strictly speaking, the later survey was only of capital cities, not entire countries as the earlier one was. This methodological problem is one of the reasons why the data should not be fetishised. That said, the actual rankings of countries or capitals are valid.

[38] Kazakhstan and Tajikistan performed very slightly better than the other Central Asian states in 2008–9 and again in 2010, scoring 2.2 and 2.0 respectively. But this still placed them among the most corrupt post-communist states, according to perception surveys. The other former Soviet states to emerge with similar low scores were Azerbaijan (1.9), Belarus (2.0) and Russia (2.1). See R. La Porta et al., 'Trust in large organisations', *The American Economic Review* 87:2 (1997), 336–7; R. La Porta et al., 'The quality of government', *The Journal of Law, Economics, and Organisation* 15:1 (1999), 224, 251, 256 and 263.

[39] A. Kupatadze, 'Organised crime before and after the Tulip Revolution: the changing dynamics of upperworld–underworld networks', *Central Asian Survey* 27:3–4 (2008), 279–99.

at the start of the millennium also revealed high levels of corruption in the two Central Asian states analysed – Kazakhstan and Kyrgyzstan – well before TI began to include them in the CPI.[40]

Organised crime in Russia

There are even fewer survey data on organised crime in Russia than there are on corruption. However, an overview of some of the most useful data, combined with references to more subjective assessments, provides enough evidence to permit the conclusion that organised crime has been a serious problem. A valuable source on the level of organised crime activity in Russia is BEEPS. Unfortunately, the first explicit question regarding organised crime was included only in 2005. According to this, some 11 per cent of Russian businesses paid protection money to gangs in the year to 2005, which accounted for 0.35 per cent of annual sales. However, BEEPS 2002 (as well as BEEPS 2005) included a question concerning organised crime as a problem of doing business. The results indicate that some 20 per cent of businesses saw it as a problem in 2005, compared with just over 20 per cent in 2002. Any apparent improvement between the two surveys was thus minimal, and within the normal margin of error, so that it is reasonable to conclude that the situation was essentially steady.[41]

Joseph Serio has provided convincing arguments as to why statistics on organised crime in Russia – though many of his points have universal applicability – must invariably be treated with extreme caution. Among the numerous reasons are definitional issues (what constitutes organised crime?), frequent changes in the composition and alignment of crime groupings, and inadequate (and hence inaccurate) police data.[42] Given this, we cite here some of the statistics provided primarily in order to demonstrate how *perceptions* of the organised crime situation in and beyond Russia are formed; it is ultimately not possible to check the veracity of most of the figures.

---

[40] See J. Anderson, *Governance and service delivery in the Kyrgyz Republic: results of diagnostic surveys* (Washington, DC: World Bank, 2002), esp. pp. 4–5, 15–17, 60–1 and 69–72; J. Anderson and A. Mukherjee, *Kazakhstan: governance and service delivery – a diagnostic report* (Washington, DC: World Bank, 2002), esp. pp. vii–xii, 14–24 and 69–73. For another highly detailed analysis of corruption in Kazakhstan see G. Shimshon, 'Corruption, institutions and development in Central Asia', MA thesis (University of Leiden, 2004).

[41] World Bank, 'Russia: BEEPS at a glance', 5.

[42] J. Serio, *Investigating the Russian Mafia* (Durham, NC: Carolina Academic Press, 2008), esp. pp. 205–28.

Detailed research by various analysts has helped to produce a picture of many of the major organised crime groupings in Russia. Thus, although the Russian Ministry of the Interior claimed that there were more than 8,000 gangs by 1996, many of these were very small, and there were by then probably only approximately twenty large ones operating in Moscow, for example. Of these, Guy Dunn identified six main ones, three of which were Chechen.[43] Similarly, while there were allegedly several hundred gangs of various sizes in St Petersburg in the 1990s, most analysts have accepted that there were really only three major ones (the Tambov, Kazan and Chechen groups).[44] Some of these have folded or assumed a lower profile, but others continued to exert significant influence through the first decade of the twenty-first century. For example, in January 2007, Russian prosecutor general Yuri Chaika announced a major investigation into the Tambov gang's alleged attempts to take control of forty major enterprises in St Petersburg,[45] and it had clearly spread to other parts of Europe. Moreover, it appears that the GFC has resulted in an *increase* in the penetration by organised crime of both the state and private enterprise.[46]

One clear indication of the security concerns of states beyond the former USSR relating to the transnational impact of Russian and Soviet organised crime was the establishment of an FBI office in Moscow in July 1994, and the special arrangement the London Metropolitan Police concluded with their Moscow counterparts shortly afterwards. In both cases, collaborative arrangements with the Russian law-enforcement agencies were proposed and concluded because of concerns in the United States and the UK respectively, about the spread of Russian organised crime into America and Britain.

Organised crime elsewhere in the former USSR

It would be possible to produce at least a chapter-length analysis of organised crime activity in each of the Soviet successor states. Since space considerations render that impossible here, the following overview must be highly selective. In terms of attempting to measure

[43] G. Dunn, 'Major Mafia gangs in Russia', in P. Williams (ed.), *Russian organised crime: the new threat?* (London: Frank Cass, 1997), pp. 65–70.
[44] See United Nations Office on Drugs and Crime, *Results of a pilot survey of forty selected organised criminal groups in sixteen countries* (Vienna: UNODC, 2002).
[45] 'Genprokuror: arestovany 25 chlenov tambovskoy OPG', *Gazeta.ru*, 16 January (2007). Available at www.gazeta.ru/news/social/2007/01/16/n_1024654.shtml
[46] Interfax-AVN, 'Rate of organised crime, corruption still not steady', cited in *Johnson's Russia List*, no. 165, 4 September (2009), item 15.

the scale, nature and impact of organised crime, it would be useful to be able to conduct experiential surveys. Unfortunately, this is much more difficult to do in the case of organised crime than with other forms of criminality. As the author of one recent attempt to gauge organised crime levels explained, 'since ordinary households are not directly victimised by organised crime, victimisation surveys cannot be used as vehicle to measure this phenomenon'.[47] On the other hand, businesses *are* often subject to pressure from organised crime, notably in the form of 'protection'. One of the few sources of reasonably hard data on organised crime in post-communist states is the 'International Crime Business Survey', conducted in 2000. This asked representatives of mainly small businesses in nine post-communist capitals, including four in the former USSR (Belarus, Lithuania, Russia and Ukraine) whether or not they had experienced intimidation or threats from crime gangs in the previous twelve months. Some of the findings were surprising. Of the four former Soviet capitals surveyed, Minsk was the one in which businesspeople were most likely to have been subjected to intimidation or extortion over the previous year, with more than 30% of businesses reporting that they had been requested to pay protection money during that period (compared to 9% in Moscow, 7% in Kiev and 3% in Vilnius).[48] This finding casts serious doubt on the notion that more authoritarian states are better able to deal with organised crime than more democratic ones.

Jan Van Dijk recently attempted to measure organised crime using a multi-angulation method, and produced a global 'Composite Organised Crime Index' of crime levels. He divided the world into sixteen regions, and concluded that Eastern Europe (mainly the former USSR), Central Asia and Transcaucasia had the highest levels of organised crime activity in the world. According to his methodology, the former Soviet countries in which organised crime was an even bigger problem than in Russia were Belarus (worst), Georgia and Ukraine. At the other end of the spectrum, organised crime was a *relatively* minor problem in Latvia and Estonia.[49]

While the scale of this is difficult to quantify, people smuggling and human trafficking have been among the major growth areas in

---

[47] J. Van Dijk, 'Mafia markers: assessing organised crime and its impact upon societies', *Trends in Organised Crime* 10:4 (2007), 40.

[48] A. Alvazzi del Frate, 'The International Crime Business Survey: findings from nine Central-Eastern European cities', *European Journal on Criminal Policy and Research* 10:2–3 (2004), 150–2.

[49] Van Dijk, 'Mafia markers', 42–3 and 45.

transnational organised crime since the early 1990s.[50] The focus here will be on trafficking, which is becoming ever more attractive to criminal gangs, for a number of reasons. One is that the punishments meted out to traffickers – on the rare occasions when they are convicted – is in most countries very mild compared with those for weapons or drug smuggling. Another is that 9/11 has led many government agencies to address weapons smuggling far more seriously than they did before the terrorist attacks on the United States; in this context, human trafficking is generally much less risky than the smuggling and illicit sale of armaments. Third, Western (particularly US) agencies have been making concerted efforts to destroy the illicit drug trade at source, by destroying opium poppy crops in Afghanistan and coca crops in Colombia. The shortage of raw materials has made it more difficult for drug traffickers, who sometimes seek an alternative 'product', supplies of which are essentially limitless and can be found almost anywhere. Desperate and impoverished people constitute one such 'product'. Finally, whereas drugs and weapons typically involve one-off sales of a given batch, the return on humans can last several years (e.g., if a trafficked woman is used for prostitution).

Most of the literature on trafficking focuses on trafficking for sexual purposes, in part because this is seen by many analysts to be the dominant form of trafficking globally. Given this, it is interesting to note that, while much of the trafficking *from* former Soviet states to non-former Soviet countries is for the purposes of sexual exploitation,[51] empirical research indicates most of the trafficking *between* and *within* former Soviet states may be for other purposes, notably cheap labour for construction, agriculture, or domestic service.[52] Apart from Russia,

---

[50] For an up-to-date analysis of the distinction between people smuggling and human trafficking see B. Buckland, 'Smuggling and trafficking: crossover and overlap', in C. Friesendorf (ed.), *Strategies against human trafficking: the role of the security sector* (Geneva: DCAF, 2009), pp. 145–74.

[51] According to German police records, cases detected revealed that the FSU states from which persons were most likely to be trafficked to Germany between 2000 and 2005, mostly for the purposes of sexual exploitation, were Russia, Ukraine, Latvia and Lithuania – see Bundeskriminalamt, *Lagebild Menschenhandel 2003 – Offene Version* (Wiesbaden: Bundeskriminalamt, 2004), p. 5; Bundeskriminalamt, *Lagebild Menschenhandel 2004 – Offene Version* (Wiesbaden: Bundeskriminalamt, 2005), p. 9. These sources reveal that 75.5% of all detected cases of trafficked persons in Germany in 2004, 80% in 2003, and a staggering 87.3% of cases in 2002 were from post-communist states; of Central and Eastern Europe (i.e. non-FSU) states, the three primary sources over this three-year period were Bulgaria, Poland and Romania.

[52] See E. Tyuryukanova, *Forced labour in the Russian Federation today: irregular migration and trafficking in human beings* (Geneva: International Labour Office: 2005), esp. pp. 10–11. An updated version of this invaluable study is available in Russian: *Prinuditel'nyi*

the main former Soviet source countries for trafficked persons beyond the former USSR are Ukraine and Moldova. Within the former USSR, the source countries for trafficked persons in Russia for all kinds of work vary according to the sector. In the case of construction, trade and prostitution, for instance, the primary sources are Ukraine and Moldova, while the largest group in agricultural work is Russians from other CIS states, and Tajikistan is the principal source country in public catering.[53]

Causes of organised crime and corruption in Russia and the former USSR

There are several reasons for the rise of both organised crime and corruption in Russia and the former USSR since the early 1990s, and they can only be briefly analysed here. Some are features that apply universally, such as the rise of the internet (rendering both cyber-crime and money-laundering easier) and the development of what Kenichi Ohmae has called the 'borderless world' as an offshoot of globalisation.[54] But Russia and some other parts of the former USSR appear to have been heavily over-represented in the growth of these forms of crime, so it is necessary to consider the specific reasons for this.

One factor that relates to globalisation but is specific to the former USSR (and other post-communist states) is that most Soviet citizens had been subject to severe restrictions on foreign travel during the communist era. Post-communism heralded several new freedoms, including the right to travel overseas. This rendered it easier for criminals to move into other countries and to link up with foreign criminal gangs. In short, this change helps to explain the *transnationalisation* of Soviet crime.

A second factor is the efficacy of the Soviet educational system. While this may not have encouraged creative thinking, its emphasis on the importance of the scientific-technical revolution meant it produced a comparatively high proportion of sophisticated mathematicians, scientists and technicians who have proved to be skilled at taking improper advantage of the Web. This again relates to globalisation. Anthony Giddens is just one of many analysts who see globalisation at least as

---

Trud v Sovremennoi Rossii: Nereguliruemaya Migratsiya i Torgovlya Lyud'mi (Geneva: International Labour Office, 2006). For a rare analysis that focuses on the trafficking of adult males in and from parts of the FSU, see R. Surtees, *Trafficking of men – a trend less considered: the case of Belarus and Ukraine* (Geneva: International Organisation for Migration, 2008).

[53] Tyuryukanova, *Forced labour*, pp. 50–4; Surtees, *Trafficking of men*, p. 10.

[54] K. Ohmae, *The borderless world* (New York: Harper Business, 1990).

much in terms of the communications revolution as the liberalisation of economics and trade.[55] There is considerable evidence that Russians, in particular, are heavily over-represented in global cyber-crime; one of their major foci is child pornography.[56] This said, Russian minister of internal affairs Rashid Nurgaliyev in June 2009 urged much closer cooperation between all CIS law enforcement agencies, since computer-based crime was a problem in many CIS states.[57]

While advanced technical training during the Soviet era helps to explain the propensity of former Soviet citizens to engage in sophisticated cyber-crime, another aspect of the Soviet legacy has also been at play. Soviet communism provided a moral code for its citizens. The collapse of the USSR meant the breakdown of that state-inspired and propagated code. While some citizens were able to replace this by turning to religion, others entered a moral vacuum. This was conducive to criminal and other forms of anti-social activity.

The collapse of the USSR also led many Soviet citizens to despondency, as they believed that their once-powerful country was now being humiliated by triumphalists, especially their decades-long principal enemies. Russians appear to have felt this more keenly than most other former Soviet citizens, many of whom could at least be proud that their nation had acquired sovereignty. Nevertheless, the USSR – but particularly Russia – had experienced either a quadruple or quintuple loss. Almost overnight, the USSR lost its outer empire (incorporating COMECON and the Warsaw Pact), the Cold War, its status as a superpower, and its role as the original model of socialism and communist power. Russia also lost its inner empire (consisting of the fourteen other republics that had once constituted the USSR). In addition to the fact that the Baltic states never joined it anyway, the CIS is a weak organisation, and can in no way be seen as even a truncated reincarnation of the USSR. People react in different ways to despondency and alienation; but anti-social behaviour is a common response.

---

[55] A. Giddens, *Runaway world* (London: Profile, 1999).
[56] Arguably the best-known Russian group allegedly playing the key role in this is the Russian Business Network – see N. Miller, 'From Russia with malice: criminals trawl the world', *Age* (Melbourne), 24 July (2007); B. Krebs, 'Shadowy Russian firm seen as conduit for cybercrime', *Washington Post*, 13 October (2007); and K-K.R. Choo, 'Organised crime groups in cyberspace: a typology', *Trends in organised crime* 11:3 (2008), esp. 280.
[57] M.A. Smith, *The Russian chronologies*, UK Department of Defence, Research and Assessment Branch (July–September 2009), available at www.da.mod.uk/.../russian-chronologies/09(13)%20MAS3.doc.pdf. For evidence of Belarusian cybercrime see P. Grabosky, *Electronic crime* (Upper Saddle River, NJ: Pearson Prentice Hall, 2007), p. 78.

Two of the salient features of post-communist countries in the early to mid-1990s were that each had a weak economy and a weak state. Both of these factors were conducive to the growth of corruption and organised crime. Weak economies typically mean high levels of unemployment; not only are many unemployed – and often desperate – people attracted to the potential gains offered by organised crime, but even employed officials may be concerned about the future, and so be tempted into corrupt activity as a way of providing for potentially hard times (the 'squirrel's nuts syndrome'). But in the case of the former USSR, a specific aspect of the unemployment requires highlighting: what happened to security police members when they found themselves jobless.

Being a communist state, the USSR had had a large security police force, of which the KGB was the best-known component. The collapse of the USSR resulted in the retrenchment of many of these officers. While some took up positions with legitimate private security companies, many were attracted to join organised crime gangs. From the perspective of such gangs, these former officers enjoyed four major advantages over others who might be interested in joining. One was that most of them were highly trained in weapons use. Second, many knew how to access weapons illegally in a weakly policed state. A third advantage was that they had first-hand knowledge about the techniques employed for detecting and fighting criminals, which was invaluable to crime gangs. A different aspect of insider knowledge, and the final point, was that these turncoats often knew which of their former colleagues with positions in the new state apparatus were most likely to be corruptible, and which were most likely to blow the whistle if approached by criminals proposing collusion.

Weak economies are often a major factor explaining weak states, since low state revenues mean that state apparatuses are seriously underfunded, and hence unable adequately to perform many of the tasks that a Weberian conception of the state would expect of them. Thus, an essential feature of most weak states is that they are unable to protect their citizens as well as functional states do. When citizens perceive the state to be incapable of providing adequate policing, some will turn to organised crime gangs for protection – for instance, of their businesses. Clearly, this enhances the role of organised crime in society. Conversely, the weakness and underfunding of the state is precisely one of the reasons for the increase in both crime and corruption; typically, the state has inadequate resources for mounting a widespread and sustained attack on either, or for paying its officers adequately.

The weaknesses so far identified can be found in many types of state. But the confusion of early transition states compounded their general weakness. Early post-communist states did not experience only *triple* transitions (economic, political, boundary-related), as is often claimed; they underwent *multiple* transitions. One of those too often overlooked was of the legal system. While many communist-era laws were overtly rejected, in many cases it took several years to replace them with laws more appropriate to the new state and its societal arrangements. This was the legislative lag of early post-communism. Laws on property became confused and promoted crime and corruption, in part because they had not been properly identified and classified.

To this point, the factors identified all relate to recent developments. But President Medvedev argued on his video blog in May 2009 that, '[u]nfortunately, Russia has a centuries-long tradition of corruption', thus explaining the contemporary phenomenon partly in terms of an age-old Russian tradition.[58] His 2009 statement was in line with his much-publicised criticism in early 2008 that Russia had a long tradition of 'legal nihilism' unequalled among European countries.[59] While this lack of respect for the law in Russia can be traced back centuries, it was exacerbated by the Soviet system. The combination of shortages of so many types of goods with large powerful bureaucracies subject to little popular control readily explains the pervasiveness both of corruption itself and of popular practices conducive to a culture of corruption, such as *blat*.[60]

Transnational crime, corruption and conflict in the former USSR

There are numerous ways in which corruption and transnational organised crime can and do contribute to conflict in the former USSR. Among the most obvious and best-documented is the violence that has occurred *between* organised crime gangs, mainly in the form of turf wars. But this peaked in the early 1990s, especially during the so-called Great Mob War of 1992–4. Already by 1995 observers were claiming that there had been a dramatic change. Thus Olga Kryshtanovskaya maintained that Russia had in microcosm what Claire Sterling had

---

[58] From *Johnson's Russia List*, no. 95, 21 May (2009), item 15.

[59] *Rossiyskaya Gazeta – Nedelya*, 24 January (2008).

[60] For a recent succinct analysis of the history of Russian corruption from the seventeenth century to the 1990s, see S. Cheloukhine, 'The roots of Russian organised crime: from old-fashioned professionals to the organised criminal groups of today', *Crime, Law and Social Change* 50 (2008), esp. 354–69. See also L. Holmes, *The end of communist power* (New York: Oxford University Press, 1993); while a detailed analysis of *blat* is A. Ledeneva's *Russia's economy of favours* (Cambridge University Press, 1998).

recently claimed typified transnational organised crime – an often tacitly agreed division of labour.[61] Kryshtanovskaya even provided a detailed summary of how the major groups had divided up the various branches of organised crime. For example, she argued, the infamous Solntsevo gang operated the illegal gambling business, while Armenian and Chechen gangs specialised *inter alia* in car theft.[62]

Even if the internecine conflict arising from turf wars has largely faded by now, there are many other ways in which corruption and transnational organised crime can contribute to conflict. These are potentially far more threatening to both the populations of former Soviet states and the global community more generally than infighting between gangs. Some are direct, others more indirect.

There is no question that the threats posed by transnational organised crime are greatly exacerbated by the *collusion* between gangs and corrupt officials. While there is still a shortage of concrete evidence on this, enough is available to permit the identification of dangers. Moreover, inferences can be made on the basis of incomplete information, analogies with the situation in other parts of the world, and reason.

In terms of direct physical threats, one of the potentially most dangerous is collusion facilitating weapons smuggling. Regarding the *actual* impact to date, a significant danger is the collusion between corrupt officials and organised crime in the smuggling and sale of conventional weapons, such as Kalashnikov AK-47 assault rifles, detonators, Fagot anti-tank missiles and RPG anti-tank grenade launchers.[63] According to the most respected Georgian newspaper, two senior Georgian military officers were in 2001 caught red-handed smuggling a large quantity of arms into Chechnya.[64] While their primary motivation may have been personal gain, another was probably the sense that they were contributing to an anti-Russian cause. If this is the case, then an even more cynical example of corrupt officials colluding with crime gangs and terrorists relates to what many Russians themselves see as their own '9/11': the Beslan school siege of September 2004. A survey conducted by the

---

[61] C. Sterling, *Crime without frontiers* (London: Warner, 1995).

[62] O. Kryshtanovskaya, 'Nelegal'nye Struktury v Rossii'', *Sotsiologicheskie issledovaniya* 8 (1995), 94–106. For a thought-provoking challenge to Kryshtanovskaya's analysis that argues against the notion of a neat division of labour between Russian crime groups, see Serio, *Investigating the Russian Mafia*, esp. pp. 214–15.

[63] For relatively recent evidence of Russian and Soviet smuggling of AK-47s, allegedly for sale to terrorists and involving military officials, see P. Hirschkorn, 'US charges 18 in Russian weapons-smuggling plot', *CNN Law Center*, 16 March (2005), available at www.cnn.com/2005/LAW/03/15/weapons.trafficking/index.html

[64] T. Wittig, 'Financing terrorism along the Chechnya-Georgia border, 1999–2002', *Global Crime* 10:3 (2009), 251–2.

Levada Center shortly after this terrorist attack revealed that more than half of the respondents blamed the tragedy in part on corrupt security officers colluding with criminal gangs and terrorists.[65] In the same month, Russian prosecutor general Vladimir Ustinov admitted that the task of combating terrorism would in the future be made even more difficult because of the high levels of collusion between Russian officials and both terrorists and crime gangs. Such collusion included both illicit arms procurement and sales, and turning a blind eye in return for bribes.[66]

But the greatest potential danger of all is posed by collusion between corrupt officials and transnational organised crime that facilitates the acquisition, smuggling and sale of nuclear materials suitable for use in nuclear weapons. Beyond the former USSR, there was more overt concern about this in the 1990s than there appears to have been in recent years,[67] despite the fact that the Federal Security Bureau announced in 2002 that attempts by criminal gangs to sell components for both nuclear and chemical weapons within the former USSR had recently intensified.[68] This reduced Western emphasis can be explained partly by the greater control the Russian state under Putin began to exert over its nuclear arsenals than it appeared to have under Yeltsin. However, it is unclear what happened to materials that in the 1990s were sold by corrupt officials to organised crime gangs and that were then smuggled out of the former USSR. While it might seem reassuring that terrorist organisations such as Al-Qaeda have not so far used dirty bombs or other weapons based on nuclear materials, it would be naïve to assume that all such smuggled materials are now out of harm's way: if state security agencies do not know the whereabouts of such materials, the latter continue to constitute a serious threat.

The references to terrorism lead to another major security risk posed by organised crime, corruption and the collusion between them. There is considerable circumstantial evidence that Chechen terrorists have become heavily involved in drug trafficking in various parts of the former USSR, including the Russian Far East. It has been claimed that

---

[65] C. Wheeler, 'Putin was set to do deal for Beslan children, says aide', *Guardian Unlimited*, 17 September (2004), available at www.guardian.co.uk/world/2004/sep/17/chechnya.russia1; *RFE/RL Newsline*, 17 September (2004), item 4.

[66] Wheeler, 'Putin was set to do deal for Beslan children, says aide'.

[67] See, for example, R. Lee, 'Recent trends in nuclear smuggling', in P. Williams (ed.), *Russian organised crime* (London: Frank Cass, 1997), pp. 109–21; T. Nelson, 'Russian realities: nuclear weapons, bureaucratic manoeuvres and organised crime', *Demokratizatsiya* 8:1 (2000), 145–59.

[68] D. Starostin, 'FSB bespokoit osmiy', *Online Vremya Novostei*, 27 September (2002), available at www.vremya.ru/2002/178/4/27502.html

Chechens have since the 1990s been funding their purchases of weapons partly from the sale of opium illegally acquired from Afghanistan.[69] Corrupt Russian officials, who turn a blind eye in return for bribes, have allegedly facilitated this. Another example of a militant politically motivated group in the former USSR allegedly becoming involved in drug trafficking to fund its activities is the IMU.[70]

While it typically poses less of a security risk than weapons or even drug smuggling, the corrupt involvement of officials in people smuggling and human trafficking may indirectly promote tensions that may develop into conflict. Thus both people smuggling and human trafficking may result in tensions between local citizens and smuggled or trafficked persons, as the latter work for rates well below those normally earned by locals performing similar tasks, thereby raising unemployment[71] and in turn the risk of alienation-related racism. And people smuggling can sometimes play a more obvious conflict-related role. Thus it is alleged that a number of law enforcement and intelligence officers in Georgia have corruptly facilitated the smuggling of persons who have subsequently become involved in terrorism.[72] A much more common phenomenon is where police officers consciously and directly collude with criminal gangs in trafficking for sexual and other purposes. For instance, Tyuryukanova's research revealed:

Cases were observed where the victim appealed to the authorities for assistance but were instead returned to their abusers. In some cases, the police made deals with pimps by not reporting them to the authorities in return for free sex with a prostitute.[73]

One of the ways in which officers of the state can indirectly collude with organised crime is through the purchase of their 'products'. If state officials purchase illicit drugs for their personal use, for example, they would necessarily be providing income to criminals. Another example, and one that has been well documented, is where military personnel use trafficked women for sexual purposes (as prostitutes). A number of such cases involving peacekeepers in Bosnia and Kosovo

---

[69] R.F. Perl, 'Taliban and the drug trade' (Washington, DC: Congressional Research Services, Library of Congress, 2001); *San Francisco Chronicle*, 4 October (2001); Wittig, 'Financing terrorism'.

[70] A. Ceccarelli, 'Clans, politics and organised crime in Central Asia', *Trends in Organised Crime* 10:3 (2007), 31.

[71] Tyuryukanova, *Forced labour*, pp. 54–6.

[72] Wittig, 'Financing terrorism', 252.

[73] Tyuryukanova, *Forced labour*, p. xix; see, too, pp. 60–3, 107, 111, 114, 115, 117, 119, 122 and 126 for concrete evidence of collusion in trafficking, mostly – but not exclusively – in connection with sex work.

have been recorded. Some of these are of soldiers from the former USSR, notably Russians.[74]

While collusion usually increases security risks and hence potential and actual conflict, it can sometimes help to *reduce* the likelihood of conflict. Reference has already been made to the decline of turf wars in Russia that allegedly resulted in part from crime gangs agreeing amongst themselves to various divisions of labour. People smuggling can reduce tensions in troubled countries; if poor, unemployed people in a transition or developing state are (illegally) able to find work in developed states and send money home, this can reduce hardship and hence the potential for unrest. At the same time, if these smuggled persons are engaged in tasks that locals are unwilling to perform, the above-mentioned scenario of tensions between locals and illegal migrants are less likely to occur. Moreover, some of the proceeds of organised crime and corruption can inject funds into an economy.[75] Since many forms of conflict are based on perceived inequalities and serious shortages, increased resources among the general population can reduce the likelihood of dissatisfaction leading to violence.

Ironically, this point about the impact of corruption and organised crime on local economies is endorsed by reference to ways in which collusion can have the *opposite* effect. Thus President Putin's advisor on Chechnya, Aslanbek Aslakhanov, argued that corruption could increase the propensity of citizens to be attracted to terrorism. Shortly after the Beslan siege, he made the point that most of the aid intended for Russia's impoverished south was being diverted into the pockets of criminals and corrupt officials.[76] If citizens believe that they are being abandoned by the state, some will be attracted to violent secessionist movements on the assumption that they will be better treated if they have their 'own' state.[77] In this type of situation, then, collusion is likely to lead to increased conflict.

As a final point, it should be noted that not all collusion that can help to reduce terrorism involves corruption. Thus, alleged Chechen organised crime boss Movladi Atlangeriev is reported to have assisted

---

[74] S. Mendelson, *Barracks and brothels: peacekeepers and human trafficking in the Balkans* (Washington, DC: CSIS Press, 2005), esp. pp. 27, 55–9. More generally on this issue see C. Corrin, 'Transitional road for traffic: analysing trafficking in women from and through Central and Eastern Europe', *Europe-Asia Studies* 57 (2005), 543–60.

[75] Van Dijk, 'Mafia markers', 52. Van Dijk explicitly cites Russia when making this point.

[76] Wheeler, 'Putin was set'. See, too, *Washington Post*, 17 September (2004), p. A27.

[77] For a recent argument to this effect by Russian Security Council secretary Nikolai Petrushev see Interfax, 25 August 2009, cited in *Johnson's Russia List*, no. 158 (2009), item 11.

Russian law enforcement agencies in their efforts to combat Chechen terrorism; there was no suggestion that Russian officials collaborated with Atlangeriev for reasons of personal gain.[78]

Conclusions

It is really only since the 1990s that the international community – in particular, the West – has taken the issues of corruption and transnational organised crime seriously as security threats. Symbolically, a watershed was reached in November 1994 at a World Ministerial Conference – held, auspiciously, in Naples – when UN secretary-general Boutros Boutros-Ghali identified transnational organised crime as potentially the most serious security threat in the contemporary world.[79] In the same year, the Organisation for Economic Co-operation and Development became the trailblazer among IOs in making the fight against transnational corruption a key priority. Its May 1994 'Recommendations on Bribery in International Business Transactions' were seen as 'the first multilateral agreement among governments to combat the bribery of foreign officials'.[80]

Fortunately, awareness of the dangers presented by these two phenomena has developed rapidly in recent years. A clear sign of this was the adoption by the UNGA of a Convention against Transnational Organised Crime in November 2000, and then of a Convention against Corruption in October 2003 (effective December 2005). However, that there was a conscious decision by the UN to adopt two separate documents, some years apart, symbolises well the fact that the international community still has a long way to go in recognising the frequent *connections* or linkages that exist between corruption and organised crime.

While corruption and organised crime are interactive, it is maintained here that the former determines the scale and nature of the latter more than vice versa. In arguing this, I fully concur with Aleksandr Gurov's statement that 'corruption is the driving force of organised crime'.[81] It follows from this that bringing the scale of corruption in Russia and elsewhere in the former USSR down to more acceptable levels – here meaning closer to average Western levels – would exert

---

[78] S. Mashkin, 'Chechenskiy avtoritet pokhishchen bez vesti', *Kommersant*, 14 April (2008).
[79] See A. Scherrer, *G8 against transnational crime* (Aldershot, UK: Ashgate, 2009), p. 43.
[80] Transparency International, *Sharpening the responses against global corruption* (Berlin: Transparency International, 1996), p. 15.
[81] A. Gurov, *Krasnaya Mafiya* (Moscow: Samotsvet, 1995), p. 283.

positive knock-on effects on organised crime. There can be no question that many forms of trafficking, whether of weapons, drugs or people, would not occur on the scale they do were it not for the involvement of corrupt officers of the state. Given this, the attempts by post-communist Russia's third president to curb corruption must be welcomed, and monitored. Medvedev himself acknowledged in late July 2009 that his anti-corruption measures had so far yielded 'only very modest results', and that it could take decades for corruption to be 'vanquished' in Russia.[82] Nevertheless, the new Russian president was extremely active during his first year in office in maintaining momentum in his fight against corruption. At last, Russia has an official definition of corruption; this one development renders it much easier to produce coherent anti-corruption laws. Of course, it was not merely a question of having anti-corruption laws passed; they also had to be implemented. In 2009, the incomes of many high-ranking government and presidential officials in Russia were published for the first time, and this occurred again in 2010.[83] Even if the president himself argued that little had been achieved, and even if some of the published figures were inaccurate, the symbolic significance of this greater transparency should not be underrated.

What other measures can be and are being taken to reduce corruption and organised crime? Some surveys suggest many Russians believe that moving towards a more authoritarian state is likely to be the most effective method for combating corruption and organised crime.[84] The questionability of this assumption has already been highlighted by reference to organised crime rates in Belarus. Further empirical analysis demonstrates that this notion is misguided. In comparative indices of corruption levels, for instance, democracies generally emerge as having far lower levels of corruption than more authoritarian systems. While this pattern applies globally, it can also be seen in microcosm in the post-communist world; the corruption rankings and scores of

[82] D. Medvedev, 'Conversation with Kirill Pozdnyakov, anchor of NTV television channel's current affairs programme *Itogovaya Programma NTV*', 26 July (2009). Available at http://archive.kremlin.ru/eng/text/speeches/2009/07/26/1132_type82916 type82917_220146.shtml

[83] 'President Medvedev marks his first anniversary in office', ITAR-TASS, 7 May (2009). Available at http://eng.tatar-inform.ru/news/2009/05/07/24870/

[84] In the July 2009 survey cited above (see fn. 8), 63 per cent of respondents indicated that they would be happy to see power concentrated in Putin's hands – while a September 2008 survey conducted by VTsIOM suggested that 30 per cent of Russians would welcome public executions as a way of combating corruption: ITAR-TASS, 18 November (2008), cited in *Johnson's Russia List*, no. 212, 19 November (2008), item 31.

the Central Asian states and Belarus noted earlier can be compared with those post-communist states that have made the most progress in democratising, providing clear evidence to this effect. Within the former USSR, the Baltic states best exemplify this point.

So what approaches should be adopted? In a recent analysis of corruption in post-communist states, I identified almost thirty different methods (many of which were then subdivided) for combating corruption.[85] While some of these approaches can also be used against organised crime, there are additional methods particularly appropriate to corruption. It would thus be impossible in a chapter of this scale and nature to provide a comprehensive listing, let alone a full analysis, of the numerous methods available. Rather, I somewhat arbitrarily highlight just a tiny number of the factors that either already are or should be contributing to a reduction in both corruption and organised-crime rates.

In cases where organised crime and corruption are transnational, international cooperation is clearly necessary. Fortunately, there are signs that international police cooperation is not merely increasing, but also improving. Police in various parts of Spain arrested several members of the St Petersburg-based Tambov organised crime gang in June 2008. The operation involved close cooperation between German, Spanish, Russian and US police authorities.[86]

Medvedev himself has argued that a key role in reducing corruption – though this also applies to organised crime – must be played by civil society. This is a point that had already been made by Russian commentators long before Medvedev came to power. Unfortunately, both the media and NGOs, two of the key components of civil society, were increasingly muzzled and hamstrung during the Putin era, which almost certainly contributed to the apparent rise in corruption during his second term as president. To the extent that Medvedev's seeming commitment to reverse his predecessor's approach towards civil society proves to be genuine, the latter should be able to play a significant and increasing role in the fight against organised crime and corruption. Although some of the current president's actions during his first eighteen months in office were questionable in terms of his putative commitment to further democratisation of Russia, his moves between mid-2009 and 2010 to reduce the level of state interference

---

[85] L. Holmes, *Rotten states?* (Durham, NC: Duke University Press, 2006): esp. pp. 211–69.
[86] 'Spain raids "major Russian gang"', *BBC News*, 13 June (2008). Available at http://news.bbc.co.uk/2/hi/europe/7453388.stm

in the activities of both domestic NGOs and small businesses, and to boost the role of small political parties, bode well.

While states can make conscious efforts to combat organised crime and corruption, the dynamism of development itself can exert powerful effects in a more abstract and less targeted way. Thus, if economies strengthen and, as a knock-on effect, states become more effective, many of the drivers of organised crime and corruption associated with the early stages of post-communist transition become less salient. Over time, property laws are passed that clarify previously opaque situations, which in turn clarifies what is meant by crime and corruption. This should render it easier for Russian and other former Soviet judiciaries to use the weight of the law to reduce these phenomena.

But a reduction in both corruption and organised crime is not solely dependent on external agencies, whether they are states, IOs, NGOs or other bodies, or even external conditions. There are also internal dynamics that are likely to contribute to this. One noted above is the tendency for former Soviet organised crime to become less violent. Another is the trend for organised crime to move increasingly into legal business activity. This pattern was observable already by the mid-1990s, as Dunn has argued.[87] But it appears to have intensified in recent years. The lines between organised and corporate crime, often somewhat blurred (globally, not just in the former USSR), are becoming even hazier.[88]

The international security threat of Russian organised crime may always have been exaggerated anyway.[89] Even if it was – and this is ultimately a matter of judgement rather than fact – we must be wary of throwing the baby out with the bathwater. The reports of violence used by Russian and other former Soviet criminals cited earlier make it abundantly clear that there has been a considerable amount of gang violence. Moreover, a substantial number of journalists, judges and law enforcement officers who were investigating both organised crime and corruption have been murdered.

[87] Dunn, 'Major mafia gangs', p. 65.
[88] On this general point see V. Ruggiero, *Organised and corporate crime in Europe* (Aldershot, UK: Dartmouth, 1996).
[89] For arguments and some evidence to this effect see J. Bäckman, *The inflation of crime in Russia* (Helsinki: National Research Institute of Legal Policy, 1998); J. Finckenauer and E. Waring, *Russian mafia in America: immigration, culture and crime* (Boston, MA: Northeastern University Press, 1998); J. Finckenauer and Yu. Voronin, *The threat of Russian organised crime* (Washington, DC: National Institute of Justice, 2001); A. Weenink and F. van der Laan, 'The search for the Russian Mafia: Central and Eastern European criminals in the Netherlands, 1989–2005', *Trends in organised crime*, 10:4 (2007), 57–76.

But the primary threat from Russian and organised crime and corruption, both within Russia and the former USSR and internationally, may be less in the form of violence and security than in the operation of economies. The more blurring there is of the boundaries between both licit and illicit economies on the one hand, and licit and illicit politics on the other, the more difficult it will be to identify and isolate both corruption and organised crime, and hence to combat them. If the GFC does result in the decline of neo-liberal economics and the return of greater state and IO regulation – where this is compatible with liberal or social democratic principles – the resulting clearer demarcation between licit and illicit economies should result in a decline in both corruption and organised crime, in the former USSR and elsewhere.

8 The transformation of war? New and old conflicts in the former USSR

Matt Killingsworth

In the final years before the USSR imploded Mikhail Gorbachev spoke about a 'coming century of peace', characterised by increased cooperation amongst great powers, the growing significance of multilateralism and the increasing illegitimacy of military force. Distinctly different from the militaristic power politics that characterised the Cold War, this order would be defined by the global spread of democracy, accord through institutional cooperation and the declining incidence of war and conflict. However, since the collapse of the USSR in 1991 and the subsequent ending of the Cold War, varying degrees of political, economic and social chaos have plagued the post-Soviet space. In fact, this space has arguably been defined by the war and conflict that has taken place there. Whereas the high-profile conflicts that took place in Rwanda and the former Yugoslavia were identified as being representative of what post-Cold War conflict would most likely continue to look like, wars in the former Soviet space, especially those in Chechnya and Georgia, have also challenged the way we think about war and conflict. With this in mind, one is therefore moved to ask whether there has been a change in the nature and character of war. If so, how significant is this change?

These questions have particular relevance to the former Soviet geopolitical space. Indeed, the former USSR serves as a microcosm for the changes that characterise the post-Cold War order: new forms of religious and ethnic secessionist violence; identity politics; and non-traditional security threats that the new Russian state has responded to in an arguably non-traditional manner. The wars in Chechnya serve as a case in point. Conversely, the 2008 Russo-Georgian conflict bears many of the hallmarks of so-called traditional warfare. Thus, while a discussion on the changing nature of conflict and warfare can certainly be framed in a broader, global context, the geopolitical significance of the former Soviet space makes a focus on this arena especially pertinent.

The aim of this chapter is to explore both competing and complementary explanations and understandings of modern war and assess their relevance in explaining and understanding the conflicts that have beset the post-Soviet republics. For much of the modern era, the interpretations of Carl von Clausewitz's *On War* dominated strategic thought. According to this traditional canon, war was fought by professional standing armies as the representatives of powerful states. War had clear political purposes, avoided targeting civilians, and once its objectives were met, hostilities were expected to cease.

In contradistinction an increasingly influential component of post-Cold War scholarship has stressed that war can no longer be interpreted within the Clausewitzian framework. The decline of the nation-state and the rise of sub- or non-state actors have led many to conclude that war is no longer a solely political contest fought between equally motivated actors. The evolution of a less clear security order inhabited by a multitude of differentiated actors means that the nature of war has changed irrevocably. In this 'new world order', war is no longer fought by regular, professional armies; it has no clear beginning and end; and its main casualties are no longer professional soldiers, but civilians.

In exploring these arguments, this chapter is presented in four parts. The first presents an overview of 'traditional', or 'old', war. The second focuses on recent writing that seeks to understand war within the broad paradigm of a globalised world. Appreciating the diverse complexity of such a paradigm, this section includes critiques of scholarship on the RMA, the so-called 'new war' literature, and understandings of war and conflict that encompass ideas of human security. The third section of the chapter assesses the relevance of the 'just war' thesis in informing us of the reasons that states (or other actors) go to war, and how these actors conduct themselves during conflict. Finally, the chapter concludes by offering some observations on how we might best understand the variety of conflicts that we have witnessed in the post-Soviet space.

From modern to post-modern war

As European sovereigns were increasingly able to stabilise borders and centralise economic and political authority during the seventeenth and eighteenth centuries, so too were they able to establish professional, standing armies. As John Keegan argues, the establishment of permanent, standing armies, via the regiment, became the device 'for securing armed forces to the state'.[1] In this respect, the evolution of the modern state is closely tied to that of the establishment of regular, professional military forces. Charles Tilley understood this when he noted that '[w]ar made the state and the state made war'.[2] During the period, the state disarmed its civilian populations, while simultaneously the scale of armed forces under its jurisdiction grew exponentially.[3] By regulating tax revenue and centralising and consolidating the political aspects of war, the state was able to further enhance its war-fighting capacity. The modern state was also able to claim to represent the collective interest. In this respect, the state came to define the 'public', and the 'public arena' became that in which force was legitimate.[4]

When considering the notion of modern conflict, the evolutionary establishment of a demarcated public and private realm is important. Patricia Owens appreciated this when she argued that war 'was for the political end of states and was justified as the legitimate means for the pursuit of state interest'.[5] She went on to note that war 'could be distinguished from less organised violence because it was defined as an activity carried out by a newly fashioned "public" entity which established the law and exceptions to the law'.[6] Thus, war fighting by agents of the state was understood not just as legitimate. Rather, it also became legal.

It is within this political environment that Clausewitz understood war. It may appear customary to include an evaluation of Clausewitz's conceptualisation of war in any discussion about conflict, the cursory sketches usually found in assessments of this type fail to appreciate the impact that *On War* has had on the discipline (as well as the practice) of international relations. And while the ordinariness of Clausewitz as a soldier has been widely acknowledged, it is also generally accepted that *On War* represents the most systematic study of nearly all facets of modern warfare.

When considering war, the writings of Clausewitz continue to offer us invaluable insights into the relationship between politics and conflict, and the former USSR is no exception here. Although writing in

---

[1] J. Keegan,. *A history of warfare* (New York: Alfred A. Knopf, 1994), p. 12.

[2] C. Tilly, 'Reflections on the history of European state-making', in C. Tilly (ed.), *The formation of national states in Western Europe* (Princeton University Press, 1975), p. 45.

[3] C. Tilly, *Coercion, capital, and European states, AD 990–1990* (Oxford, UK: Blackwell, 1990), p. 69.

[4] M. Weber, *From Max Weber: essays in sociology*, trans. and ed. H.H. Gerth and C. Wright Mills (London: Routledge, 1991), p. 71.

[5] P. Owens, 'Distinctions, distinctions: "public" and "private" force?' *International Affairs* 84 (2008), p. 983.

[6] Ibid.

the nineteenth century, his claim that 'war is act of policy ... [it] cannot be divorced from political life, and whenever this occurs in our thinking about war the many elements that connect the two elements are destroyed, and we are left with something pointless and devoid of sense' remains astute.[7]

Similarly, his observations on the character or nature of war continue to be relevant. Clausewitz famously defined war as 'an act of force to compel our enemy to do our will', which is 'nothing but the continuation of policy with other means'.[8] In this respect, Clausewitz understood war as a rational act. He also saw that war was dangerous and unpredictable. Although it was fought by professional armies, war took place in an environment in which things were likely to go wrong:

> Everything in war is very simple, but the simplest thing is very difficult [...] countless minor incidents – the kind you can never really foresee – combine to lower the general level of performance, so that one always falls short of the intended goal [...] The military machine is basically very simple and very easy to manage. But we should bear in mind that none of its components is of one piece: each part is composed of individuals, every one of whom retains his potential of friction.[9]

'Friction' was thus the environment in which all war took place. Here, Clausewitz knew that the intrinsic nature of war was for things not to always go as planned. Thus, while understanding the reasons for going to war as rational, Clausewitz appreciated the moral and psychological aspects of fighting war. According to Clausewitz, understandings of war that fail to 'reckon with and give value to moral qualities' are deficient, for moral qualities 'constitute the spirit that permeates war as a whole'.[10]

There are parts of *On War* that might be regarded as confusing or even contradictory, but one area in which Clausewitz was explicit was in regard to the relationship between ends and means in war. In relation to tactics, 'the means are fighting forces trained for combat; the end is victory'.[11] Elaborating on the relationship between politics and war, he wrote that 'the political object is the goal, war is the means of reaching it, and means can never be considered in isolation from their purpose'.[12] Thus, wars are fought with clear political outcomes in mind. Hence, when these outcomes are reached, or victory is secured, war no longer needs to be fought. But, as Michael Howard notes, the key to victory

---

[7] C. von Clausewitz, *On War*, trans. M.E. Howard and P. Paret (Princeton University Press, 1976), pp. 605–7.

[8] Ibid., p. 983.   [9] Ibid., pp. 119–21.   [10] Ibid., p. 184.

[11] Ibid., pp. 142–3.   [12] Ibid., p. 81.

is politics: 'the most splendid of victories was nothing in itself unless it was the means to the attainment of a political end'.[13]

While the end is political, the means (the battle) is also important. Clausewitz wrote that warring parties need to be prepared and willing to engage in overwhelming force; 'the whole of military activity must relate directly or indirectly to the engagement'.[14] Victory, quite simply, is the defeat of the enemy. Clausewitz wrote briefly on what he called 'minimal war' which consisted of 'threatening the enemy, with negotiations held in reserve'.[15] But it is clear from *On War* that victory gained through such actions was unsatisfactory. Victory was best achieved through focusing attacks on what Clausewitz called the enemy's centre of gravity, which represented a 'hub' of power and movement that an adversary relied upon.[16] Such an attack, he argued, should be relentless:

If the enemy is thrown off balance, he must not be given time to recover. Blow after blow must be struck in the same direction; the victor, in other words, must strike with all of his strength and not just against a fraction of the enemy's. Not by taking things the easy way [...] but by constantly seeking out his centre of power, by daring all to win all, will one really defeat the enemy.[17]

Such sentiments might appear little more than barbaric and brutal. But this is the point. As a soldier, Clausewitz knew war was bloody and nasty:

We are not interested in generals who win wars without bloodshed. The fact that slaughter [*die Schlacht*] is a horrifying spectacle must make us take war more seriously, but not provide an excuse for gradually blunting our swords in the name of humanity. Sooner or later, someone will come along with a sharp sword and hack off our arms.[18]

Understanding war as an act of force that compelled your enemy to do your will led Clausewitz to conclude that wars will tend to escalate to extremes of 'absolute war'. This, for Clausewitz, was the logic of war, indeed the nature of war. Elaborating on this point, Howard notes that one cannot compel one's enemy without destroying their power to resist: 'so long as he has any capacity for resistance left, you are logically bound to destroy it'.[19] Thus there was 'no stopping place short of the extreme'.[20]

---

[13] M.E. Howard, *Clausewitz* (Oxford University Press, 1983), p. 37.
[14] Clausewitz, *On War*, p. 95.   [15] Ibid., p. 604.
[16] Ibid., pp. 595–6.   [17] Ibid., p. 596.
[18] Ibid., p. 260.   [19] Howard, *Clausewitz*, p. 49.
[20] Ibid. Although not explicit in Clausewitz's work, this idea of 'absolute war' is assumed to be undertaken by great powers. Thus, war should be understood as symmetrical in that it is undertaken by parties of roughly equivalent standing and stature.

Clausewitz asserted that war has two key aspects: subjective and objective. The former comprised those qualities common to all warfare in all periods – namely, violence and bloodshed. The latter encompassed the actual, dynamically changeable, highly variable detail of warfare. Clausewitz explained it thus:

War is more than a true chameleon that slightly adapts its characteristics to a given case. As a total phenomenon its dominant tendencies always make war a paradoxical trinity, composed of primordial violence, hatred and enmity, which are regarded as blind natural force; of the play of chance and probability within which the creative spirit is free to roam; and of its element of subordination, as an instrument of policy, which makes it subject to reason alone.[21]

Since *On War* was first published, Clausewitz's influence on the way strategists have thought about war has as much to do as anything else with the way that conflicts – especially the two world wars in the twentieth century – were played out. According to Hugh Smith, the First World War 'epitomised war as Clausewitz understood it'.[22] Fought by powerful armies representing states in space somewhat removed from the civilian population, the 'Great War' was characterised by bloody battles. It consumed much of the apparatus of the state, with 'armies requiring a large, disciplined and trained workforce, a constant supply of material and complex systems of management'.[23] And although it was a different war in many respects, especially with regards to technology, the Second World War can also be understood within a Clausewitzian framework. It was the 'total war' that the conflict of 1914–18 had threatened to become. Anything identified as contributing to the enemy's war effort became a legitimate target. It was a protracted and bloody conflict, won by defeating armies on the ground. Both the world wars were thus still recognisable as 'modern', in the Clausewitzian sense.[24] In many respects, the unprecedented and massive mobilisation of state resources in each case represented a logical endpoint to Clausewitz's ideas.

However, the Cold War environment presented new challenges to the Clausewitzian framework. In particular, the advent of nuclear weapons jeopardised the 'natural limits on violence and the prospects for imposing further political controls that Clausewitz believed kept all actual wars from mounting to horrible, senseless "absolute" extremes'.[25]

[21] Ibid., p. 101.
[22] H. Smith, *On Clausewitz: a study of military and political ideas* (Basingstoke, UK: Palgrave MacMillan, 2005), p. 239.
[23] Ibid., p. 239.   [24] Ibid., p. 242.
[25] M. Mandelbaum, *The nuclear question: the United States and nuclear weapons, 1946–1976* (Cambridge University Press, 1979), p. 4.

Though this is not the place to elaborate on nuclear strategy during the Cold War, it is valuable to examine how Clausewitz's ideas might inform our understanding of why, aside from so-called 'proxy' wars, the Cold War remained cold.

Thankfully, direct conflict between the post-1945 superpowers did not eventuate. It is difficult to imagine how such a war could have remained non-nuclear. However, this is certainly not to say the advent of nuclear weapons rendered all war obsolete. Indeed, the Cold War was characterised by so-called proxy wars, or (as the United States chose to describe them) low-intensity conflicts. What the advent of nuclear weapons has done so far is render major war among great powers effectively obsolete. Russia has certainly attempted to make this a cornerstone of its own post-Cold War nuclear strategy, shifting to a 'first use if necessary' doctrine in the face of a US-developed NMD shield that threatens to render the Russian deterrent obsolete. And in spite of the 2010 New Start Agreement between Washington and Moscow, it is clear that both former president Putin and President Medvedev continue to regard nuclear weapons as a vital Russian strategic asset.

In the Clausewitzian context, what lessons for the way we understand war can be drawn from the conflicts that have sprung up on the territory of the former USSR since its collapse? To begin with, and as with many non-traditional conflicts involving insurgents or guerrilla movements, Clausewitz's observations about the friction and the 'fog' of war remain accurate interpretations of the constantly shifting alliances, networks and enemies faced by Russian forces in the two wars in Chechnya. The difficulty of obtaining accurate intelligence and the inability of Russian forces to consistently hold ground in the first war (repeated in the temporary and often pyrrhic victories over rebel forces led by Aslan Maskhadov in the second conflict) underscored the problem of maintaining effective command and control over any battlefield, much less one that was conducted between asymmetrical actors. Likewise, the requirement that morality should not get in the way of the successful prosecution of war was certainly visible in the conduct of each side in the wars in Chechnya, with atrocities committed not only as a necessary evil to reach victory, but also as a way to clearly communicate the will of the protagonists to win at all costs.

There is logic as well in assessing the 2008 war in Georgia, which was a more traditional interstate conflict over territory and resources, within a Clausewitzian framework. It was certainly 'politics by other means', as both sides sought to gain advantage over the other, with Moscow seeking to weaken Tbilisi both physically (by cementing its grip over the separatist regions of South Ossetia and Abkhazia), as well as ideationally (by linking Georgia's behaviour to the 'nationalities' question, in which Russia was exercising its legitimate right to protect its citizens). For his part, Mikhail Saakashvili sought to turn Russia's 'invasion' to his advantage, repeatedly pressing for his nation to be fast-tracked for NATO membership.

However, there are aspects of Clausewitz's thinking that have not held up well over time. The complex ethnic and political tensions that were the triggers for conflict in Moldova, and between Armenia and Azerbaijan over Nagorno-Karabakh, may have also had raw material objectives, but this was only part of the picture. It can be argued that the link between transnational terrorism and organised crime, which has flourished in the post-Soviet space, fits poorly within the massified conception of war envisaged by Clausewitz. With this in mind, it is reasonable to question not only the continuing relevance of Clausewitz, and how his writing might inform our understanding of post-Cold War conflict. We should also ask whether, as it has been suggested in a number of quarters, the nature and character of post-Cold War conflict has changed to such an extent as to require new frameworks through which to understand war.

'New war' meets hot and frozen conflicts

The end of the Cold War and the subsequent UN-sponsored cooperation in Kuwait was thought to have ushered in a 'new world order', in which great power war, and hence mass war casualties, could be regarded as a thing of the past. Linked to this, the end of the Cold War was reflective of greater systemic change in international relations, where states were no longer the most important actors, and the multiple forces of globalisation had rendered much of the state's heavily mechanised armed forces redundant. This thinking is perhaps best represented by Rupert Smith, whose views on war, as it was traditionally conceived, are unequivocal:

War as cognitively known to most non-combatants, war as battle in a field between men and machinery, war as a massive deciding event in a dispute in international affairs: such war no longer exists [...] It is now time to recognise that a paradigm shift in war has undoubtedly occurred: from armies with comparable forces doing battle on a field to strategic confrontation between a range of combatants, not all of which are armies, and using different types of weapons, often improvised. The old paradigm was that of interstate industrial war. The new one is the paradigm of war amongst the people.[26]

Smith's observations are part of a broader range of writing that stresses the difference between Clausewitzian (or 'old') wars, and so-called 'new' war. Pointing to wars in Bosnia–Herzegovina, Rwanda, Somalia and Liberia, and Chechnya and Sierra Leone, the new war literature argues that the prevalence of old, state-based war has decreased, while the number of civil wars, as well as wars between non-state entities, has increased.[27]

New wars, according to their proponents, need to be understood within the broader context of globalisation. According to the most prominent new war theorist, Mary Kaldor, 'the intensification of global interconnectedness – political, economic, military and cultural – and the changing character of political authority' is transforming the nature of war.[28] Kaldor argues that new wars can be contrasted with old wars in terms of means, ends and the way in which they are financed. From this perspective, the blurring of the distinction between public and private, the declining influence of the state and the subsequent effects that this has on ideas of identity, territory and governance renders Clausewitzian war redundant.

With regards to means, a distinction is drawn between the way the old and new wars are organised. In the past, war had been centrally organ-ised, controlled and fought on behalf of the state. In contrast, new wars are fought by highly decentralised groups, 'such as paramilitary units, local warlords, criminal gangs, police forces, mercenary groups and also regular armies, including breakaway units from regular armies'.[29] The method of war fighting is also thought to be 'new'. Whereas 'old wars' were characterised by large battles, new wars are distinguished by the avoidance of large-scale battles. New war is thought to consist of roll-ing skirmishes, objectives advanced through control of the population, population displacement and violence directed against civilians. The new war literature emphasises that force is no longer directed 'against

---

[26] R. Smith, *The utility of force: the art of war in the modern world* (London: Allen Lane, 2005), pp. 1–3.

[27] M. Kaldor, *New and old wars*, 2nd edn (Stanford University Press, 2006); C. Allen, 'Warfare, endemic violence and state collapse in Africa', *Review of African Political Economy*, 26 (1999); W. Shawcross, *Deliver us from evil: peacekeepers, warlords, and a world of endless conflict* (New York: Simon and Schuster, 2000); and H. Münkler, *The New Wars* (Oxford: Polity, 2005).

[28] Kaldor, *New and old wars*, p. 4.   [29] Ibid., p. 7.

the enemy's armed force, but against the civilian population, the aim being to either drive it from it a certain area [...] or to force it to supply and support certain armed groups on a permanent basis'.[30] Here, a further distinction relates to ideas of conduct during war. Whilst old wars were fought with at least a tacit appreciation of the norms and codified laws of war, new wars are notable for their barbarism, violence and total disregard for established norms and laws.

As well as highlighting distinctions in means, the new war thesis also draws distinctions about objectives in violent conflict. Whereas old war was fought for purely political ends, a feature of new war, according to Donald Snow, is 'the essential divorce of war from politics. In this style, war is not so clearly the continuation of politics by other means.'[31] Pursuing a related theme, Martin Van Creveld argues that it is 'preposterous [...] to think that, just because some people wield power, they act like calculating machines that are un-swayed by passions. In fact, they are no more rational than the rest of us.'[32]

Those who advocate viewing war through the prism of new economic rationales also argue that wars should no longer be understood as an extension of politics. According to this view, war can be seen as a continuation of *economics* by other means.[33] As Jan Angstrom points out, 'this does not necessarily mean that wars are caused by economic shortcomings but rather that the conduct, and continuation, of the war is determined by economic incentives'.[34] And, while conceding that personal enrichment might not be the primary motivating factor for going to war, a final group of new war theorists nonetheless charges that the economy of war making has changed. While old wars were financed by states out of traditional revenue streams, new wars are financed in an entirely different manner. They draw on more unorthodox and often ad hoc measures such as looting, robbery, pillage, extortion and hostage taking, as well as more complex means such as arms and drug trafficking, oil smuggling and money laundering. In the post-Cold War era, warring parties have often been forced to develop their own means of

---

[30] H. Münkler, *The new wars* (Oxford: Polity, 2005), p. 14.

[31] D. Snow, *Distant thunder: patterns of conflict in the developing world* (London: M.E. Sharpe, 1997), p. 129.

[32] Van Creveld, *The transformation of war*, p. 157.

[33] D. Keen, 'Incentives and disincentives for violence', in M. Berdal and D. Malone (eds.), *Greed and grievance: economic agendas in civil war* (Boulder, CO: Lynne Rienner Publishers, 2000), p. 27 (emphasis in original).

[34] J. Angstrom, 'Introduction: debating the nature of modern war', in I. Duyvesteyn and J. Angstrom (eds.), *Rethinking the nature of war* (London: Frank Cass, 2005), p. 11.

economic sustainability. Reflecting the logic of globalisation, 'this has often meant moving beyond the state in pursuit of wider alternative economic networks'.[35] Kalevi Holsti has extended this, drawing links between the breakdown of state and economic motives, to claim that war (especially in the developing world), might in fact be neo-medieval:

> The new medievalism is demonstrated most dramatically in the nature of armed conflict in these states. War has become de-institutionalised in the sense of central controls, rules, regulations, etiquette and armaments. Armies are rag-tag groups frequently made up of teenagers paid in drugs, or not paid at all. In the absence of authority and discipline, but in keeping with the interests of the warlords, 'soldiers' discover opportunities for private enterprises of their own.[36]

Despite the apparent prevalence of new wars, a number of authors have questioned the relevancy of the distinction made between old and new wars, with many questioning the novelty of new wars. As Edward Newman has observed, '[m]uch of this is not new: all of the factors that characterise new wars have been present, to varying degrees, throughout the last 100 years. The actors, objectives, spatial context, human impact, political economy, and social structure of conflict have not changed to the extent argued in the new wars literature.'[37] Regarding civil wars, Newman points out that rather than increasing, as claimed in the new war literature, the quantitative incidence of civil war has in fact declined since 1992.[38] Stathis Kalyvas goes further, suggesting that the distinction between 'old' civil wars and 'new' civil wars is invalid due to the shortcomings of data in contemporary war, and ignorance of historical detail in relation to earlier wars.[39]

For other critics, the emphasis that the new war literature places on the breakdown between the public and the private sectors, and the subsequent ramifications this has for understanding conflict, is also flawed. For instance, Patricia Owens argues that 'public-private distinctions shift and change as an effect of political power', and that 'there is clear historical and sociological evidence to support the conceptual claim

---

[35] M. Duffield, 'Globalisation, transborder trade and war economies', in M. Berdal and D. Malone (eds.), *Greed and grievance: economic agendas in civil wars* (Boulder, CO: Lynne Rienner Publishers, 2000), pp. 73–4.

[36] K. Holsti, 'The coming chaos? Armed conflict in the world's periphery', in T.V. Paul and J. Hall (eds.), *International order and the future of world politics* (Cambridge University Press, 1999), p. 304.

[37] E. Newman, 'The 'new wars' debate: a historical perspective is needed', *Security Dialogue* 35 (2004), 179.

[38] Ibid., 180.

[39] S.N. Kalyvas, '"New" and "old" civil wars: a valid distinction?', *World Politics* 54 (2001), 99.

that a variety of public-private distinctions are made and remade during war'.[40] Reflecting a theme that is present in most of the critiques of the new war thesis, Owens suggests that debates about political violence 'should be understood historically as the transnational constitution and circulation of military and economic power'.[41]

The strongest critiques of the new war literature are those that question the underpinning idea of the new war thesis; that new wars should be understood within the context of globalisation. Here it is true that globalisation as a term suffers from definitional imprecision. The 'totalising' pretensions of the term limit its use as an analytical tool. When used in such a way, efforts to understand individual cases and specific mechanisms are invariably flawed. Not only is the term itself problematic, as Mats Berdal notes, so too is the extent to which economic aspects of globalisation are inherently conflict-generating. For Berdal, an emphasis on economic motivations does not adequately explain why people resort to violence; greater attention should be paid to historical and cultural roots.[42]

Indeed, while it is undeniably the case that certain aspects of conflict have changed, the new war literature exaggerates much of this change. First, one must be wary of claims pointing to the broader phenomenon of globalisation as a facilitator of a new type of war. Second, one must also be wary of frameworks premised on the declining power of the state. The violence in the post-Soviet space clearly demonstrates the state's continued capacity and ability to fight wars. Finally, echoing Newman and Kalyvas, the old/new war distinction is a false dichotomy. Much of that pronounced as 'new' reflects an evolution in the nature and character of warfare, while that pronounced as 'old' remains current.

The wars in Chechnya are an explicit example in favour of viewing war through a lens that reflects their status rather than their root causes. One could potentially make the case that Chechnya was an example of new war, given that it seemed on the surface to encompass new actors, new methods, new economics and new objectives that were based on identity, and hence fundamentally different to the political goals of traditional war. But here too one can question to what extent such observations really were new at all. The civilian casualties caused in Chechnya were exceeded significantly during the strategic bombing campaigns of the Second World War, and both sides of that conflict

---

[40] Owens, 'Distinctions, distinctions', 988.   [41] Ibid.
[42] M. Berdal, 'How "new" are "new wars"? Global economic change and the study of civil war', *Global Governance* 9 (2003), 477–502.

behaved barbarically towards non-combatants at times. By the same token, the notion that the war in Chechnya was associated with new economics linked to transnational crime (rather than state taxation policies) neglects the fact that looting, the hoarding of art treasures and the establishment of black markets for guns, money and drugs have accompanied any site of conflict from Berlin to Baghdad. One can even ask whether the new radicalised identities of combatants in Chechnya was the primary driver for war. Although Shamil Basaev, Ibn-al Khattab and Dokka Umarov are painted as radical Islamists fighting for a legitimate alternative identity, so too can one paint the struggle as essentially a self-determination campaign: in other words, for the wholly traditional (or 'old') notion of statehood and sovereignty. A virtually secular sense of nationalism was certainly the reason Maskhadov (and, earlier, Jokhar Dudayev) fought.

The 'new war' literature stands as the most prominent attempt to recast our understanding of organised conflict. But applied more directly to conflict in the post-Soviet space, the application of 'hot' and 'frozen' conflict are potentially much more appropriate attempts to enrich our understanding of the changed nature of war. At the time of writing, the on-and-off-again wars in Trans-Dniester, Abkhazia, South Ossetia and Nagorno-Karabakh remained largely unresolved. Reflective of this, the conflicts that have beset this area are often collectively referred to – as they are, indeed, by other contributions in this volume – as 'frozen' conflicts. The term is not only designed to reflect the static nature of these conflicts, but also the idea that if left alone, they will remain in stasis.[43] Furthermore, the term also suggests that the conflicts are not only unresolvable, but that it is in the interests of one or more of the warring parties for the conflict to remain frozen.[44]

Even so, using the idea of 'frozen' conflicts leads to many of the same problems faced by the 'new war' framework. As Dov Lynch points out, so-called frozen conflicts are in fact dynamic, so understanding them as frozen leads to ill-informed policy decisions.[45] And while they are elaborated on further in other chapters in this volume, the conflicts witnessed in Uzbekistan, Chechnya and Abkhazia remind us that war remains a complex phenomenon. In this respect, by reducing any episode of political violence to a 'new' war, or a 'hot' or 'frozen' conflict, is unhelpful, doing little more than adding new metaphors.

---

[43] See O. Antonenko, 'A war with no winners', *Survival* 50 (2008), pp. 23–36.
[44] See C. Welt, 'The thawing of a frozen conflict: the internal security dilemma and the 2004 prelude to the Russo-Georgia war', *Europe-Asia Studies* 62 (2010), 63–97.
[45] D. Lynch, 'Separatist states and post-Soviet conflicts', *International Affairs* 78 (2002), 831–48.

Human security

Assessments of conflict that are premised on the changed role of the state also imply the need to reassess traditional understandings of security. Such reassessments often point to the areas of the world beset by new wars, and argue that dominant statist conceptions exacerbate insecurity, creating what Kaldor calls a 'security gap'.[46] Arguably, traditional conceptions of security – in other words, those that are premised on military defence of territory – ignore broader conceptions, specifically those concerned with individual or 'human' security (as opposed to state security). In response to the so-called security gap, 'human security [...] reorients security and thinking and policy around the individual as the referent object'.[47] More specifically, the Commission on Human Security (CHS), convened in 2001, suggests that human security

> means protecting people from critical and pervasive threats and situations, [and] building on their strengths and aspirations. It also means giving people the building blocks of survival, dignity and livelihood. Human security connects different types of freedoms – freedom from want, freedom from fear and freedom to take action on one's own behalf.[48]

Kaldor argues that the human security approach aims 'to both stabilise conflicts and address the sources of insecurity'.[49] This should not be thought of as superseding state security but rather, as Matthew Weinert suggests, 'human security complements, not displaces, state security'.[50] In an increasingly interconnected world, where states are becoming gradually more integrated into layers of global governance, advocates of human security thus argue that the 'need for classic state security policies is likely to come to complement the more urgent human security tasks, rather than the other way around'.[51]

However, the human security framework is of limited use, especially when war breaks out. The concept, as Newman points out, is 'normatively attractive, but analytically weak. Through a broad human security lens, anything that presents a critical threat to life and livelihood

---

[46] M. Kaldor, *Human security*, p. 10.

[47] E. Newman, 'A normatively attractive but analytically weak concept', *Security Dialogue* 35 (2004), 358.

[48] Commission on Human Security, 'Outline of the Report of the Commission on Human Security' (2008). Available at http://ochaonline.un.org/Reports/tabid/2186/language/en-US/Default.aspx

[49] Kaldor, *Human security*, p. 191.

[50] M.S. Weinert, 'From state security to human security', in P. Hayden (ed.), *The Ashgate research companion to ethics and international relations* (Farnham, UK: Ashgate, 2009), p. 155.

[51] Kaldor, *Human security*, p. 196.

is a security threat, whatever the source.'[52] In this respect, it presents few insights into rationales for going to war. The especially vague and imprecise language adopted by the CHS certainly does not assist those in search of analytical precision. To be fair, the literature on human security does raise valid questions about the relationship between the individual and the state, and in turn questions the idea of state sovereignty. The human security approach, with its focus on the citizen, reverses the traditional role of the citizenry supporting Westphalian notions of territorial sovereignty and legitimacy.[53] Instead of people serving the state, the state must serve and support those from whom its legitimacy is drawn.

But even this is problematic. The human security critique of 'traditional' approaches sees the state as amoral and divorced from human interaction. Yet the state has never been the unitary actor that particularistic, Waltzian constructs might suggest. The human security framework also suffers from much the same problems as the new war thesis. Founded as it is on a broad conception of globalisation that has as its core tenet the declining power or influence of the sovereign nation-state, it has limited explanatory value when exploring examples of state-versus-state war. Similarly, considering its focus on non-traditional security threats, human security provides limited analytical value when discussing wars fought for 'traditional' reasons such as territory.[54] This was certainly the case in the war between Russia and Georgia, in which the discourse on human rights was used and abused on both sides. Moscow argued strenuously that it was protecting its citizens, while a storm of protest emanated from Tbilisi that the security of its people – not to mention Georgian democracy – was under assault.

The revolution in military affairs and 'spectator war'

While it is not part of the thinking on new wars, the debate surrounding the so-called revolution in military affairs (RMA) also suggests that there is something distinctively new about the way that wars are fought. Somewhat similarly to the new wars literature, the RMA literature implicitly suggests that alterations to the character of warfare may be of such proportions that the nature of warfare itself has been

---

[52] Newman, 'A normatively attractive but analytically weak concept', 358.
[53] Ibid.
[54] For an engaging discussion on the practical limitations of human security, see M. McDonald, 'Human security and the construction of security', *Global Society* 16 (2002), 277–95.

transformed.[55] Pinpointing the 1991 Gulf War as the beginning of much of the discussion on the RMA, Colin McInnes notes, 'for although some of the technologies had been used during conflicts in the 1980s [...] the Gulf War saw the widespread and deliberate exploitation of leading edge technologies [providing] the first hard evidence of a technological revolution'.[56] In particular, the use of precision-guided weapons, and the ability, via mounted cameras on the planes from whence they were dispatched, for the viewer to watch these weapons 'sail unerringly into hapless vehicles [or buildings] singled out for destruction' only served to reinforce the idea that we were witnessing something very 'new' in the way that wars could be fought.[57] That the RMA has been embraced by those responsible for military strategy is demonstrated by the fact that of the total munitions used in the 1991 Gulf War, 9 per cent of them were precision guided, while in 2003 the Coalition of the Willing had used 68 per cent precision-guided munitions.[58]

More specifically, the driving force behind the current RMA is related to information processing. This has three main components. First, information dominance, comprising a network of sensor systems, 'promises to disperse the fog of war for friendly commanders and thicken it for the enemy'.[59] Second, precision weapons promise to make warfare 'more efficient than ever, and to make desired strategic outcomes almost guaranteed'.[60] Third, 'information technology allows for the networking of all aspects of the military organisation [...] that generates a net effect far greater than the sum of its parts'.[61]

Advocates of the RMA believe that 'the technologies of the information age should allow military power to be employed to its maximum efficiency with speed, precision, and minimum human cost. There is no need to target civilians nor even to hit them inadvertently.'[62] The new technologies that form the centrepiece of the RMA thus not only change the way that war is fought, but also alter the way that victory is attained. Following the logic of the RMA, the increased reliance

---

[55] D. Lonsdale, *The nature of war in the information age: Clausewitzian future* (London: Frank Cass, 2004).

[56] C. McInnes, *Spectator-sport war: the West and contemporary conflict* (Boulder, CO: Lynne Rienner Publishers, 2002), p. 119.

[57] J.M. Beier, 'Outsmarting technologies: rhetoric, revolutions in military affairs, and the social depth of warfare', *International Politics* 43 (2006), 268.

[58] Cited in Angstrom, 'Introduction: debating the nature of modern war', p. 16.

[59] B. Loo, 'Introduction: revolutions in military affairs: theory and applicability to small armed forces', in B. Loo (ed.), *Military transformation and strategy* (Abingdon, UK: Routledge, 2009), p. 2.

[60] Ibid.   [61] Ibid., p. 3.

[62] L. Freedman, 'The changing forms of military conflict', *Survival* 40 (1998), 44.

on 'smart' weapons would ideally lead to quick, clean victories with minimal collateral damage. Similarly, the heavy reliance on technology would limit not only the theatre of war, but require fewer ground troops.

While it is undeniable that technological advances have changed the way wars are fought, the 'revolution' that RMA literature alludes to is thus far limited to the United States, which, 'through precision firepower delivered from altitude by aircraft, cruise missiles or unmanned aerial vehicles (UAVs or 'drones') [...] currently own regular warfare'.[63] Thus, the RMA sheds little light on changes in the reasons that wars are fought. This is especially the case when observing wars in the post-Soviet space, particularly given the capability gaps between the former republics of the USSR (including even Russia), and the much more developed militaries fielded by Western nations. Furthermore, while the RMA represents the type of war that powerful states are best suited to winning, McInnes points out that this 'creates an incentive for enemies to fight precisely the sort of war that [such states do] *not* want to become engaged in'.[64] Finally, the idea that war can be clean is naïve. As Chechnya demonstrates, war remains a bloody enterprise where combatants still seek victory by inflicting the most amount of damage possible on their enemies.

Just war and the laws of war

As the modern state assumed control over the means for fighting war, there also developed, at first tacitly, then later through formal international agreements, understandings about how war was to be fought:

> To distinguish war from mere crime, it was defined as something waged by sovereign states and by them alone. Soldiers were defined as personnel licensed to engage in armed violence on behalf of the state [...] They were supposed to fight while only in uniform, carrying their arms 'openly' [...] They were not supposed to resort to 'dastardly' methods such as violating truces, taking up arms again after they had been wounded or taken prisoner [...] The civilian population was supposed to be left alone, 'military necessity' permitting.[65]

The evolution of the codified laws of war was informed by the just war tradition. While Mark Evans notes that 'just war theory's ability to influence political leaders and military combatants has always been questioned', the idea of defence of sovereignty, elaborated on by Hugo

---

[63] Gray, *War, peace and international relations*, p. 242.
[64] McInnes, *Spectator-sport war*, p. 139.
[65] Van Creveld, *The transformation of war*, pp. 40–1.

Grotius in *The Laws of War and Peace* (1625) remains a centrepiece of legitimising the use of force.[66] For this reason alone, it is worth exploring the ways in which the just war tradition, in terms of how wars are legitimised, inform our ability to evaluate conflicts in the post-Soviet sphere.

A further reason is provided by Alex Bellamy. Engaging with Michael Walzer's idea of the 'war convention', he suggests that the just war tradition does more than provide a framework for judgement. Rather, 'it can also constrain and enable certain types of activity'.[67] And, as Walzer points out, while 'chivalry may be dead', nonetheless 'fighting unfree, professional soldiers [...] remain sensitive to those limits and restraints that distinguishes their life's work from mere butchery'.[68]

The just war tradition is understood to comprise two components: *jus ad bellum* (or when it is right to fight) and *jus in bello* (the right way to conduct war). While certainly not the first to write on these ideas, St Augustine drew clear distinctions between the two components, arguing that while resorting to the use of force might be regrettable, it could be justified under certain circumstances, including using force as sparingly as possible and force being deployed by legitimate civil authorities. It is these ideas that continue to inform codified laws of war. Here, contemporary understandings of the right to use force are contained in the UN Charter. More specifically, article 2(4) explicitly forbids the use of force; a generally agreed-upon fundamental rule of international relations to which there are only two exceptions. As set out under Article 51 of the Charter, states are permitted to defend themselves against acts of aggression; and under Article 39, the UN Security Council has the right to authorise actions of collective enforcement.

Aside from the right to use force, there is a further set of criteria underpinning the idea of *jus ad bellum*. The first of these concerns right intention to resort to the use of force. While perhaps somewhat dated, this criterion does serve as a guide or reference point to make judgements on 'good' wars (those fought for the common good) and 'bad' wars (those fought for the sake of fighting or territorial aggrandisement). The second criterion suggests that the war must be fought for a just cause. According to Mark Evans, 'the justice of the cause is sufficiently great as to warrant warfare and does not negate countervailing

---

[66] M. Evans, 'Moral theory and the idea of just war', in M. Evans (ed.), *Just war theory: a reappraisal* (Edinburgh University Press, 2005), p. 5.

[67] A. Bellamy, *Just wars: from Cicero to Iraq* (Cambridge University Press, 2006), p. 2.

[68] M. Walzer, *Just and unjust war: a moral argument with historical illustrations*, 4th edn (New York: Basic Books, 2006), p. 45.

values of equal or greater weight'.[69] Just causes are generally under-stood to constitute, among other factors, acts of self-defence, defence of others and punishment of wrongdoers. While Walzer argues 'that when fighting breaks out, there must always be some state against which the law can and should be enforced', it is not uncommon for both parties to claim that their cause is just.[70]

A third criterion concerns proportionality of ends – or, as Evans puts it, 'on the basis of available knowledge and reasonable assessment of the situation' it is necessary to be 'as confident as one reasonably can of achieving one's just objective without yielding longer term conse-quences that are worse than the status quo'.[71] This is closely related to a fourth criterion concerning a reasonable expectation of success. A fifth criterion asks whether warfare is genuinely a last resort. This does not necessarily mean that all avenues short of force have been exhausted, but rather that 'actors carefully evaluate all the different strategies that might bring about the desired end, selecting force if it appears to be the only feasible strategy for these ends'.[72] Finally, war must be conducted by the right authority (following a proper declaration), so that 'one must have the *right* to wage war'.[73] In the pre-modern era, declaring war was the right of sovereign princes. In the modern era, the sovereign state is the entity that has the right to fight wars. This said, the question of who has the right to declare wars currently remains debatable. Positivist legal interpretations, guided by the UN Charter, argue that states act-ing in self-defence, or actions permitted by the UN Security Council, are the only legitimate means of declaring war.

With regards to declaring war, Evans makes an important point when he suggests that not only should the declaration be publically defended, but subsequently, one must 'be prepared to be politically account-able for the conduct and aftermath of the war'.[74] With this in mind, it appears that it is to wars undertaken by the sovereign nation-state that the just war tradition is most applicable. This is further underscored by Bellamy, who notes that a declaration 'clearly marks the transition from peace to war and hence the type of legal rules that ought to be applied'.[75]

Whereas there are some vagaries with the laws and norms associated with *jus ad bellum*, the legal and moral rules that form the foundation

---

[69] Evans, 'Moral theory and the idea of just war', p. 12.
[70] Walzer, *Just and unjust war*, p. 59.
[71] Evans, 'Moral theory and the idea of just war', p. 12.
[72] Bellamy, *Just wars*, p. 123.
[73] Evans, 'Moral theory and the idea of just war', p. 13 (emphasis in original).
[74] Ibid.   [75] Bellamy, *Just wars*, p. 127.

of *jus in bello* are clearer. The four Geneva Conventions (1949) widely assumed to hold the status of customary law, granted wide-ranging protections to non-combatants, the injured and the sick, and prisoners of war. Recognising limits to the conventions, between 1974 and 1977 states negotiated additional protocols. The first Geneva Protocol strengthened the distinction between combatants and non-combatants, insisting that 'the civilian population as such, as well as individual civilians, shall not be the object of attack. Acts or threats of violence the primary purpose of which is to spread terror among the civilian population are prohibited.'[76] Article 51 also focused on the issue of discriminatory force, outlawing attacks 'which may be expected to cause incidental loss of civilian life, injury to civilians, damage to civilian objects, or a combination thereof'. Finally, the first Protocol insisted that military force be directed only at military objectives, defined in the Protocol as 'those objects which by their nature, location, purpose or use make an effective contribution to military action and whose total or partial destruction, capture or neutralisation, in the circumstances ruling at the time, offers a definite military advantage'.[77]

Of particular relevance to the conflicts discussed in this volume is the second Geneva Protocol. Arguing that 'the only provision applicable to non-international armed conflicts before the adoption of the present Protocol was Article 3 common to all four Geneva Conventions of 1949', Protocol II has the specific aim of extending 'the essential rules of the law of armed conflicts to internal wars'.[78] As explained in the Protocol's introductory text, 'Article 3 proved to be inadequate in view of the fact that about 80% of the victims of armed conflicts since 1945 have been victims of non-international conflicts and that non-international conflicts are often fought with more cruelty than international conflicts.'[79] Essentially, Protocol II sought to regulate how states might respond to internal insurgents. However, as Bellamy notes, 'Protocol II offered states considerable latitude in deciding whether or not a particular insurgency could be labelled an "armed conflict".'[80]

---

[76] Protocol Additional to the Geneva Conventions of 12 August 1949, and relating to the Protection of Victims of International Armed Conflicts (Protocol I), 8 June (1977), Article 51. Available at www.icrc.org/ihl.nsf/WebART/470–750065?OpenDocument

[77] Protocol Additional to the Geneva Conventions of 12 August 1949, and relating to the Protection of Victims of International Armed Conflicts (Protocol I), 8 June (1977), Article 52. Available at www.icrc.org/ihl.nsf/WebART/470–750067?OpenDocument

[78] Protocol Additional to the Geneva Conventions of 12 August 1949, and relating to the Protection of Victims of Non-International Armed Conflicts (Protocol II), 8 June (1977), Introduction. Available at www.icrc.org/ihl.nsf/INTRO/475?OpenDocument

[79] Ibid. [80] Bellamy, *Just wars*, p. 110.

Protocol II is especially pertinent when examining the two wars in Chechnya (1994–6 and 1999–2000). Vladimir Galtiskii, a former captain in the Russian military, argues 'that events in Chechnya [...] should be classified as an internal armed conflict, in the course of which it is obligatory to adopt Article 3, common to all four Geneva Conventions [...] and Protocol II [...] in its entirety'.[81] However, even if these wars were classified in the way Galtiskii suggests, despite significant evidence that Russian forces have been responsible for systematic atrocities and war crimes, especially in Chechnya, its international prestige has apparently not suffered much.[82]

Herein lies the problem with the laws of war. The just war tradition and codified laws of war seem more suited to making judgements about conflict once it has concluded, rather than limiting the actions of actors during the conflict. While the advent of the ICC might go some way to remedying this problem, the anarchical nature of international politics and the absence of an authoritative global judicial presence mean that Bellamy is correct when he notes that the just war tradition, including codified laws of war, 'creates the possibility for the meaningful discussion about the legitimacy of war [...] but it cannot determine political outcomes or judgements in every case'.[83]

Conclusions

As the USSR was one of the Cold War superpowers, understanding war and conflict in the Soviet space was a comparatively straightforward task. For international relations theorists, war and conflict (or the lack thereof), was easily understood within the then-dominant realist paradigm. States were the dominant actors in the international system and their actions were determined and understood primarily through the lens of power and the national interest. The advent of nuclear weapons and the evolution of mutually assured destruction ensured that an uneasy balance of power existed between the superpowers. Direct conflict between the United States and the USSR would inevitably result in nuclear Armageddon; wiser heads prevailed and Gaddis's 'Long Peace' endured until 1991. And although the events of 9/11 accelerated its momentum, the implosion of the USSR inspired questions regarding long-held assumptions about sources of insecurity and possible

---

[81] Cited in M. Evangilista, *The Chechen wars: will Russia go the way of the Soviet Union?* (Washington, DC: Brookings Institution, 2002), p. 142.
[82] Ibid., p. 140.
[83] Bellamy, *Just wars*, p. 3.

resultant ramifications about the nature and character of warfare. In a post-Cold War, globalised world, are previously held assumptions about the nature and character of war still relevant?

It is clear that organised conflict no longer entirely reflects that described by Clausewitz. Wars are no longer primarily fought between powerful states. Nor are they primarily fought by well-organised, centrally funded and centrally commanded professional military apparatuses. Likewise, the continuing evolution of just war norms, particularly the strengthening of the Geneva Conventions and the establishment of the ICC, suggests a changing perception in what is and what is not legitimate with regards to conduct during war. Thus, a change in the character of warfare is discernible, even if this has reached the territory of the former USSR only unevenly.

Likewise, the changed security environment might also have given rise to changes in the reasons for going to war outside traditional, narrow interpretations of the national interest. The Chechen wars were framed variously as being part of the broader 'war on terror' (thus the argument that combatants should not be afforded protections under the Geneva Conventions or Geneva Protocols), a civil war and a conventional war. The 2008 war in Georgia was presented as humanitarian intervention (protecting the rights of Russians). While much of this was highly disingenuous, the very fact that such rationales were presented is representative of some change.

However, the degree to which these changes are caused or facilitated by globalisation or rapid advances in military technology is debatable. It is also difficult to know to what degree the just war tradition regulates conduct during war. The actions of the Russian military in both Chechnya and Georgia suggest that they have a limited effect. The failure to prosecute any members of the military for what were widely regarded as war crimes in Chechnya strengthens this conclusion. By the same token, scholarship that focuses on the decreasing capacity of states to wage war is exaggerated, as the events in Georgia during 2008 demonstrated. It is clear that the state maintains both the ability and the wherewithal to conduct traditional, Clausewitzian wars. Similarly, ideas of human security, premised as they are on a particular understanding of globalisation, fail to appreciate the continuing relevance of so-called traditional warfare. As such, Clausewitz's insights into war remain remarkably valuable. While some aspects of the *character* of warfare (or how war is fought) might have changed, the *nature* of warfare (or the reasons actors go to war, and generally who does the fighting) has not changed. Furthermore, it is unlikely to change soon since 'its nature as organised violence for political goals survives untouched by radical shifts in political forms, motives for conflict or technology'.[84] Thus, the conflicts we have witnessed in the former Soviet territories are best seen as reflecting evolutions, in contrast to views that see them as revolutions.

---

[84] C. Gray, 'Clausewitz rules, OK? The future is the past – with GPS', *Review of International Studies* 25 (1999), 169.

9 Conclusions: the future of conflict in the former USSR

Matthew Sussex

It is rare that specific conclusions about a book's subject matter can be drawn from an edited collection of this type. Certainly, the contributors to this volume would not agree on a rank order of causes for the different conflicts that have occurred on the territory of the former USSR. Nor would we necessarily agree on which of the wars since 1991 are more significant than others, and we would not be able to articulate a common position on the most appropriate way to resolve conflict in the former Soviet space. Such is the nature of academic discourse. So too is it the nature of war itself, which can be prompted by myriad structural, political, economic, social, ideational and technological forces, sometimes in easily recognisable patterns, and sometimes not. Yet it is instructive that all the chapters in this book find common ground on one key area: the prospects for future conflict. Each contribution explicitly notes that the conditions that can give rise to conflict have not been ameliorated in the two decades since the collapse of the USSR. In fact, it can be argued that they have actually grown more acute in some cases. There are several reasons for this, each of which has been addressed in more detail in specific chapters. Perhaps the most significant has been the inability of former Soviet states – whether due to material weakness, failure to construct appropriate domestic and regional institutions, competing interests, polarised identities, or a mix of these – to address the root causes of regional conflict.

The obvious inference to be drawn from this is that conflict will remain a fact of life in the geopolitical space once occupied by the USSR. But this prompts new questions, which – at the risk of over-speculation – should nonetheless be addressed, based on what we know about the type, frequency and causes of war in the region. For instance, what form will conflict in the former USSR take in the future? What will be its primary drivers? What effect will conflict have on broader global power configurations? And, finally, in what areas might the conditions for war be lessened, and is there any evidence that this is occurring?

As a conclusion to this book, in this final chapter I offer an assessment of future prospects for conflict in the former USSR. In evaluating the arenas in which war might persist I draw on the central themes that this volume's contributors have grappled with. These include (but are certainly not limited to) power, state building, territory and crime, the blurry nature of internal and external politics, and spongy norms relating to nationalism, sovereignty and identity. I survey both less likely outcomes, like renewed Russian imperialism and great power war, as well as more likely scenarios such as failed states, resource wars and the reignition of frozen conflicts. In doing so, I do not intend to prescribe specific policy choices for Russia, Ukraine or any other past republic of the USSR to help prevent conflict. This subject regularly comes up in the scholarly literature, and it seems (to me at least) that analysts and experts have been making broadly similar prescriptions for regional order since the mid-1990s, to little real effect.[1] These well-intentioned studies often neglect the fact that the former Soviet states lack the material capacity to achieve deep and rapid change. Some also do not take into account the perverse incentives for various players to actually *encourage* conditions that create instability and discord.[2] And still other assessments are either far too concerned with apportioning blame for war, or have too much faith in the power of interdependence, institutions and ideas to ameliorate the anarchical forces that were unleashed when the USSR collapsed.[3]

'Restoring' Russia via imperial conquest

There are four clear reasons why one of the most catastrophic scenarios for future conflict in the former USSR – the restoration of a Russian empire by force – is thankfully one of the most unlikely. First, if Russia intends to forcibly reintegrate the 'near abroad', it has already missed any small chance it had to do so. Second, if the past two decades have

---

[1] On this point see – amongst many others – Trenin, 'Russia reborn'; S. Blank, *Towards a new Russia policy* (Washington, DC: US Army War College, 2008); Z. Brzezinski, 'The premature partnership', *Foreign Affairs* 73 (1994), 67–82; D. Trenin, 'Russia leaves the West', *Foreign Affairs* 85 (2006), 87–96; and A. Arbatov, 'Russia's foreign policy alternatives'.

[2] For instance, this includes A. Freireynch, 'The enemy is at the gates: Russia after Beslan', *International Affairs* 81 (2005), 141–61; C. Hagel, 'A Republican foreign policy', *Foreign Affairs* 83 (2004), 74–6; C. Bildt, 'The Baltic litmus test', *Foreign Affairs* 73 (1994), 72–9; and D. Remnick, 'Can Russia change?', *Foreign Affairs* 76 (1997), 35–49.

[3] See, for instance, Y. Timoshenko, 'Containing Russia', *Foreign Affairs* 86 (2007), 65–82; S. Garnett, 'Russia's illusory ambitions', *Foreign Affairs* 76 (1997), 61–76; and C.A. Kupchan and C.C. Kupchan, 'The promise of collective security', *International Security* 20 (1995), 52–61.

taught us anything about Russian military power, it is that what remains of the once-vaunted Red Army has trouble securing its own borders, much less the capability to launch wars of aggrandisement. Third, the risks of either broader conflict or crippling isolation due to the international pariah status Russia would earn from resurgent imperialism would be far too great. Finally, and probably most importantly, Russia has no need to recreate a broader Russian empire while it is able to occupy a position of relative primacy in the region.

During the radicalisation of Russian politics that occurred soon after the constitutional crisis of 1992–3, many feared that 'Weimar Russia' would give way to a far right with new imperial ambitions. The view that transitional democracies were apt to adopt militaristic foreign policies was popular,[4] especially as Boris Yeltsin was forced to rule effectively by decree in the face of a fractious parliament. This was assisted by the prominence of Vladimir Zhirinovsky, the 'clown prince' of Russian politics, whose misnamed Liberal Democratic Party of Russia (LDPR) won 25 per cent of the vote in the parliamentary elections of 1993. Announcing a foreign policy doctrine titled *Plevok na Zapad* ('Spitting on the West'),[5] Zhirinovsky's stunts were viewed in the West with alarm, especially since the LDPR's electoral success gained it spots on Duma committees. The LDPR chairman of the Committee on Geopolitics, Alexei Mitrofanov, argued in favour of forcing Ukraine and Belarus to reintegrate with Russia.[6] Other radical groups preaching a combination of neo-fascism and anti-Semitism also became prominent. They included the Russian National Bolsheviks whose chief ideologue, Aleksandr Dugin, was later to claim to be a confidante of Vladimir Putin.[7] Even the KPRF that dominated the 1995 Duma elections became essentially a right-wing organisation, suggesting NATO was establishing a *cordon sanitaire* around Russia.[8] But in the event,

---

[4] One of the most important publications on this topic was E. Mansfield and J. Snyder, 'Democratisation and war', *Foreign Affairs* 74 (May–June, 1995), 79–97.

[5] V. Zhirinovsky, *Plevok na Zapad* (Moscow: Liberal'no-demokraticheskaia partiia Rossii, 1995).

[6] Mitrofanov wrote a nationalistic screed on geopolitical issues in 1997, which was a fairly typical far-right account of the need for renewed Russian imperialism. See A. Mitrofanov, *Shagi Novoi Geopolitiki* (Moscow: Russkii Vestnik, 1997). For other statements on LDP foreign policy see *Khvatit grabit' Rossiiu: pogranichnaia politika i natsional'nye interesy Rossii* (Moscow: LDP, 1995); and V. Zhirinovsky, *S tankami i pushkami ili bez tankov i pushek* (Moscow: Liberal'no-demokraticheskaia partiia Rossii, 1995).

[7] Dugin envisaged the recreation of the USSR, but this time as an empire without any pretence that it was comprised of sovereign republics. See A. Dugin, *Geopolitika* (Moscow: Arktogaia, 1995).

[8] *Sovetskaya rossiya*, 22 April (1997), p. 1.

the entire political spectrum shifted to the right. Far from being lone stalwarts of a strong Russia battling against a weak and incompetent government, the LDPR and KPRF found the government adopting a pragmatic nationalist approach centred on notions of spheres of influence, a rejection of NATO expansion, and a reassertion of Russian national interests in the near abroad. By the time Putin took over as president in 2000, a consensus on foreign affairs was firmly emplaced, and the moment for a 'red-brown' alliance to take control had passed.

Yet ideas alone, both radical and mainstream, cannot alter reality without the physical capability to do so. In spite of a military modernisation campaign aimed at creating a leaner and more efficient armed force, in 2010 Russian military expenditure only amounted to 3.3% of global spending.[9] This ranked it well below the PRC (which accounted for about 6% of global military expenditure) and a long way behind the United States, which was responsible for nearly 50% of world military spending. Russia's army shrank over the period 1991–9 from 3.2 million to 1.2 million personnel, including reservists and conscripts,[10] and dwindled again between 2000 and 2010 to around 850,000 active servicemen and servicewomen. The poor repair of Russia's navy makes it unable to project power, an inefficient logistics train makes resupplying its army hugely problematic, and patchy servicing of tanks and armoured vehicles means that many front-line groups are frequently unable to take the field at even half their notional combat strength. If Russia were serious about reintegrating former Soviet republics, a rearmament campaign of at least 10–15 years would be necessary. This would give ample strategic warning time for threatened nations to form counterbalancing alliances with external partners.

In addition to lacking the capacity or the will to recreate the territory of the USSR (in Putin's words, anyone believing it could return 'has no brain'), the risks of conquest are simply too great in the post-Cold War era. Whilst much of Russian strategic policy relies on creating energy dependency (and hence vulnerability) amongst its neighbours and Western powers alike, it is similarly vulnerable to source diversification, especially by the EU. Even a partial sanctions regime, with the United States and EU participating in a limited moratorium on purchasing Russian energy, would quickly send the Russian economy into free-fall. Thus, while Russia may not be sensitive to raw economic

---

[9] Stockholm International Peace Research Institute, *SIPRI Yearbook, 2010* (Stockholm: SIPRI, 2010).

[10] This followed Yeltsin's decree, 'On priority measures for reforming the Russian Federation armed forces and improving their structure', *Rossiskaya gazeta*, July 19 (1997), p. 5.

interdependence at present, this is only because it does not overstep what the West considers to be its place in the post-Cold War order. And although the West is prepared to put up with Russian regional primacy, the prospect of a world held to ransom by an energy superstate covering the entire territory of the USSR would not be tolerated.

Indeed, Russia has very little reason to try to restore the USSR. As Roger Kanet notes in chapter 2 of this volume, the consequences of a neo-imperial Russian foreign policy are not synonymous with a desire for formal conquest. In the post-Cold War era, neo-imperialism has come to mean 'empire lite' rather than traditional definitions that stipulate the possession of foreign territories. The limits on Russian primacy evident in the constrainment strategies pursued by external actors, in addition to the multi-vector foreign policies favoured by Russia's closest friends in the CSTO, indicate that any likelihood of a renewed push for a formal Russian empire is extremely remote.

Conflict between major powers on the territory of the former USSR

Before even considering the prospects for major war occurring between large powers in the former Soviet space, one should ask: which large powers? And for what purpose? It is very difficult to conceive of any large-scale conventional war erupting spontaneously in the former USSR except perhaps by accident, or as the product of a smaller conflict that then escalates and spirals out of control. Notwithstanding the ongoing problematic relationship between Russia and NATO, for reasons relating to material capabilities outlined above, Russia would be foolish to actively seek war with the United States or its allies. A range of factors, from nuclear deterrence and the US NMD shield, not to mention the sheer enormity of the human and economic costs that would be incurred by each side, make such an eventuality highly unlikely. We can also discount war between Russia and Japan (over what issues?) since there is not enough traction in either weak irredentist disputes like the one over the Kurile Islands, or contests over trade routes to justify large-scale conflict.

Some analysts have speculated that two scenarios could involve major powers directly in the former Soviet space: war between Russia and the PRC over territory and resources; or war between the United States and the PRC on former Soviet territory for the same reasons.[11] However, a

---

[11] See, for example, Z. Khalizad and I.O. Lesser (eds.), *Sources of conflict in the twenty-first century: regional futures and US strategy* (Santa Monica, CA: RAND, 1998), p. 300; and W. Lacquer, 'Once more with feeling', *Society* 33 (1995), 32–41.

number of conditions would have to be met in order to bring about either of these conflicts. In both instances, the PRC would have to physically invade Siberia, the Far East or the Central Asian states in a bid to seize control over mineral and energy assets, and either the United States or Russia (or both) would have to respond with force. Assuming that the current vectors of the People's Liberation Army's modernisation programme continue, Beijing will doubtless have the capability to carry out a military operation on the territory of the former USSR. The PRC has also long maintained that it has an area of interest in the Far East, and Russian strategists have worried about the dramatic demographic disparities between a heavily populated northern PRC and a correspondingly depopulated south-east Russia.

But for war to occur this would also have to assume a total breakdown of the SCO, which symbolises much about the diplomatic and economic bridges that have been built between Moscow and Beijing. And whilst the PRC's appetite for energy continues to grow, it already has access to significant oil and gas exports from the former USSR, often in partnership with CIS states, and sometimes outbidding Russia to secure them. Deepening a stable and mutually advantageous Russo-Chinese relationship is very much in Beijing's interests as it quietly goes about building national power. Indeed, those worried about Chinese expansionism tend to be much more concerned about the PRC becoming more assertive in the South China Sea, muscling in on the oil and gas deposits around the Spratly and Paracel Islands, and threatening to dominate the strategic choke-point of the Malacca Strait, through which some 75 per cent of Asia's hydrocarbon imports flow.[12]

With respect to either great power war, or violent Russian imperialism, the chances of major conflict happening spontaneously on the former territory of the USSR are slim. However, those interested in the security politics of the former USSR should not interpret this as comforting. In fact, it simply reinforces what we have already learnt about conflict in the post-Cold War era: that sustained interstate war, especially amongst large powers, has largely given way – even if only temporarily – to episodes of political violence that occur locally, transnationally and asymmetrically on the intra-state level. The triggers for the wars that occurred over Chechnya, between Armenia and Azerbaijan, between Russia and Georgia over the status of South Ossetia and Abkhazia, and

---

[12] I. Storey, 'China's "Malacca dilemma"', *Jamestown Foundation China Brief* 6 (2006). Available at www.jamestown.org/programs/chinabrief/single/?tx_ttnews%5Btt_news%5D=31575&tx_ttnews%5BbackPid%5D=196&no_cache=1

in the ethnic discord that erupted in Kyrgyzstan in 2010 are much more diffuse than those that lead to conventional interstate conflict. They are based on issues that are more deeply seated within political communities, and hence they are much more difficult to resolve conclusively. Given that the causes that have already led to conflict in the former USSR have not been addressed, the chances of these types of conflicts flaring or recurring remain all too likely.

The reignition of frozen conflict in Russia

It is axiomatic that the now-frozen separatist conflicts on Russian territory still frequently heat up and erupt into violence. In contrast, other separatist conflicts – for instance, over Northern Ireland, the Basque region of Spain, East Timor or even Sri Lanka – have ended more or less decisively. In Northern Ireland the Good Friday Agreement hammered out between the British government, Sinn Fein and the IRA, and Ulster loyalists resulted in power-sharing that has been largely respected by all but the most extreme fringe elements of Northern Irish society. In Spain, Eta effectively abandoned the struggle for a free Basque country after the Zapatero government carried out a series of high-profile arrests in Spain and France, and succeeded in decapitating its leadership.[13] As the same time, popular support for its political wing, Batasuna, plummeted below 10 per cent.[14] In East Timor, the long struggle for self-determination by the Fretelin organisation was only settled after pro-Indonesian militia went on a rampage in the lead-up to a referendum on independence. This prompted the Australian-led International Force for East Timor (INTERFET) taskforce to intervene, and paved the way for East Timorese statehood. In contrast, in Sri Lanka the independence campaign by the Tamil Tigers was crushed by military offensives from Colombo, compressing an organisation that had once held large swathes of territory – and even possessed its own air force – into ever-smaller enclaves until its leaders ultimately capitulated.

With the exception of East Timor, which resulted in the creation of a brand new state in the international system, the outcomes of each of these conflicts demonstrate what Martin Van Creveld identified

[13] V. Mallett, 'Suspected ETA chief held in Pyrenees raid', *Financial Times*, 17 November (2008), p. 8.

[14] 'Supporters of Batasuna will launch a new party', *Spain Review*, 7 February (2011). Available at www.spainreview.net/index.php/2011/02/07/supporters-of-batasuna-will-launch-a-new-political-party

as two clear ways for governments to win counter-insurgency cam-paigns.[15] The first, Van Creveld suggested, was the 'long' strategy.[16] This required a commitment by the government to a lengthy struggle, utilising minimum force and not deploying massive numbers of troops: preferably, in fact, turning control over counter-terrorism efforts to local police forces. But at the same time, as in Northern Ireland, it also meant engaging in a 'hearts and minds' campaign, investing in public goods and services as well as developing infrastructure and creating jobs at the site of conflict. Alternatively, for Van Creveld, and as the final stages of the Sri Lankan campaign against the Tamils highlighted, one could envisage a 'quick win' strategy. This had to be completely ruthless, employ overwhelming force, wedge opposition forces politic-ally, and be guided by a willingness not to let niceties such as concerns for human rights intervene.

The situation in Chechnya is the product of neither of these strat-egies. Instead, it is a classic example of the frozen conflicts on Russia's edges. Despite fighting Chechen rebels to a standstill, Russia's first war in Chechnya was a public relations disaster. Its second war, spearheaded by Putin, coincided with 9/11. Putin used this to great advantage in his diplomacy with the United States by arguing that he was fighting radi-cal Islamic terrorism inside Russia's borders. Yet the war accomplished little more than subduing rebels, instead of pacifying them entirely. The use of massive force by the Russian military bore a resemblance to Van Creveld's quick victory strategy. But it missed political opportunities to split effectively pro-secular fighters for self-determination such as Aslan Maskhadov away from more radical elements of the Chechen insur-gency like Shamil Basaev, the man blamed for the Beslan school siege of 2004 and numerous other atrocities.[17] Instead, the Kremlin tarred Maskhadov and Basaev with the same brush and put bounties on both of their heads.[18] When it announced it had finally killed Basaev in 2006, a year after it had earlier engineered the assassination of Maskhadov, it only succeeded in muddying the conflict by giving Chechens interested in independence no alternative but to continue fighting, whether or not they had become radicalised in the process.

---

[15] Van Creveld, *The transformation of war.*
[16] 'Russian bounties sow distrust among Chechen rebels', *STRATFOR Global Intelligence Briefs*, 16 March (2005).
[17] On Basaev see M. Sussex, 'Beslan's lessons: is pre-emption better than cure?' *Australian Journal of International Affairs* 58 (2004), 414–18.
[18] M. Van Creveld, *The changing face of war: combat from the Marne to Iraq* (New York: Random House, 2007), p. 268.

Moscow's strategy of Chechenisation similarly did little to remove the root causes that had prompted the war in the first place. By playing divide-and-rule, transferring favours between rival warlords, and by forcing Ramzan Kadyrov to rely on continued patronage by the Kremlin, Putin was able to enforce order upon Chechnya. In fact, by 2007 it was clear that Russia had won the war. Grozny's airport was modernised, a massive construction effort was undertaken to rebuild the city itself, and restaurants and internet cafes opened in its centre. But the fighters that remained in the mountainous regions of the province still carried out harassing attacks against security forces, and prominent officials or businessmen still ran the risk of extortion or kidnapping if they ventured away from strongly fortified areas. The ethnic, religious and political schisms that beset Chechnya thus still await resolution, and similar tensions can be found in neighbouring Russian republics. Indeed, Basaev had attempted to broaden the war in 1999 with his 'raid' into Dagestani territory. This makes the triggers for renewed conflict in the Caucasus still very much live.

And yet it is difficult to see how Moscow could have kept Chechnya part of Russia without using significant military assets and then keeping local elites on their toes with a seemingly arbitrary system of patronage. There was (and still is) a legitimate fear that the question of Chechen independence is linked to the question of continued Russian sovereignty. The spectre of one breakaway republic succeeding in gaining independence is that it could start a domino effect with the potential to lead to the complete fragmentation of the Russian state along ethnic lines. In such circumstances a divided Russia would not only be excluded from a resource-rich and strategically sensitive southern flank (which it could ill afford to lose in any case), but it would also face the prospect of chronic and widespread – rather than localised – instability within its borders. Such an eventuality would lead to lawlessness away from centres of Russian authority. In tightly controlled bastions of Russian power, the temptation would be for an authoritarian crackdown. As Leslie Holmes has argued in this volume, each of these conditions would be perfect for crime and corruption to skyrocket. Meanwhile, any newly independent ex-Russian microstates would lack critical political and economic cohesion. This in turn would raise the prospect of state failure, creating a deluge of displaced people, and plunging the Eurasian order into anarchy.

Separatism, state failure and anarchy

In addition to the frozen conflicts in Russia, there are other separatist conflicts in the former USSR that have the potential to thaw into bloodshed. At the time of writing, it had been nearly a decade since the Key West talks that were thought to have broken the deadlock in efforts to resolve the conflict between Armenia and Azerbaijan over the disputed status of Nagorno-Karabakh. The presidents of Armenia and Azerbaijan have continued to face significant internal political risks in negotiating a comprehensive settlement that would permit a referendum to take place in Karabakh, and withdraw Armenian forces from the surrounding territory. The ceasefire line that stretches for roughly 100 miles has some 20,000 soldiers facing off against each other, in a situation that may be less heavily militarised, but is nonetheless reminiscent of the demilitarised zone separating South Korea from the Democratic People's Republic of Korea. As Thomas de Waal has observed, the BTC pipeline runs just 12 miles away from the line of contact in Karabakh, there is an unmonitored zone of Armenian-held Azerbaijani territory that borders Iran, and the ceasefire line itself is monitored by only six unarmed observers from the OSCE.[19] This makes the region strategically very important indeed, especially given that Georgia and Russia lie to the north, with troubled recent histories of their own.

As in Nagorno-Karabakh, the situation in Abkhazia and South Ossetia is still tense. As this volume has demonstrated, the reasons for the Russo-Georgian war over the breakaway regions in 2008 remains contested. Many blame Georgia's president, Mikhail Saakashvili, for starting the conflict, based on an initial misreading of Russia's willingness to get involved. Once the conflict was underway, Saakashvili turned the campaign into a media circus, deliberately overplaying the threat to Georgian sovereignty as part of his government's efforts to join the NATO alliance. Yet one can also point the finger at the Kremlin, which clearly used the issue of Russian citizenship to make arguments for intervention on human rights grounds (which it had some cause to do) when other national interests were also at play. For supporters of the R2P, as Kernen and Sussex have noted in chapter 5, Russian efforts to justify retaliation on the basis of legitimate responses to human rights violations was a cynical adaptation of legal instruments intended to relieve suffering.

Whichever side is to blame for the 2008 war, South Ossetia and Abkhazia remain in limbo. Each territory endures with Russian military support, but their 'independence' remains partial and contested. Should either emerge as sovereign entities they would arguably be failed

---

[19] T. de Waal, 'Armenia and Azerbaijan are at it again', *National Interest*, 30 March (2011). Available at http://nationalinterest.org/commentary/armenia-azerbaijan-at-it-again-5087

states in the making without significant international support. The most logical – and proximate – state to proffer that support is Russia itself, which has resisted calls for it to support formal referenda on statehood in the separatist regions. Even so, it has failed to successfully use multi-lateral mechanisms to shore up perceptions of legitimacy in its actions, given the refusal of its other CSTO partners to recognise the independence of Abkhazia and South Ossetia.

A similarly problematic situation exists in respect to Trans-Dniester, which remains unrecognised by any major formal international legal entity, even after nearly two decades since the brief war between Moldova and the region that stalemated after Russian mediation in 1992. The region's security remains underpinned by the presence of 2,500 Russian peacekeepers, and, despite offers of significant concessions towards regional autonomy in exchange for Trans-Dniester returning to Moldova, the region has continued to hold out for independence, gaining a reputation as a hub for organised crime and corruption in the process. For its part, Moscow has reiterated its support for Moldovan sovereignty, but it also has a stake in upholding the status quo. Mediation of the stalemate has also been affected by the frequent political clashes around Tiraspol, which have created a state of affairs where it is difficult over any sustained period to track which political forces are actually in control, and thus who should be invited to the bargaining table.

There is still a significant possibility that independence movements – if pushed more firmly – might cause the 'frozen' conflicts in the former USSR to erupt into war. Whilst the problem of Trans-Dniester is probably the least difficult to resolve, there are few prospects for a solution in the short term. The only really stable enclave in post-Soviet territory is the area housing the Russian Black Sea Fleet in the Crimea around Sevastopol, and even this arrangement continues to rankle with Ukrainian nationalists as a highly visible reminder of the Soviet past. When one considers that Central Asia has also been prominent in being the site for ethnic clashes between Kyrgyz and Uzbeks, it is clear that separatism, the potential for state failure and anarchy in sensitive areas of Eurasia must also be considered likely triggers of future wars in the post-Soviet space.

Resource wars

Conflicts over resources tend to happen in areas where rising demand meets dwindling availability. Yet this is paradoxically not the case in the former USSR. Rather than representing a problem of resource shortages, the key consideration has been control over supply. As has already been well documented in this volume and elsewhere, it is possible to frame any of the wars in the former USSR as resource wars. This is because they have all been at least partly struggles linked to oil, gas and minerals. This was true of the two wars in Chechnya, in which the transport of energy across Chechen territory was an important issue for Russia. In the conflict over Nagorno-Karabakh, resources have also been drivers for war, and they have been most prominent in Russia's repeated use of gas supplies as a weapon against Ukraine, Georgia and even its close ally, Belarus.

More generally, in most wars one can locate motivations linked to territory and resources. But the conflicts in the former USSR – and the chance of more of them in the future – are especially indicative of this phenomenon. While much scholarly attention has been devoted to the potential for conflict over energy in the Middle East, particularly after the notional global 'peak oil' phase is reached in the next twenty to fifty years, it should not be forgotten that Russia and Central Asia are perhaps just as important, while the Caucasus stands at a geographical crossroads between Europe, the Middle East and Asia. It is little wonder, under the circumstances, that this region of the world received so much attention in early twentieth-century geopolitical thought.

That thinking may be needed again. In the international system of the twenty-first century, consistent and reliable access to oil and gas at a fair price equals security. By the same token, the ability to control the supply of those resources equals power and influence. Russia's strategic calculations have certainly centred upon that logic. Its energy-security policy seeks to ensure Moscow retains as much control as possible over the extraction, processing, transport and price of oil and gas originating in the former USSR. Its establishment of strong trading ties with Central Asian states have allowed it to play a central role in the exploitation of easily extracted gas reserves without having to engage in the prohibitively expensive task of trying to service demand from hard-to-reach sources on its own territory.

So concerned have Medvedev and Putin been with maintaining Russia's position as an energy powerhouse that they have been prepared to exacerbate international tensions by claiming ownership of much of the Arctic, and they plan to establish military bases along the Arctic frontier. Russia's National Security Strategy of 2009 states clearly that Russia expects war over possession of energy resources along its borders within a decade. In its analysis of security threats up to 2020, the document notes that 'the presence and potential escalation of armed conflicts near Russia's national borders', in the absence of agreements between Russia and its neighbours, constitute 'the major threats to Russia's interests'.[20] It goes on to suggest that as a direct result of resource competition 'it cannot be ruled out that military force could be used to resolve emerging problems that would destroy the balance of forces near the borders of Russia and her allies'.[21]

Many have criticised the stance taken by Russia in its dealings with neighbours and extra-regional states over the issue of energy. US vice-president Joe Biden issued a strong condemnation in 2009, in which he alleged that Russia would soon have to make hard choices about its national security, and loosen its grip on former Soviet republics.[22] His remarks resulted in a storm of outrage in Moscow, but Biden was right in one sense: Russian primacy in its own region is tentative and seems to be gradually slipping, in spite of the advances it has made in rebuilding national power from the nadir of the late 1990s. The willingness of Central Asian states to deal with the PRC (sometimes in preference to Russia), the desire of Georgia and Ukraine to embed themselves in Western alliance structures (not to mention institutions of economic and political union), and disagreements with Belarus all point to the conclusion that Russia's neighbours are not prepared to become Russia's vassals.

But whether Biden is right on the broader issue of eventual Russian capitulation to Western interests is as yet unclear. Indeed, the Bismarckian approach adopted by Putin and Medvedev on matters of territorial sovereignty and access to vital strategic resources is to an extent understandable. Caught in an unenviable position between a wealthy EU and a rising PRC, with massive territory and resources of its own but with a dwindling population base, and with global power undergoing a massive reorientation from West to East, Russia can ill afford a foreign policy that relies upon the good graces of others.[23]

The foreign and security policy community in Russia is nothing if not pragmatic, and its decision-makers are aware that any full-scale alignment with the PRC would result in Russia taking the role of junior partner. The history of Russian engagement with the West is also a cautionary tale for Russian strategic-policy managers who might consider a

---

[20] Security Council of the Russian Federation, *National Security Strategy of the Russian Federation up to 2020*, 12 May (2009). Available at www.scrf.gov.ru/documents/99.html

[21] Ibid.

[22] For Biden's interview, conducted by the *Wall Street Journal*, see P. Spiegle, 'Biden says weakened Russia will bend to the US', *Wall Street Journal*, 25 July (2009), p. A1.

[23] A similar point is made by A.C. Lynch, 'The realism of Russian foreign policy', *Europe-Asia Studies* 53 (2001), 7–31.

renewed push into the 'Common European Home'. Attempting to bed down its control over energy in the CIS area therefore makes sense, at least for the moment. A future global role as a pivot state in a multipolar world order, using energy as its strategic currency, is perhaps the most achievable near-term prospect for Russia, and would open up its policy space to significant flexibility. This means, however, that the resources Moscow seeks to secure will also be resources that are contested: by Russia, by other former Soviet republics and potentially even by extra-regional great powers.

Final observations: mitigating war in the former USSR?

The conflicts that have occurred on the territory of the former USSR over the past two decades reveal just how far-reaching social, economic and ethnic forces can be when they are released from a unifying power structure. This book noted in its introductory chapter that although few observers lament the passing of the USSR, even fewer would argue that the area of its former geographical footprint is more secure today than it was under communism. Nationalism, separatism and a desire for self-determination have all played a role in exacerbating the local, transnational and interstate security challenges that exist in the former Soviet space. So too have weak governance structures, the economic paralysis of the 1990s, radical Islam and polarised identities, along with the resurgence of the great power image after Vladimir Putin took over from Boris Yeltsin, which coincided with the sudden strengthening of the Russian economy.

There are many ways to mitigate war, and one can seek to do so at a variety of levels. In this book and in many others, calls can be found for economic development, education opportunities, improved regulation to tackle organised crime, the provision of incentive structures to the disenfranchised to prevent radicalisation, dialogue between people and nations to calm the fires of nationalism, and the creation of new multilateral institutions to promote confidence and trust at the international level. And yet none of these measures are completely reliable, especially in isolation. Education means little without subsequent opportunities for stable employment. Economic development can encourage clientism, or aid paradoxes in which measurable results from assistance funding never eventuate. Dialogues to understand difference can become dialogues of the deaf that produce nothing meaningful in terms of agreements, policy or peace. And while multilateral institutions can indeed create trust and reciprocity, in international politics there is nothing to guarantee that they might not also be used as instruments of hegemony.

Given the weakness that has gripped the former USSR it is perhaps remarkable that there have not been more wars, and it is equally remarkable that those conflicts that have occurred remained relatively contained. But it is equally true that the forces that can create war are still to be found in abundance in the former Soviet space. Unfortunately, there has been little progress made on constructing robust security architecture to fill this void. Where there have been attempts to do so, whether in the context of Medvedev's EST proposals, the EU's engagement agenda or the Obama administration's offer to strengthen dialogue with NATO, states have continued to view each other with suspicion. Mistrust has also been the dominant characteristic over a host of other regional problems, from Nagorno-Karabakh to Ossetia, to attempts to clamp down on organised crime. As long as this is not rectified – and there is little evidence to say that it will be, at least for the foreseeable future – the prospects for conflict, competition and war in the former USSR will remain high.

Many will find these conclusions grim, or at the very least pessimistic. Such a perception is doubtless exacerbated by the fact that the deliberate focus of this book has been on conflict rather than on the prospects for peace. But false optimism is arguably more dangerous than misplaced prudence. At any rate, it means that surprises are much more likely to be pleasant ones. It is certainly my hope, and my fellow contributors' hope, that events in former USSR will lead us to become pleasantly surprised more often in the future.

Bibliography

'Abashidze resigns; Saakashvili's next target – Abkhazia', *Pravda.ru*, 22 June (2007). Available at http://english.pravda.ru/world

'Abkhaz leader rules out being part of Georgia', BBC Monitoring, Former Soviet Union, transcribed 30 April (2008) from Channel One TV (Russia), 30 April (2008).

'Abkhazia appeals to world organisations over independence', BBC Monitoring, Former Soviet Union, transcribed 7 March (2008) from ITAR-TASS, 7 March (2008).

'Abkhazia, South Ossetia want independence', *Kavkaz Center News Agency*, 18 February (2008). Available at www.kavkaz.org.uk

Acharya, A., 'The Association of Southeast Asian Nations: "security community" or "defence community"', *Pacific Affairs* 64 (1991), 159–78.

   Constructing a security community in Southeast Asia: ASEAN and the problem of regional order, 2nd edn (New York: Taylor & Francis, 2009).

Adler, E., and Barnett, M., *Security communities* (Cambridge University Press, 2008).

Adyasov, I., '2010: a milestone for CIS', *RIA Novosti*, 29 December (2010).

Agreements on the Creation of the Commonwealth of Independent States Signed in December 1991/January 1992 (London: Russian Information Agency/ Novosti, 1992).

Akehurst, M., 'The use of force to protect nationals abroad', *International Relations* 5 (1977), 3–23.

Akihiro, I. (ed.), *Eager eyes fixed on Eurasia*, vol. 1: *Russia and its neighbors in crisis* (Sapporo: Slavic Research Centre, Hokkaido University, 2007).

   Eager eyes fixed on Eurasia, vol. 2: *Russia and its eastern edge* (Sapporo: Slavic Research Centre, Hokkaido University, 2007).

Akiner, S., *Central Asia: a new arc of crisis?* (London: Royal United Services Institute, 1993).

   'Melting pot, salad bowl – cauldron? Manipulation and mobilisation of ethnic and religious identities in Central Asia', *Ethnic and Racial Studies* 20 (1997), 362–98.

Allen, C., 'Warfare, endemic violence and state collapse in Africa', *Review of African Political Economy* 26 (1999), 367–84.

Allison, R., 'Regionalism, regional structures and security management in Central Asia', *International Affairs* 80 (2004), 463–83.

'Russia resurgent: Moscow's campaign to "coerce Georgia to peace"', *International Affairs* 84 (2008), 1145–71.

Alvazzi del Frate, A., 'The International Crime Business Survey: findings from nine Central-Eastern European cities', *European Journal on Criminal Policy and Research* 10:2–3 (2004), 150–2.

Alvazzi del Frate, A., and van Kesteren, J., *Criminal victimisation in urban Europe: key findings of the 2000 International Crime Victim Surveys* (Turin: UNICRI, 2004).

Ambrosio, T., *Authoritarian backlash: Russian resistance to democratisation in the former Soviet Union* (Aldershot, UK: Ashgate, 2008).

'Catching the "Shanghai Spirit": how the Shanghai Cooperation Organisation promotes authoritarian norms in Central Asia', *Europe–Asia Studies* 60 (2008), 1321–44.

Anders, R.B., and Kofman, M., 'European energy security: reducing volatility of Ukraine-Russia natural gas pricing disputes', *Strategic Forum*, Institute for National Strategic Studies (Washington, VA: National Defence University, 2011).

Anderson, J., *Governance and service delivery in the Kyrgyz Republic: results of diagnostic surveys* (Washington, DC: World Bank, 2002).

Anderson, J., and Mukherjee, A., *Kazakhstan: governance and service delivery – a diagnostic report* (Washington, DC: World Bank, 2002).

Angstrom, J., 'Introduction: debating the nature of modern war', in I. Duyvesteyn and J. Angstrom (eds.), *Rethinking the nature of war* (London: Frank Cass, 2005), pp. 1–27.

Angus Reid Global Monitor, 'Half of Russians yearn for superpower status', 4 February (2008), reprinted in *Johnson's Russia List*, no. 2008-24, 4 February (2008).

Antonenko, O., 'A war with no winners', *Survival* 50 (2008), 23–36.

Arbatov, A., 'Russia's foreign policy alternatives', *International Security* 18 (1993), 5–43.

'Russian foreign policy thinking in transition', in Vladimir Baranovsky (ed.), *Russia and Europe: the emerging security agenda* (Oxford University Press, 1997), pp. 135–59.

Arbatov, A., Chayes, A., Chayes, A., and Olson, L. (eds.), *Managing conflict in the former Soviet Union: Russian and American perspectives* (Cambridge, MA: MIT Press, 1997).

Arvedlund, E.E., 'Pipeline done, oil from Azerbaijan begins flowing to Turkey', *New York Times*, 26 May (2005), p. C6.

Aslund, A., Bogetik, Z., Sutela, P., and Carothers, T., 'Russia's response to the Financial Crisis', Carnegie Endowment for International Peace, 4 May (2010). Available at www.carnegieendowment.org/events/?fa=eventDetail&id=2895

Atkin, M., 'Tajikistan: a president and his rivals', in S.N. Cummings (ed.), *Power and change in Central Asia* (London: Routledge, 2002), pp. 97–114.

Auty, R.M., 'Transition to mid-income democracies or to failed states?', in R.M. Auty and I. de Soysa (eds.), *Energy, wealth and governance in the Caucasus and Central Asia* (London: Routledge, 2006), pp. 3–16.

Auty, R.M., and de Soysa, I., 'Incentives to reform in the Caucasus and Central Asian political states', in R.M. Auty and I. de Soysa (eds.), *Energy, wealth and governance in the Caucasus and Central Asia* (London: Routledge, 2006), pp. 135–51.

Aviutsky, V., 'The South Ossetia conflict', *Défense nationale et sécurité collective* (October 2008), 41.

Ayoob, M., 'State-making, state-breaking and state failure: explaining the roots of third world insecurity', in L. Van de Goor, K. Rupeshinge and P. Sciarone (eds.), *Between development and destruction: an enquiry into the causes of conflict in post-colonial states* (Basingstoke, UK: Macmillan, 1996), pp. 67–86.

Babus, S.W., 'Democracy-building in Central Asia post-September 11', in D.L. Burghart and T. Sabonis-Helf (eds.), *In the tracks of Tamerlane: Central Asia's path to the twenty-first century* (Washington, DC: National Defence University Center for Technology and National Security Policy, 2004), pp. 115–38.

Bäckman, J., *The inflation of crime in Russia* (Helsinki: National Research Institute of Legal Policy, 1998).

Badiou, A., *The century*, trans. Alberto Toscano (Cambridge: Polity, 2007).

Barany, Z., *Democratic breakdown and the Russian military* (Princeton University Press, 2007).

Barber, T., 'Georgia fears impact of Kosovo crisis', *Financial Times*, 7 December (2007).

Barnard, A., 'Russians confident that nation is back', *New York Times*, 15 August (2008).

Bates, R.H., *Prosperity and violence: the political economy of development* (New York: W.W. Norton, 2001).

Beier, J.M., 'Outsmarting technologies: rhetoric, revolutions in military affairs, and the social depth of warfare', *International Politics* 43 (2006), 266–80.

Beissinger, M., 'The persistence of empire in Eurasia', *NewsNet: News of the American Association for the Advancement of Slavic Studies* 48 (2008), 1–8.

Beissinger, M., and Young, C. (eds.), *Beyond state crisis? Post-colonial Africa and post-Soviet Eurasia in comparative perspective* (Washington, DC: Woodrow Wilson Center Press, 2002).

Bellamy, A., *Just wars: from Cicero to Iraq* (Cambridge University Press, 2006).

Benard, C., 'Central Asia: "apocalypse soon" or eccentric survival?', in A.M. Rabasa, C. Benard, P. Chalk, C.C. Fair, T. Karaski, R. Lal, I. Lesser and D. Thaler (eds.), *The Muslim world after 9/11* (Santa Monica, CA: Rand Corporation, 2004), pp. 321–66.

Berdal, M., 'How "new" are "new wars"? Global economic change and the study of civil war', *Global Governance* 9 (2003), 477–502.

Berryman, J., 'Russia, NATO enlargement and the new "lands in between"', in R.E. Kanet (ed.), *A resurgent Russia and the West: the European Union, NATO and beyond* (Dordrecht, The Netherlands: Republic of Letters Press, 2009), pp. 161–85.

Bertsch, G.K, Craft, C., Jones, S.A., and Beck, M. (eds.), *Crossroads and conflict: security and foreign policy in the Caucasus and Central Asia* (New York: Routledge, 2000).

Bhadrakumar, M.K., 'Russia takes control of Turkmen (world?) gas', *Asia Times*, 30 July (2008). Available at www.atimes.com/atimes/Central_Asia/JG30Ag01.html

Bildt, C., 'The Baltic litmus test', *Foreign Affairs* 73 (1994), 72–9.

Blakelely, R., *State terrorism and neoliberalism: the north in the south* (London: Routledge, 2009).

Blank, S., 'Putin's twelve-step program', *The Washington Quarterly*, 25 (2002), p. 150.

'Russia's real drive to the south', *Orbis* 29 (1995), 369–86.

'Toward a new Chinese order in Asia: Russia's failure', *National Bureau of Asian Research, Special Report* 26 (March 2011).

Towards a new Russia policy (Washington, DC: US Army War College, 2008).

'The US-Russian military agenda: the past as prologue', in A. Cohen (ed.), *Russia and Eurasia: a realistic policy agenda for the Obama administration*, Heritage Special Report, 27 March (2009), pp. 13–17.

Blum, D., 'Conclusion: is disintegration inevitable and why should we care?', in D. Blum (ed.), *Russia's future: Consolidation or disintegration?* (Boulder, CO: Westview, 1994), pp. 147–8.

Bluth, C., and Kassenov, O., 'The "game" of security in Central Asia', in Y. Kalyuzhnova and D. Lynch (eds.), *The Euro-Asian world: a period of transition* (Basingstoke, UK: Macmillan, 2000), pp. 28–44.

Bobbitt, P., *Terror and consent: the wars for the twenty-first century* (London: Allen Lane, 2008).

Bochkarev, D., 'European gas prices: implications of Gazprom's strategic engagement with Central Asia', *Pipeline and Gas Journal* 236 (June 2009), 15–22.

Bohr, A., 'The Central Asian states as nationalising regimes', in G. Smith (ed.), *Nation-building in the post-Soviet borderlands: the politics of national identities* (Cambridge University Press, 1998), pp. 139–66.

Bonner, A., 'Georgian losses and Russia's gain', *Middle East Policy* 15 (Winter 2008), 81–90.

Bova, R., 'Democratisation and the crisis of the Russian state', in G. Smith (ed.), *State-building in Russia: the Yeltsin legacy and the challenge of the future* (Armonk, NY: M.E. Sharpe, 1999), pp. 17–40.

Bremmer, I., 'Post-Soviet nationalities theory: past, present, and future', in I. Bremmer and R. Taras (eds.), *New states, new politics: building the post-Soviet nations* (Cambridge University Press, 1997), pp. 3–28.

Bremmer, I., and Taras, R. (eds.), *New states, new politics: building the post-Soviet nations* (Cambridge University Press, 1997).

Brown, A., *The Gorbachev factor* (Oxford University Press, 1996).

'Perestroika and the end of the Cold War', *Cold War History* 7 (February 2007), 1–17.

Brzezinski, Z., 'An agenda for NATO', *Foreign Affairs* 88 (September–October 2009), 2–20.

'The premature partnership', *Foreign Affairs* 73 (1994), 67–82.

Buckland, B., 'Smuggling and trafficking: crossover and overlap', in C. Friesendorf (ed.), *Strategies against human trafficking: the role of the security sector* (Geneva: DCAF, 2009), pp. 145–74.

Bueno de Mesquita, B., Smith, A, Siverson, R.M, and Morrow, J.D., *The logic of political survival* (Cambridge, MA: MIT Press, 2003).

Bugajski, J., *Cold peace: Russia's new imperialism* (Westport, CT: Praeger, 2007).

Bundeskriminalamt, *Lagebild Menschenhandel, 2003 – Offene Version* (Wiesbaden: Bundeskriminalamt, 2004).

Lagebild Menschenhandel, 2004 – Offene Version (Wiesbaden: Bundeskriminalamt, 2005).

Bush, G.H.W., 'Toward a new world order' (Washington, DC: US Government Printing Office, 1990).

Buzan, B., and Waever, O., *Regions and powers: the structure of international security* (Cambridge University Press, 2003).

Buzan, B., Waever, O., and de Wilde, J., *Security: a new framework for analysis* (Boulder, CO: Lynne Rienner Publishers, 1997).

Caldwell, L.T., 'Russian concepts of national security', in R. Legvold (ed.), *Russian foreign policy in the twenty-first century and the shadow of the past* (New York: Columbia University Press, 2007), pp. 326–30.

Casier, T., 'The clash of integration processes? The shadow effect of the enlarged EU on its Eastern neighbours', in K. Malfliet, L. Verpoest and E. Vinokurov (eds.), *The CIS, the EU and Russia* (Basingstoke, UK: Palgrave Macmillan, 2007), pp. 73–94.

'The new neighbours of the European Union: the compelling logic of enlargement?', in J. DeBardeleben (ed.), *The boundaries of EU enlargement: finding a place for neighbours* (Basingstoke, UK: Palgrave Macmillan, 2008), pp. 19–32.

Ceccarelli, A., 'Clans, politics and organised crime in Central Asia', *Trends in Organised Crime* 10:3 (2007), 19–36.

Central Bank of the Russian Federation, 'Main macroeconomic indicators' (2000). Available at www.cbr.ru/eng/statistics/credit_statistics

Centre for Strategic and International Studies (CSIS), 'Overview', Russia/Eurasia Program, Caucasus Initiative (2009). Available at www.csis.org/ruseura/caucasus

Cerny, P.G., *Rethinking world politics: a theory of transnational neopluralism* (Oxford University Press, 2010).

Chayes, A., and Chayes, A. (eds.), *Preventing conflict in the post-communist world: mobilising international and regional organisations* (Washington, DC: Brookings Institution, 1996).

Cheloukhine, S., 'The roots of Russian organised crime: from old-fashioned professionals to the organised criminal groups of today', *Crime, Law and Social Change* 50 (2008), 353–74.

'China, Russia to enhance mutual investment', *China Daily*, 27 March (2009). Available at www.chinadaily.com.cn/china/2009–03/27/content_7625216.htm

'China/Russia: focus on pipelines during Medvedev visit', Radio Free Europe/Radio Liberty (RFE/RL), 29 May (2008).

China National Petroleum Corporation (CNPC), 'CNPC in Kazakhstan' (n.d.). Available at www.cnpc.com.cn/eng/cnpcworldwide/euro-asia/kazakhstan

Chivers, C.J., 'Russia warns it may back breakaway republics in Georgia', *New York Times*, 16 February (2008).

'UN inquiry concludes that Russian jet downed Georgian reconnaissance drone', *New York Times*, 27 May (2008), p. A6.

Choo, K.-K.R., 'Organised crime groups in cyberspace: a typology', *Trends in Organised Crime* 11:3 (2008), 270–95.

Chun, H., 'Russia's energy diplomacy toward Europe and Northeast Asia'. Unpublished paper presented at the II WISC Conference, Ljubljana, Slovenia, 5–6 July (2008).

'CIS unrecognised states to coordinate policy in Georgia's Abkhazia', BBC Monitoring, Trans Caucasus, 1 November (2007), transcribed by B. Kernen, Regnum News Agency, 1 November (2007).

Clausewitz, C. von., *On war*, trans. M.E. Howard and P. Paret (Princeton University Press, 1976).

Collier, P., *The bottom billion: why the poorest countries are failing and what can be done about it* (Oxford University Press, 2007).

Wars, guns and votes: democracy in dangerous places (London: Bodley Head, 2009).

Collins, K., 'Clans, pacts and politics in Central Asia', *Journal of Democracy* 13 (2002), 137–52.

Colton, T.J., *Yeltsin: a life* (New York: Basic Books, 2008).

Colton, T.J., and Tucker, R.C. (eds.), *Patterns in post-Soviet leadership* (Boulder, CO: Westview, 1995).

Commission on Human Security, 'Outline of the Report of the Commission on Human Security' (2008). Available at http://ochaonline.un.org/Reports/tabid/2186/language/en-US/Default.aspx

'The Commonwealth of Independent States', *Inventory of international non-proliferation organisations and regimes* (Washington, DC: Center for Nonproliferation Studies, 2008).

Conley, J.M., *Indo-Russian military and nuclear cooperation: lessons and options for US policy in South Asia* (Lanham, MD: Lexington Books, 2001).

'A conversation with Sergei Lavrov' (New York: Council on Foreign Relations, 28 September 2008). Available at www.cfr.org/un/conversation-sergey-lavrov/p17384

Coppieters, B., and Levgold, R. (eds.), *Statehood and security: Georgia after the rose revolution* (Cambridge, MA: MIT Press, 2005).

Corrin, C., 'Transitional road for traffic: analysing trafficking in women from and through Central and Eastern Europe', *Europe-Asia Studies* 57 (2005), 543–60.

Crabtree, S., and Esipova, N., 'Georgians favour ongoing cooperation among CIS countries', *Gallup News*, 25 August (2009).

Craft, P., 'Stanford Professor Michael McFaul pushes for "Democracy in Russia" proposal', *Stanford Review*, 17 April (2009).

Crosston, M., *Shadow separatism: implications for democratic consolidation* (Aldershot, UK: Ashgate, 2004).

Crow, S., 'Russian Federation faces foreign policy dilemmas', *RFE/RL Research Report* 1:10 (1992).

'CSTO launches situation containment exercises', *Russia Today*, 25 October (2010).

'CSTO to rush aid to Kyrgyzstan', 17 June (2010). Available at www.natomission. ru/en/security/article/security/artnews/99

Cummings, S.N., *Kazakhstan: centre-periphery relations* (London: Royal Institute of International Affairs, 2000).

(ed.), *Power and change in Central Asia* (London: Routledge, 2002).

Dale, C., 'The case of Abkhazia (Georgia)', in L. Jonson and C. Archer (eds.), *Peacekeeping and the role of Russia in Eurasia* (Boulder, CO: Westview, 1996), pp. 121–38.

Danilov, D., 'Russia's role', *A question of sovereignty: the Georgia-Abkhazia peace process*, *Accord* 7 (September 1999). Available at www.c-r.org/our-work/ accord/georgia-abkhazia/russias-role.php

Dawisha, K., and Parrot, B., *Russia and the new states of Eurasia: the politics of upheaval* (Cambridge University Press, 1994).

De Haas, M., 'SCO summit demonstrates its growing cohesion', *Power and Interest News Report*, 14 August (2007).

'Deklaratsiya Moskovskoi Sessii Soveta Kollektivnoi Bezopasnosti ODKB', Moscow, 5 September (2008). Available at www.kremlin.ru/events/ articles/2008/08/205859/205904.shtml

de Waal, T., 'Armenia and Azerbaijan are at it again', *National Interest*, 30 March (2011). Available at http://nationalinterest.org/commentary/ armenia-azerbaijan-at-it-again-5087

Demes, P., Gyarmati, I., Krastev, I., Liik, K., and Vondra, A., *Why the Obama administration should not take Central and Eastern Europe for granted*. Policy Brief, The German Marshall Fund of the United States, 13 June (2009).

'Deputy speaker says West provoking Russia into recognising breakaway republics', BBC Monitoring, Former Soviet Union, transcribed 20 February (2008) from ITAR-TASS, 20 February (2008).

Deyermond, R., *Security and sovereignty in the former Soviet Union* (Boulder, CO: Lynne Rienner Publishers, 2008).

Dibb, P., 'The bear is back', *American Interest* 2 (2006), 78–85.

Dobbs, M., '"We are all Georgians"? Not so fast', *Washingtonpost.com*, 7 August (2008), p. B01.

'Doktrina informatsionnoi bezopasnosti Rossiiskoi Federatsii', *Rossiiskaia gazeta*, 28 September (2000), pp. 3–4. Available at www.scrf.gov.ru/ Documents/Degree/2000/09–09.html

Donaldson, R., and Nogee, J., *The foreign policy of Russia: changing systems, enduring interests* (Armonk, NY: M.E. Sharpe, 1999; 3rd edn 2005).

Duffield, M., *Global governance and the new wars: the merging of development and security* (London: Zed Books, 2001).

'Globalisation, transborder trade and war economies', in M. Berdal and D. Malone (eds.), *Greed and grievance: economic agendas in civil wars* (Boulder, CO: Lynne Rienner Publishers, 2000), pp. 69–90.

Dugin, A., *Geopolitika* (Moscow: Arktogaia, 1995).

Dunlop, J., *Russia confronts Chechnya: roots of a separatist conflict* (Cambridge University Press, 1998).

Dunn, G., 'Major Mafia gangs in Russia', in P. Williams (ed.), *Russian organised crime: the new threat?* (London: Frank Cass, 1997), pp. 65–70.

'Dushanbinskaya Deklaratsiya Glav Gosudarstv Chlenov ShOS', Dushanbe, 27–8 August (2008). Available at www.kremlin.ru/events/articles/2008/ 09/206197/206216.shtml

Dzidzoev, V.D., and Dzugaev, K.G., *Yuzhnaya Osetiya v retrospektive gruzino-osetinskikh otnoshenii* (Tskhinval: Vladikavkaz Research of the Russian Academy of Sciences and the Tibilov South Ossetian State University, 2007).

'Eastern Europe, America and Russia: pipedreams', *The Economist*, 26 January (2008), pp. 50–2.

Ebel, R., and Menon, R. (eds.), *Energy and conflict in Central Asia and the Caucasus* (Lanham, MD: Rowman & Littlefield, for The National Bureau of Asian Research, 2000).

EIA (US Energy Information Administration) report on Russia (last updated November 2010). Available at www.eia.doe.gov/cabs/russia/Full.html

Ellingsen, T., and Gleditsch, N.P., 'Democracy and armed conflict in the third world', in K. Volden and D. Smith (eds.), *Causes of conflict in third world countries* (Oslo: International Peace Research Institute, 1997), pp. 69–81.

Engvall. J., *Kyrgyzstan: the Anatomy of a Failed State* (Uppsala: Central Asia-Caucasus Institute, Silk Road Studies Program, 2006).

Erofeyev, V., 'A promising pariah on the Black Sea; Abkhazia', *The International Herald Tribune*, 29 June (2006).

Esman, M., 'Diasporas and international relations', in G. Sheffer (ed.), *Modern diasporas in international politics* (New York: St Martin's Press, 1986), pp. 333–49.

European Security and Defence Assembly, Assembly of WEU, 'Russia's defence policy', 5 June (2008). Available at www.assembly-weu.org/en/ documents/sessions_ordinaires/rpt/2008/2008.php

Evangilista, M., *The Chechen wars: will Russia go the way of the Soviet Union?* (Washington, DC: Brookings Institution, 2002).

Evans, G., 'Russia in Georgia: not a case of the responsibility to protect', *New Perspectives Quarterly* 25 (2008), 53–55.

Evans, G., and Sahnoun, M., 'The responsibility to protect', *Foreign Affairs* 81 (2001), 99–108.

Evans, M., 'Moral theory and the idea of just war', in M. Evans (ed.), *Just war theory: a reappraisal* (Edinburgh University Press, 2005), pp. 1–24.

Eyl-Mazzega, M-A., 'The gas crisis between the Ukraine and Russia: one crisis too far that obliges a humiliated Europe to react', *European Issues* 125, *Les Policy Papers de la Fondation Robert Schuman*, 26 January (2009). Available at www.robert-schuman.org/question_europe.php?num=qe-125

Fearon, J., and Laitin, D., 'Ethnicity, insurgency, and civil war', *American Political Science Review* 97 (2003), 75–90.

'Federal Law of the Russian Federation on the procedure of exit from the Russian Federation and entry into the Russian Federation', adopted 15 August (1996). Available at www.imldb.iom.int/viewDocument. do?id=%7B927CB59B-EC52–4DA5-B353–2463C835A8E3%7D

Feinstein, L., and Slaughter, A-M., 'A duty to prevent', *Foreign Affairs* 83 (2004), 136–46.

Finckenauer, J., and Voronin, Y., *The threat of Russian organised crime* (Washington, DC: National Institute of Justice, 2001).

Finckenauer, J., and Waring, E., *Russian mafia in America: immigration, culture and crime* (Boston, MA: Northeastern University Press, 1998).

'The Foreign Policy Concept of the Russian Federation', approved by the president of the Russian Federation, V. Putin, 28 June (2000), reprinted in *Johnson's Russia List*, no. 4403, 14 July (2000).

'The Foreign Policy Concept of the Russian Federation: 30/07/2008' (2008). Available at www.maximsnews.com/news20080731russiaforeignpolicy-concept10807311601.htm

Freedman, L., 'The changing forms of military conflict', *Survival* 40 (1998), 39–56.

Freire, M.R., *Conflict and security in the former Soviet Union: the role of the OSCE* (Aldershot, UK: Ashgate, 2003).

Freireynch, A., 'The enemy is at the gates: Russia after Beslan', *International Affairs* 81 (2005), 141–61.

Friedman, G., 'Georgia and the balance of power', *New York Review of Books*, 25 September (2008).

Fuller, L., 'Analysis: domestic pressure on Abkhaz president intensifies', Radio Free Europe/Radio Liberty (RFE/RL), 6 June (2008).

Gaddis, J.L., *The long peace: inquiries into the history of the Cold War* (Oxford University Press, 1989).

Gadzhiev, K.S., *Geopolitika kavkaza* (Moscow: Mezhdunarodnye otnosheniya, 2001).

Galloway, J., 'A bad neighbour in a bad neighbourhood', *Miami Herald*, 17 August (2008).

Galtung, F., 'Measuring the immeasurable: boundaries and functions of (macro) corruption indices', in C. Sampford, A. Shacklock, C. Connors and F. Galtung (eds.), *Measuring corruption* (Aldershot, UK: Ashgate, 2006), pp. 101–30.

Galtung, J., ' Violence, peace, and peace research', *Journal of Peace Research* 6 (1969), 167–91.

Garnett, S., 'Russia's illusory ambitions', *Foreign Affairs* 76 (1997), 61–76.

Gazprom, 'Gazprom and SOCAR sign agreement on Azerbaijani gas purchase and sale terms', 29 June (2009). Available at www.gazprom.com/press/news/2009/june/article66713

Geddes, B., *Politician's dilemma: building state capacity in Latin America* (Berkeley: University of California Press, 1994).

Gegeshidze, A., 'Post-war Georgia: resetting Euro-Atlantic aspirations?', *Caucasus Analytical Digest* 5 (2009), 5–9.

Gel'man, V., 'Iz ognya da v polymya? Dinamika postsovetskikh rezhimov v sravnitel'noi perspektive', *Polis* (2007), 81–108.

'Genprokuror: arestovany 25 chlenov tambovskoy OPG', *Gazeta.ru*, 16 January (2007). Available at www.gazeta.ru/news/social/2007/01/16/n_1024654.shtml

George, J.A., 'The dangers of reform: state building and national minorities in Georgia', *Central Asian Survey* 28 (2009), 135–54.

'Expecting ethnic conflict: the Soviet legacy and ethnic politics in the Caucasus and Central Asia', in A.E. Wooden and C.H. Stefes (eds.), *The politics of transition in Central Asia and the Caucasus: enduring legacies and emerging challenges* (London: Routledge, 2009), pp. 75–102.

'Minority political inclusion in Mikhail Saakashvili's Georgia', *Europe-Asia Studies* 60 (September 2008), 1151–75.

'Georgia: how a tiny breakaway province could become the new Cold War frontline: while Georgia hopes to join NATO, its rebel Abkhazia area is being wooed by Russia', *The Guardian*, 17 April (2008).

'Georgia and Russia: gather round the gorge', *The Economist*, 17 May (2008), p. 20.

'Georgia: South Ossetian call for recognition; cites "Kosovo precedent"', Radio Free Europe/Radio Liberty (RFE/RL), 6 March (2008).

'Georgian President tells Russia to forget "caricature" images of past', *Rustani-2 TV* (Georgia), 6 May (2006).

'Georgian pundit views policy in South Ossetia, relations with Russia, Turkey', BBC Monitoring, Trans Caucasus, transcribed 24 July (2007) from *24 Saati*, 23 July (2007).

'Georgia's South Ossetia possibly recognised in 2008 – separatist leader', *Regnum News Agency* (Russia), 20 February (2008).

Giddens, A., *Runaway world* (London: Profile, 1999).

Giragosian, R., 'Georgian planning flaws led to campaign failure', *Jane's Defence Weekly*, 15 August (2008).

'Shifting security in the South Caucasus', *Connections: The Quarterly Journal* 6 (2007), 100–6.

Gittings, J., 'Bush claims Russia and China as allies', *Guardian*, 22 October (2001). Available at www.guardian.co.uk/world/2001/oct/22/china.afghanistan

Giuliano, E., 'Secessionism from the bottom up: democratisation, nationalism and local accountability in the Russian transition', *World Politics* 58 (2006), 276–310.

Gleason, G., *The Central Asian states: discovering independence* (Boulder, CO: Westview, 1997).

Global Legal Group, 'International comparative legal guide to gas regulation 2011' (2011). Available at www.iclg.co.uk/khadmin/Publications/pdf/4183.pdf

Goldman, M. (ed.), *Global studies: Russia, the Eurasian republics, and Central/Eastern Europe*, 10th edn (Dubuque, IA: McGraw-Hill/Dushkin, 2005).

The piratisation of Russia: Russian reform goes awry (London: Routledge, 2003).

Goldthau, A., 'Resurgent Russia? Rethinking Energy Inc', *Hoover Institution Policy Review* 147, 26 January (2008).

Gorbachev, M., 'The common European home', 6 July (1989). Available at www.coe.int/aboutcoe/index.asp?page=nosInvites&sp=gorbachev

Gorbachev, M., and Ikeda, D., *Moral lessons of the twentieth century: Gorbachev and Ikeda on Buddhism and Communism* (London: I.B. Tauris, 2005).

Grabosky, P., *Electronic crime* (Upper Saddle River, NJ: Pearson Prentice Hall, 2007).

Graham, T., 'US-Russian relations: the challenge of starting over', reprinted in *Ekspert*, March (2009). Available at www.expert.ru/printissues/expert/2009/09/vozmozhnost_nachat_snachala

Gray, C., 'Clausewitz rules, OK? The future is the past – with GPS', *Review of International Studies* 25 (1999), 161–82.

  War, peace and international relations: an introduction to strategic history (London: Routledge, 2007).

Grzymala-Busse, A., and Luong Jones, P., 'Reconceptualising the state: lessons from post-communism', *Politics & Society* 30 (2002), 529–44.

Gulette, D., 'Theories on Central Asian factionalism: the debate in political science and its wider implications', *Central Asian Survey* 26 (2007), 373–87.

Gurev, V., 'The Georgian theme', *International Affairs* (Moscow) 52 (2005), 96–101.

Gurov, A., *Krasnaya Mafiya* (Moscow: Samotsvet, 1995).

'Hacker "stole 130m credit card numbers"', *Independent*, 19 August (2009), p. 27.

Hagel, C., 'A Republican foreign policy', *Foreign Affairs* 83 (2004), 74–6.

Hahn, G.M., 'The *Jihadi* insurgency and the Russian counterinsurgency in the North Caucasus', *Post-Soviet Affairs* 24 (January–March 2008), 1–39.

  Russia's Islamic challenge (New Haven, CT: Yale University Press, 2007).

Hahn, M., 'Moscow achieves success with Kazakh oil deal', *Power and Interest News Report*, 29 May (2007).

Hale, H.E., and Taagepera, R., 'Russia: consolidation or collapse?', *Europe-Asia Studies* 54 (2002), 1101–25.

Hancock, K.J., 'Russia: great power image versus economic reality', *Asian Perspectives* 31 (2007), 71–98.

'Head of Georgian Church warns Russia against recognising breakaway regions', BBC Monitoring, Trans Caucasus, transcribed 17 February (2008) from *Rustavi-2 TV* (Georgia), 17 February (2008).

Heathershaw, J., *Post-conflict Tajikistan: the politics of peacebuilding and the emergence of legitimate order* (London: Routledge, 2009).

Hedenskog, J., Konnander, V., Nygren, B., Oldberg, I., and Pursiainen, C. (eds.), *Russia as a great power: dimensions of security under Putin* (Abingdon UK: Routledge, 2005).

Hegre, H., Ellingsen, T., Gates, S., and Gleditsch, N.P., 'Toward a democratic civil peace? Democracy, political change, and civil war, 1816–1992', *American Political Science Review* 95 (2001), 33–48.

Helms, Senator J., 'Amend the ABM Treaty? No, scrap it', *The Wall Street Journal*, 22 January (1999).

Herd, G., ' Russia: systemic transformation or Federal collapse?', *Journal of Peace Research* 36 (1999), 259–69.

'Hilary Clinton's invitation to Russia sounds like a belch of the Cold War', *Pravda*, 24 February (2010). Available at http://english.pravda.ru/world/americas/24–02–2010/112349-russia_nato-0

Hirschkorn, P., 'US charges 18 in Russian weapons-smuggling plot', *CNN Law Center*, 16 March (2005). Available at www.cnn.com/2005/LAW/03/15/weapons.trafficking/index.html

Hodess, R., 'Bribe payers index 2008' (Berlin: Transparency International, 2008).

Hoffman, D., 'Russia is sinking into the void of a "failed state"', *International Herald Tribune*, 27 February (1999), p. 1.

Holmes, L., 'Crime, organised crime and corruption in post-communist Europe and the CIS', *Communist and Post-Communist Studies* 42:2 (2009), 265–87.

The end of communist power (New York: Oxford University Press, 1993).

Rotten states? (Durham, NC: Duke University Press, 2006).

Holsti, K., 'The coming chaos? Armed conflict in the world's periphery', in T.V. Paul and J. Hall (eds.), *International order and the future of world politics* (Cambridge University Press, 1999), pp. 283–310.

Peace and war: armed conflicts and international order, Cambridge Studies in International Relations (Cambridge University Press, 1991).

Horowitz, B., 'IKEA and the graft factor', *Moscow Times*, 23 July (2009).

Howard, M.E., *Clausewitz* (Oxford University Press, 1983).

Hughes, J., *Chechnya: from nationalism to jihad* (Philadelphia: University of Pennsylvania Press, 2007).

'Managing secession potential in the Russian Federation', *Regional & Federal Studies* 11 (2001), 36–68.

Hughes, J., and Sasse, G. (eds.), *Ethnicity and territory in the former Soviet Union: regions in conflict* (London: Frank Cass, 2001).

Human Rights Watch '"Bullets were falling like rain": the Andijan massacre, May 13, 2005' (2005). Available at http://hrw.org/reports/2005/uzbekistan0605

Ibraimov, S., 'China-Central Asia trade relations: economic and social patterns', *China and Eurasia Forum Quarterly* 7 (2009), 47–59.

Ikenberry, G.J., *After victory: institutions, strategic restraint and the rebuilding of order after major wars* (Princeton University Press, 2001).

'Intelligence brief: Poland fumes over Russian-German projects: meeting in Lithuania to counter Russian influence in FSU', *Power and Interest News Report*, 2 May (2008).

Interfax, 'Grazhdane Putinu: zdes' u vas nedorabotki', 27 July (2009). Available at www.interfax.ru/business/txt.asp?id=92162&sw=%CB%E5%E2%E0%E4%E0&bd=23&bm=7&by=2009&ed=30&em=7&ey=2009&secid=0&mp=0&p=1

International Crisis Group, 'Georgia and Russia: clashing over Abkhazia', *Europe Report* 193, 5 June (2008). Available at www.crisisgroup.org/en/regions/europe/caucasus/georgia/193-georgia-and-russia-clashing-over-abkhazia.aspx

'Kyrgyzstan on the edge', *Asia Briefing* 55, 9 November (2006). Available at www.crisisgroup.org/en/regions/asia/central-asia/kyrgyzstan/B055%20Kyrgyzstan%20on%20the%20Edge.aspx

'Kyrgyzstan: a faltering state', *Asia Report* 109, 16 December (2005). Available at www.crisisgroup.org/en/regions/asia/central-asia/kyrgyzstan/109-kyrgyzstan-a-faltering-state.aspx

'Tajikistan: on the road to failure', *Asia Report* 162, 12 February (2009). Available at www.crisisgroup.org/en/regions/asia/central-asia/tajikistan/162-tajikistan-on-the-road-to-failure.aspx

'Uzbekistan: Stagnation and Uncertainty', *Asia Briefing* 67, 22 August (2007). Available at www.crisisgroup.org/en/regions/asia/central-asia/ uzbekistan/B062-uzbekistan-stagnation-and-uncertainty.aspx

'Interv'yu Dmitriya Medvedeva telekanalam "Rossiya", Pervomu, NTV', Sochi, 31 August (2008). Available at www.kremlin.ru/text/appears/ 2008/08/205991.shtml

Isaacs, R., 'Between informal and formal politics: neopatrimonialism and party development in post-Soviet Kazakhstan', PhD thesis (Oxford Brookes University, 2009).

Isachenkov, V., 'Russia strengthens gas grip', *MiamiHerald.com*, 19 January (2008).

Jervis, R., 'From balance to concert: a study of international security cooperation', *World Politics* 38 (October 1985), 58–79.

Johnson, R., *Oil, Islam and conflict: Central Asia since 1945* (London: Reaktion Books, 2007).

Johnson's Russia List, no. 95, 21 May (2009), item 15.

Johnson's Russia List, no. 97, 26 May (2009), item 10.

Johnson's Russia List, no. 121, 1 July (2009), item 5.

Johnson's Russia List, no. 158, 26 August (2009), item 11.

Johnson's Russia List, no. 165, 4 September (2009), item 15.

Johnson's Russia List, no. 212, 19 November (2008), item 31.

Johnson's Russia List, no. 4403, 14 July (2000).

Jonson, L., and Archer, C. (eds.), *Peacekeeping and the role of Russia in Eurasia* (Boulder, CO: Westview, 1996).

Judt, T., *Reappraisals: reflections on the forgotten twentieth century* (London: Penguin, 2009).

Kagan, R., 'Putin makes his move', *Washington Post*, 11 August (2008). Available at www.washingtonpost.com/wp-dyn/content/article/2008/08/10/ AR2008081001871.html

Kalachova, I., 'Poverty and welfare trends in Ukraine over the 1990s', *UNICEF Country Papers*, UNICEF Innocenti Research Centre (Florence: UNICEF, 2002).

Kaldor, M., *Human security: reflections on globalisation and intervention* (Cambridge: Polity, 2007).

New and old wars: organised violence in a global era (Cambridge: Polity, 2001; 2nd edn 2006).

Kalyvas, S.N., '"New" and "old" civil wars: a valid distinction?', *World Politics* 54 (2001), 99–118.

Kanet, R.E. (ed.), *Resolving regional conflicts* (Champaign, IL: University of Illinois Press, 1998).

Russia: re-emerging great power (Basingstoke, UK: Palgrave Macmillan, 2007).

'The Russian Federation', in E.A. Kolodziej and R.E. Kanet (eds.), *Coping with conflict after the Cold War* (Baltimore, MD: The Johns Hopkins University Press, 1996), pp. 60–86.

'Zwischen konsens und konfrontation: Rußland und die Vereinigten Staaten', *Osteuropa* 51 (2001), 509–21.

Kanet, R.E., and Freire, M.R. (eds.), *Russia and its neighbours* (New York: Routledge, in press).

Kanet, R.E., and Homarac, L., 'The US challenge to Russian influence in Central Asia and the Caucasus', in R.E. Kanet (ed.), *Russia: re-emerging great power* (Basingstoke, UK: Palgrave Macmillan, 2007), pp. 173–94.

Kanet, R.E., and Ibryamova, N.V., 'La sécurité en Europe centrale et orientale: un système en cours de changement', *Revue d'Études Comparatives Est-Ouest* 33 (2002), 179–203.

'Verpaßte Gelegenheiten? Amerikanisch-Russische Beziehungen in den 90er Jahren', *Osteuropa* 51 (2001), 985–1001.

Kanet, R.E., and Kozhemiakin, A.V. (eds.), *The foreign policy of the Russian Federation* (London: Macmillan Publishers, 1997).

Kang, D., 'The theoretical roots of hierarchy in international relations', *Australian Journal of International Affairs* 58 (2004), 337–52.

'Why China's rise will be peaceful: hierarchy and stability in the East Asian region', *Perspectives on Politics* 3 (2005), 551–4.

Kassianova, A., 'Russia: still open to the West? Evolution of the state identity in the foreign policy and security discourse', *Europe-Asia Studies* 53 (2001), 821–39.

Keegan, J., *A history of warfare* (New York: Alfred A. Knopf, 1994).

Keen, D., 'Incentives and disincentives for violence', in M. Berdal and D. Malone (eds.), *Greed and grievance: economic agendas in civil war* (Boulder, CO: Lynne Rienner Publishers, 2000), pp. 19–42.

Khachatrian, H., 'Russian moves in Caucasus energy and power sectors could have geopolitical impact', *Eurasia Insight*, 25 September (2006).

Khalizad, Z., and Lesser, I.O. (eds.), *Sources of conflict in the twenty-first century: regional futures and US strategy* (Santa Monica, CA: RAND, 1998).

Khvatit grabit' Rossiiu: pogranichnaia politika i natsional'nye interesy Rossii (Moscow: LDP, 1995).

Kim, L., 'Putin's biggest failure is fight against Russian corruption, poll shows', 12 August (2010). Available at www.bloomberg.com/news/2010-08-12/putin-s-biggest-failure-is-fight-against-russian-corruption-poll-shows.html

Klare, M.T., *Rising powers, sinking planet: the new geopolitics of energy* (New York: Metropolitan Books, 2008).

Kleveman, L., *The new great game: blood and oil in Central Asia* (London: Atlantic Books, 2003).

Kolstoe, P., *Russians in the former Soviet republics* (Bloomington: Indiana University Press, 1995).

'Kontseptsiia natsional'noi bezopasnosti Rossiiskoi Federatsii', *Nezavisimoe voennoe obozrenie*, 11 July (2000). Available at http://nvo.ng.ru/concepts/2000–01–14/6_concept.html

'Konseptsiya natsional'noi bezopasnosti', *Rossiiskaya gazeta*, 26 December (1997), pp. 4–5.

Konseptsiya vneshnei politiki Rossiiskoi Federatsii, 12 July (2008).

'Kontseptsiya vneshnei politiki Rosiiskoi Federatsii', *Diplomaticheski Vestnik* (special issue), January (1993).

'Korruptsiya popravila prezidenta', *Kommersant*, 28 July (2009).

Kosachëv, K., 'Rezhimy prikhodyat i ukhodyat: Mif, budto Rossiya oderzhima zhelaniem vernut' Gruziyu v sferu svoego vliyaniya', *Rossiiskaya gazeta*, 3 March (2009).

Koselleck, R., 'Historical criteria of the modern concept of revolution', in R. Koselleck (ed.), *Futures past: on the semantics of historical time*, trans. Keith Tribe (Cambridge, MA: MIT Press, 1985 [1979]), pp. 39–54.

Kozhemiakin, A.V., and Kanet, R.E., 'Russia as a regional peacekeeper', in R.E. Kanet (ed.), *Resolving regional conflicts* (Champaign: University of Illinois Press, 1998), pp. 225–39.

Kozhokin, E.M., 'Georgia-Abkhazia', in J.A. Azrael and E.A. Payin (eds.), *US and Russian policymaking with respect to the use of force*, conference report (RAND Centre for Russian and Eurasian Studies, RAND Corporation, September 1995).

Kramer, A.E., 'Central Asia on front line in energy battle', *New York Times*, 20 December (2007), pp. C1, C6.

Krasner, S., *Sovereignty: organised hypocrisy* (Princeton University Press, 1999).

'Think again: sovereignty', *Foreign Policy* 121 (2001), 20–9.

Krebs, B., 'Shadowy Russian Firm Seen as Conduit for Cybercrime', *Washington Post*, 13 October (2007).

'Three indicted in identity theft case', *Washington Post*, 18 August (2009), p. A11.

Kremenyuk, V., *Conflicts in and around Russia* (New York: Praeger, 1994).

Kreutz, A., *Russia in the Middle East: friend or foe?* (Santa Barbara, CA: Praeger Security International/Greenwood Press, 2006).

Kryshtanovskaya, O., 'Nelegal'nye Struktury v Rossii'', *Sotsiologicheskie issledovaniya* 8 (1995), 94–106.

Kucera, J., 'The CSTO, forthcoming as ever, on Kyrgyzstan', *Eurasianet*, 6 May (2010). Available at www.eurasianet.org/node/61003

'US blocking NATO-CSTO cooperation', *Eurasianet*, 12 February (2011). Available at www.eurasianet.org/node/62882

Kupatadze, A., 'Organised crime before and after the Tulip Revolution: the changing dynamics of upperworld-underworld networks', *Central Asian Survey* 27:3–4 (2008), 279–99.

Kupchan, C.A., and Kupchan, C.C., 'Concerts, collective security and the future of Europe', *International Security* 16 (1991), 114–61.

'The promise of collective security', *International Security* 20 (1995), 52–61.

Kurtbag, O., 'EU's response to the Georgia crisis: an active peace broker or a confused and divided actor?' *Journal of Central Asian and Caucasian Studies* 3 (2008), 58–74.

La Porta, R., Lopez-de-Silanes, F., Shleifer, A., and Vishny, R.W., 'The quality of government', *The Journal of Law, Economics, and Organisation* 15:1 (1999), 222–79.

'Trust in large organisations', *The American Economic Review* 87:2 (1997), 336–7.

Laitin, D.D., *Identity in formation: the Russian-speaking populations in the near abroad* (Ithaca, NY: Cornell University Press, 1998).

Lantier, A., 'US oil pipeline politics and the Russia-Georgia conflict', *World Socialist Web Site*, 21 August (2008). Available at www.wsws.org/articles/2008/aug2008/pipe-a21.shtml

Lapidus, G.W., 'Ethnicity and state-building: accommodating ethnic differences in post-Soviet Eurasia', in M. Beissinger and C. Young (eds.), *Beyond state crisis? Postcolonial Africa and post-Soviet Eurasia in comparative perspective* (Washington, DC: Woodrow Wilson Center Press, 2002), pp. 323–58.

Laquer, W., *The last days of Europe: epitaph for an old continent* (New York: Thomas Dunne Books, 2007).

'Once more with feeling', *Society* 33 (1995), 32–41.

Layne, C., 'The war on terrorism and the balance of power: the paradoxes of American hegemony', in T.V. Paul, J. Wirtz and M. Fortmann (eds.), *Balance of power: theory and practice in the twenty-first century* (Stanford University Press, 2004), pp. 103–27.

Ledeneva, A., *Russia's economy of favours* (Cambridge University Press, 1998).

Lee, R., 'Recent trends in nuclear smuggling', in P. Williams (ed.), *Russian organised crime* (London: Frank Cass, 1997), pp. 109–21.

Lewis, D., *The temptations of tyranny in Central Asia* (London: Hurst, 2008).

Lieven, A., 'Balkan unrest remains a recipe for disaster', *Financial Times*, 14 January (2008).

Chechnya: tombstone of Russian power (New Haven, CT: Yale University Press, 1998).

'Empire's aftermath: a comparative perspective', in S.N. Cummings (ed.), *Power and change in Central Asia* (London: Routledge, 2002), pp. 24–41.

Lo, B., *Russian foreign policy in the post-Soviet era: reality, illusion and mythmaking* (Basingstoke, UK: Palgrave Macmillan, 1997).

Lobjakas, A., 'NATO lacks the stomach for South Caucasus fight', *Caucasus Analytical Digest* 5 (2009), 2–4.

Lomsadze, G., 'Georgia: treading carefully on the matter of Kosovo independence', *Eurasianet*, 21 February (2008). Available at www.eurasianet.org/departments/insight/articles/eav022108a.shtml

Lonsdale, D., *The nature of war in the information age: Clausewitzian future* (London and New York: Frank Cass, 2004).

Loo, B., 'Introduction: revolutions in military affairs: theory and applicability to small armed forces', in B. Loo (ed.), *Military transformation and strategy* (Abingdon, UK: Routledge, 2009), pp. 1–12.

Lucas, E., *The new Cold War* (New York: Palgrave MacMillan, 2008).

Luong Jones, P., *Institutional change and political continuity in post-Soviet Central Asia: power, perceptions, and pacts* (Cambridge University Press, 2002).

'Introduction: politics in the periphery: competing views of Central Asian states and societies', in P. Luong Jones (ed.), *The transformation of Central Asia: states and societies from Soviet rule to independence* (Ithaca, NY: Cornell University Press, 2004), pp. 1–26.

Lynch, A.C., 'The realism of Russian foreign policy', *Europe-Asia Studies* 53 (2001), 7–31.

Lynch, D., *Engaging Eurasia's separatist states: unresolved conflicts and de facto states* (Washington, DC: United States Institute of Peace Press, 2004).

Russian peacekeeping strategies in the CIS, 1992–1997: the cases of Georgia, Moldova and Tajikistan (New York: St Martin's Press, 2000).

'Separatist states and post-Soviet conflicts', *International Affairs* 78 (2002), 831–48.

Mackinlay, J., and Cross, P. (eds.), *Regional peacekeepers: the paradox of Russian peacekeeping* (New York: United Nations University Press, 2003).

MacKinnon, M., *The new Cold War: revolutions, rigged elections and pipeline politics in the former Soviet Union* (New York: Carroll and Graf Publishers, 2007).

Makinder, H., 'The geographical pivot of history', *The Geographical Journal*, April (1904).

Maksutov, R., 'The Shanghai Cooperation Organisation: a Central Asian perspective', SIPRI Project Paper, August (2006). Available at www.sipri. org/contents/worldsec/Ruslan.SCO.pdf/download

Malashenko, A., *Islam dlya Rossii*, Carnegie Endowment for International Peace (Moscow: Rosspen, 2007).

Mallett, V., 'Suspected ETA chief held in Pyrenees raid', *Financial Times*, 17 November (2008), p. 8.

Malone, D., 'The High Level Panel and the Security Council', *Security Dialogue* 36 (2005), 370–72.

Mandelbaum, M., *The nuclear question: the United States and nuclear weapons, 1946–1976* (Cambridge, MA: Cambridge University Press, 1979).

Mann, M., 'The autonomous power of the state: its origins, mechanisms and results', *Archives Européennes de Sociologie* 25 (1983), 187–213.

Mansfield, E., and Snyder, J., 'Democratisation and war', *Foreign Affairs* 74 (May–June 1995), 79–97.

'Democratisation and the danger of war', *International Security* 20 (1995), 5–38.

Markedonov, S., 'Abkhazia in geopolitical game in the Caucasus', *RIA Novosti*, 13 August (2007). Available at www.gab-ibn.com/IMG/pdf/Ge3-_Abkhazia_In_Geopolitical_Game_In_The_Caucasus.pdf

'The paradoxes of Russia's Georgia policy', *Russia in Global Affairs* 2 (April–June 2007).

Markowitz, L., 'How master frames mislead: the division and eclipse of nationalist movements in Uzbekistan and Tajikistan', *Ethnic and Racial Studies* 32 (2009), 716–38.

The micro-foundations of rebellion and repression: rents, patronage, and law-enforcement in Tajikistan and Uzbekistan (Seattle, WA: The National Council for Eurasian and East European Research, 2008).

Mashkin, S., 'Chechenskiy avtoritet pokhishchen bez vesti', *Kommersant*, 14 April (2008).

McDermott, R.N., 'Russia's conventional armed forces after the Georgia war', *Parameters: US Army War College Quarterly* 39 (2009), 65–80.

McDonald, M., 'Human security and the construction of security', *Global Society* 16 (2002), 277–95.

McFaul, M., 'The fourth wave of democracy and dictatorship: noncooperative transitions in the postcommunist world', in M. McFaul and K.

Stoner-Weiss (eds.), *After the collapse of communism: comparative lessons of transition* (Cambridge University Press, 2004), pp. 58–95.

McFaul, M., and Stoner-Weiss, K., 'The myth of Putin's success', *Foreign Affairs* 87 (2008), 68–84.

McInnes, C., *Spectator-sport war: the West and contemporary conflict* (Boulder, CO: Lynne Rienner Publishers, 2002).

McLaughlin, D., 'Georgian president claims Russia set on ousting him', *Irish Times*, 7 August (2010). Available at www.irishtimes.com/newspaper/world/2010/0807/1224276378730.html

McMillan, J., Sokolsky, R., and Winner, A.C., 'Toward a new regional security architecture', *Washington Quarterly* 23 (2004), 161–75.

McSweeney, B., 'Identity and security: Buzan and the Copenhagen School' (review essay), *Review of International Studies* 22 (1996), 81–93.

Mearsheimer, J., 'The false promise of international institutions', *International Security* 19 (1994/5), 5–49.

The tragedy of great power politics (New York: W.W. Norton, 2001).

Medvedev, D., 'Conversation with Kirill Pozdnyakov, anchor of NTV current affairs programme *Itogovaya Programma NTV*', 26 July (2009). Available at http://archive.kremlin.ru/eng/text/speeches/2009/07/26/1132_type82916type82917_220146.shtml

'Poslanie Federal'nomu Sobraniyu Rossiyskoy Federatsii'. Available at http://news.kremlin.ru/transcripts/1968

'Stenograficheskii otchet o vstreche s uchastnikami mezhdunarodnogo kluba "Valdai"', Moscow, 12 September (2008).

Melvin, N.J., 'Patterns of centre-regional relations in Central Asia: the cases of Kazakhstan, the Kyrgyz Republic and Uzbekistan', *Regional & Federal Studies* 11 (2001), 165–93.

Mendelson, S., *Barracks and brothels: peacekeepers and human trafficking in the Balkans* (Washington, DC: CSIS Press, 2005).

Menon, R., and Motyl, A., 'The myth of Russian resurgence', *The American Interest* 2 (2007), 96–101.

Menon, R., Federov, Y., and Nodia, G. (eds.), *Russia, the Caucasus, and Central Asia* (New York: M.E. Sharpe, 1999).

Menon, R., and Spruyt, H., 'Possibilities for conflict and conflict resolution in post-Soviet Central Asia', in B. Rubin and J. Snyder (eds.), *Post-Soviet political order: conflict and state building* (London: Routledge, 1998), pp. 104–27.

Miller, N., 'From Russia with malice: criminals trawl the world', *Age* (Melbourne), 24 July (2007).

Mitrofanov, A., *Shagi Novoi Geopolitiki* (Moscow: Russkii Vestnik, 1997).

'Moscow to prevent Ukraine's, Georgia's NATO accession', *RIA Novosti*, 8 April (2010). Available at http://en.rian.ru/russia/20080408/104105506.html

Motyl, A., 'After empire: competing discourses and inter-state conflict in post-imperial Eastern Europe', in B. Rubin and J. Snyder (eds.), *Post-Soviet political order: conflict and state building* (London: Routledge, 1998), pp. 14–33.

Motyl, A., Ruble, B., and Shevtsova, L. (eds.), *Russia's engagement with the West: transformation and integration in the twenty-first century* (New York: M.E. Sharpe, 2005).

Münkler, H., *The new wars* (Oxford: Polity, 2005).

Munro, N., *Russia votes* (Centre for the Study of Public Policy, University of Aberdeen). Available at www.russiavotes.org/president/presidency_performance.php?PHPSESSID=ec4620a625f8c4d5d8c90fe50dcdf4ff

Naumkin, V.V., *Militant Islam in Central Asia: the case of the Islamic Movement of Uzbekistan* (Berkeley: Berkeley Program in Soviet and Post-Soviet Studies, 2003). Available at http://repositories.cdlib.org/iseees/bps/2003_06-naum

Nelson, T., 'Russian realities: nuclear weapons, bureaucratic manoeuvres and organised crime', *Demokratizatsiya* 8:1 (2000), 145–59.

Newman, E., 'The 'new wars' debate: a historical perspective is needed', *Security Dialogue* 35 (2004), 173–89.

'A normatively attractive but analytically weak concept', *Security Dialogue* 35 (2004), 358–59.

Nichol, J., 'Russia-Georgia conflict in South Ossetia: context and implications for US interests', *CRS Report for Congress* (Washington, DC: Congressional Research Service, 24 October 2008).

Nodia, G., 'The conflict in Abkhazia: national projects and political circumstances', in B. Coppieters, G. Nodia and Y. Anchabadze (eds.), *The Georgians and Abkhazians: the search for a peace settlement* (Brussels: Vrije University, 1998).

Normark, P., 'Time is ripe for Russian policy change towards Georgia', European Rim Policy and Investment Council, *Perihelion Articles*, 16 February (2003). Available at www.erpic.org/perihelion/articles2003/february.georgia

Nygren, B., 'Putin's attempts to subjugate Georgia: from sabre-rattling to the power of the purse', in R.E. Kanet (ed.), *Russia: re-emerging great power* (Basingstoke, UK: Palgrave Macmillan, 2007), pp. 107–23.

'Putin's use of energy resources with respect to CIS countries'. Unpublished paper presented at the Seventh International CISS Millennium Conference, Buçaco, Portugal, 14–16 June (2007).

The rebuilding of greater Russia: Putin's foreign policy toward the CIS countries (Abingdon, UK: Routledge, 2007).

O'Connor, K., *Intellectuals and apparatchiks. Russian nationalism and the Gorbachev revolution* (Lanham, MD: Lexington Books, 2006).

Ohmae, K., *The borderless world* (New York: Harper Business, 1990).

'Oil over troubled waters', *The Economist*, 28 May (2005), p. 54.

O'Kane, R.H.T., 'A probabilistic approach to the causes of coups d'état', *British Journal of Political Science* 11 (1981), 287–308.

Olcott, M., *Central Asia's second chance* (Washington, DC: Carnegie Endowment for International Peace, 2005).

'Velika li ugroza dzhikhada v Tsentral'noi Azii? *Pro et Contra* 13 (2009), 39–52.

Oldberg, I., 'Foreign policy priorities under Putin: A *Tour d'Horizon*', in R. Hedenskog, V. Konnander, B. Nygren, I. Oldberg and C. Pursiainen (eds.), *Russia as a great power: dimensions of security under Putin* (Abingdon, UK: Routledge, 2005), pp. 29–56.

'Russia's great power ambitions and policy under Putin', in R. Kanet (ed.), *Russia: re-emerging great power* (Basingstoke, UK: Palgrave Macmillan, 2007), pp. 13–30.

'Open letter to the Obama Administration from Central and Eastern Europe', Radio Free Europe/Radio Liberty (RFE/RL), 16 July (2009). Available at www.rferl.org/content/An_Open_Letter_To_The_Obama_ Administration_From_Central_And_Eastern_Europe/1778449.html

Orange, R., 'Death tolls in southern Kyrgyzstan violence mounts to 23', *The Telegraph*, 11 June (2010). Available at www.telegraph.co.uk/news/ worldnews/asia/kyrgyzstan/7820518/Death-toll-in-southern-Kyrgyzstan-violence-mounts-to-23.html

OSCE/ODIHR, *Preliminary findings on the events in Andijan, Uzbekistan, 13 May 2005* (Warsaw: Office for Democratic Institutions and Human Rights, 2005). Available at www1.osce.org/documents/odihr/2005/06/15233_en.pdf

Owens, P., 'Distinctions, distinctions: "public" and "private" force?' *International Affairs* 84 (2008), 977–90.

Ozhiganov, E., 'The Republic of Georgia: conflict in Abkhazia and South Ossetia', in A. Arbatov, A. Chayes, A.H. Chayes and L. Olson (eds.), *Managing conflict in the former Soviet Union, Russian and American perspectives* (Cambridge, MA: MIT Press, 1997), pp. 341–400.

Pamir, A.N., 'Energy and pipeline security in the Black Sea and Caspian Sea regions: challenges and solutions', in O. Pavliuk and I. Klympush-Tsintsadze (eds.), *The Black Sea region: cooperation and security building* (Armonk, NY: M.E. Sharpe, 2003), pp. 123–55.

Pannier, B., 'Central Asia: Beijing flexes economic muscle across region', Radio Free Europe/Radio Liberty (RFE/RL), 29 May (2008).

Papp, D.S., 'The former Soviet Republics and the Commonwealth of Independent States', in D.J. Murray and P.R. Viotti (eds.), *The defence policies of nations: a comparative study* (Baltimore, MD: Johns Hopkins University Press, 1994) pp. 119–232.

Perl, R.F., 'Taliban and the drug trade' (Washington, DC: Congressional Research Services, Library of Congress, 2001).

Perlo-Freeman, S., and Stålenheim, P., 'Military expenditure in the South Caucasus and Central Asia', in A.J.K. Bailes, B. Hagelin, Z. Lachowski, S. Perlo-Freeman, P. Stålenheim and D. Trofimov (eds.), *Armament and disarmament in the Caucasus and Central Asia* (Stockholm International Peace Research Institute, 2003), pp. 7–20.

Peterson, A., and Ziyadov, T., 'Azerbaijan and Georgia: playing Russian roulette with Moscow' (Washington, DC: Central Asia-Caucasus Institute, October 2007).

Philip, C., and Halpin, T., 'Russia in nuclear threat to Poland', *The Times*, 16 August (2008). Available at www.timesonline.co.uk/tol/news/world/ europe/article4543744.ece

'Poland wants talks with Russia, Germany on pipeline', *RFE/RL Newsline*, 8 January (2008).

Popjanevski, J., 'Parliamentary elections in Abkhazia: opposition on the rise?', *Central Asia-Caucasus Analyst*, 2 July (2007).

Poppe, E., and Hagendorn, L., 'Types of identification among Russians in the "near abroad"', *Europe-Asia Studies* 53 (2001), 57–71.

Powell, R., 'The inefficient use of power: costly conflict with complete information', *American Political Science Review* 98 (2004), 633–48.

'President Medvedev marks his first anniversary in office', ITAR-TASS, 7 May (2009). Available at http://eng.tatar-inform.ru/news/2009/05/07/24870/

'Press conference with Sergei Lavrov', Russian Federation mission to the United Nations, September (2008). Available at www.mid.ru/rus_fp_e_17.html

Price Waterhouse Coopers, 'Guide to doing business and investing in Uzbekistan' (2010). Available at www.pwc.com/uz/en/assets/pdf/UZ_DBG_2010.pdf

Prichner, H. Jr., *Reviving greater Russia? The future of Russia's borders with Belarus, Georgia, Kazakhstan, Moldova and Ukraine* (Lanham, MD: University Press of America, 2005).

Primakov, Y., 'Russia, the West and NATO', *Obschaya gazeta*, 37, 22–7 September (1996).

Prinuditel'nyi Trud v Sovremennoi Rossii: Nereguliruemaya Migratsiya i Torgovlya Lyud'mi (Geneva: International Labour Office, 2006).

Protocol Additional to the Geneva Conventions of 12 August 1949, and relating to the Protection of Victims of International Armed Conflicts (Protocol I), 8 June (1977), Article 51. Available at www.icrc.org/ihl.nsf/WebART/470–750065?OpenDocument

Protocol Additional to the Geneva Conventions of 12 August 1949, and relating to the Protection of Victims of International Armed Conflicts (Protocol I), 8 June (1977), Article 52. Available at www.icrc.org/ihl.nsf/WebART/470–750067?OpenDocument

Protocol Additional to the Geneva Conventions of 12 August 1949, and relating to the Protection of Victims of Non-International Armed Conflicts (Protocol II), 8 June (1977). Available at www.icrc.org/ihl.nsf/INTRO/475?OpenDocument

'Putin focuses on domestic policy in state-of-nation address to Russian Parliament', RTR Russia TV, Moscow, 25 April (2005), BBC Monitoring, Former Soviet Union, trans. in *Johnson's Russia List*, no. 9130, 25 April (2005).

Putin, V., 'President's speech to the Federal Assembly', BBC Monitoring, Former Soviet Union, April (2005).

First person: an astonishingly frank self-portrait by Russia's President Putin, with N. Gevorkyan, N. Timakova and A. Kolesnikov, trans. C.A. Fitzpatrick (London: Hutchinson, 2000).

Rapoport, A. (ed.), 'Introduction', in C. von Clausewitz, *On War* (London: Penguin, 1968 [1832]).

Rashid, A., *Descent into chaos: the world's most unstable region and the threat to global security* (London: Penguin, 2009).

Jihad: the rise of militant Islam in Central Asia (New Haven, CT: Yale University Press, 2002).

Reitman, A., 'EU and Russia tackle thorny issues at Samara summit', *EU Observer*, 18 May (2005). Available at http://euobserver.com/9/24088

Remnick, D., 'Can Russia change?', *Foreign Affairs* 76 (1997), 35–49.

'Results of public opinion polls, December 2008–February 2009', *The Monitoring of Public Opinion: Economic and Social Changes (VTsIOM)* (January–February 2009), p. 54. Available at http://wciom.com/fileadmin/user_upload/file_monitoring/2009_1%2889%29_11_Contents.pdf

RFE/RL Newsline, 17 September (2004), item 4.

Riaño, J., and Hodess, R., 'Bribe payers index 2008' (Berlin: Transparency International, 2008).

Rice, S.E., and Patrick, S., *Index of state weakness in the developing world* (Washington, DC: Brookings Institution, 2008).

Robinson, N., 'The global economy, reform and crisis in Russia', *Review of International Political Economy* 6 (1999), 531–64.

'Patrimonial political economy and the global economy'. Paper delivered to the ISA-ABRI Joint International Meeting, Rio de Janeiro (2009). Available at www.allacademic.com/meta/p381097_index.html

'Russia: limiting the impact of crisis in a post-communist transitional economy', in J. Robertson (ed.), *Power and politics after financial crisis: rethinking foreign opportunism in emerging markets* (Basingstoke, UK: Palgrave Macmillan, 2008), pp. 212–28.

Russia: a state of uncertainty (London: Routledge, 2002).

'State-building and international politics: the emergence of a "new" problem and agenda', in A. Hehir and N. Robinson (eds.), *State-building; theory and practice* (London: Routledge, 2007), pp. 1–28.

Roeder, P.G., 'From hierarchy to hegemony: the post-Soviet security complex', in D.A. Lake and P.M. Morgan (eds.), *Regional orders: building security in a new world* (University Park: Penn State University Press, 1997).

Rondelli, A., *Russia and Georgia: relations are still tense* (Luleå, Sweden: CA&CC Press AB Publishing House, 2006). Available at www.ca-c.org/c-g/2006/journal_english

Roper, S., 'Regionalism in Moldova: the case of Trans-Dniester and Gaugazia', *Regional & Federal Studies* 11 (2001), 101–22.

Rossiyskaya Gazeta – Nedelya, 24 January (2008).

Roy, O., *The new Central Asia: the creation of nations* (London: I.B. Tauris, 2000).

Rozman, G., Nosov, M.G., and Watanabe, K. (eds.), *Russia and East Asia: the twenty-first century security environment* (Armonk, NY: M.E. Sharpe for East/West Institute, New York, 1999).

'Rubezh 2008: the first large-scale CSTO exercise', *Partnership for Peace Information Management System*, 24 July (2008).

Rubin, B., 'Central Asia wars and ethnic conflicts – rebuilding failed states', Human Development Report Office Occasional Paper (New York: United Nations Development Program, 2004).

Ruggiero, V., *Organised and corporate crime in Europe* (Aldershot, UK: Dartmouth, 1996).

Rukavishnikov, V., 'Choices for Russia: preserving inherited geopolitics through emergent global and European realities', in R.E. Kanet (ed.), *Russia: re-emerging great power* (Basingstoke, UK: Palgrave Macmillan, 2007), pp. 54–78.

Rukhadze, V., 'Abkhazia and South Ossetia – Russia's never-ending game', Abkhazia Institute for Social and Economic Research, 8 July (2007). Available at www.abkhazia.com/research-blogs/politics/535-abkhazia-and-south-ossetia-russias-never-ending-game

Russell, J., *Chechnya: Russia's war on terror* (New York: Routledge, 2007).

'Russia attacks "provocative" Georgia after ministerial talks', BBC Monitoring, Former Soviet Union, transcribed 30 August (2007) from Russian Ministry of Foreign Affairs website, 30 August (2007).

'Russia: Moscow warns Georgia, Ukraine; brushes off Abkhaz mediation offer', Radio Free Europe/Radio Liberty (RFE/RL), 7 June (2008). Available at www.rferl.org/featuresarticleprint/2008/06

'Russian bounties sow distrust among Chechen rebels', *STRATFOR Global Intelligence Briefs*, 16 March (2005).

'Russian PM threatens to review relations with EU', *RIA Novosti*, 23 March (2008). Available at http://en.rian.ru/russia/20090323/120699757.html

'Russia's Foreign Policy Concept', *International Affairs* 40 (Moscow) (1993).

'Russia's Medvedev attacks Belarus President Alexander Lukashenko', *BBC News*, 4 October (2010). Available at www.bbc.co.uk/news/world-europe-11469027

'Russia's new military doctrine declares USA and NATO key potential enemies', trans. D. Sudakov, *Pravda.ru*, 19 September (2006). Available at http://english.pravda.ru/russia/kremlin/19-09-2006/84521-russia_doctrine-0/

Rutland, P., 'Putin's path to power', *Post-Soviet Affairs* 16 (2000), 313–54.

Sagramoso, D., *Russian imperialism revisited* (London: Routledge, 2010).

Sakwa, R., (ed.), *Chechnya: from past to future* (London: Anthem Press, 2005).
  The dual state in Russia: factionalism and the Medvedev succession (Cambridge University Press, 2010).
  'Introduction: why Chechnya?', in R. Sakwa (ed.), *Chechnya: from past to future* (London: Anthem Press, 2005), pp. 1–20.
  '"New Cold War" or "twenty years' crisis?" Russia and International Politics', *International Affairs* 84 (2008), 241–67.
  Putin: Russia's choice, 2nd edn (London and New York: Routledge, 2008).
  'The regime system in Russia', *Contemporary Politics* 3 (1997), 7–25.
  Russian politics and society, 4th edn (London: Macmillan, 1997).

Sakwa, R., and Webber, M., 'The Commonwealth of Independent States, 1991–1998: stagnation and survival', *Europe-Asia Studies* 51 (1999), 367–92.

San Francisco Chronicle, 4 October (2001).

Sasse, G., *The Crimea question: identity, transition, and conflict* (Cambridge, MA: Harvard University Press, 2007).

Satarov, G., 'Corruption, Western and Russian', in Y. Senokosov and E. Skidelsky (eds.), 'Corruption in Russia', *Russia on Russia* 4 (Moscow School of Political Studies and Social Market Foundation, 2001).
  Diagnostika rossiyskoy korruptsii: sotsiologicheskiy analiz (Moscow: INDEM, 2002).
  Vo skol'ko raz uvelichilas' korruptsiya za 4 goda: rezul'taty novogo issledovanija Fonda INDEM (Moscow: INDEM, 2005). Available at www.anti-corr.ru/projects.htm#2005

Schatz, E., 'Framing strategies and non-conflict in multi-ethnic Kazakhstan', *Nationalism and Ethnic Politics* 6 (2000), 71–94.

Modern clan politics and beyond: the power of 'blood' in Kazakhstan (Seattle: University of Washington Press, 2004).

Scherrer, A., *G8 against transnational crime* (Aldershot, UK: Ashgate, 2009).

Scott, M., and Solvyov, D., 'Medvedev says Russia will rebuff aggression', 9 May (2009). Available at http://uk.reuters.com/article/2009/05/09/us-russia-parade-idUKTRE5480NM20090509

Secrieru, S., *Illusion of power: Russia after the South Caucasus battle*, CEPS Working Document No. 311, February (2009).

Security Council of the Russian Federation, *National Security Strategy of the Russian Federation up to 2020*, 12 May (2009). Available at www.scrf.gov. ru/documents/99.html

Segal, G., 'East Asia and the "constrainment" of China', *International Security* 20 (1996), 107–35.

Serio, J., *Investigating the Russian Mafia* (Durham, NC: Carolina Academic Press, 2008).

Shain, Y., and Barth, A., 'Diasporas and international relations theory', *International Organisation* 57 (2003), 449–79.

Shaw, M., *War and genocide: organised killing in modern society* (Cambridge: Polity, 2003).

'War and globality: the role and character of war in the global transition', in H-W. Yeong (ed.), *The new agenda for peace research* (Aldershot, UK: Ashgate, 1999), pp. 61–80.

Shawcross, W., *Deliver us from evil: peacekeepers, warlords, and a world of endless conflict* (New York: Simon & Schuster, 2000).

Shearman, P., and Sussex, M., 'Globalisation, "new wars" and the war in Chechnya', in R. Sakwa (ed.), *Chechnya: from past to future* (London: Anthem Press, 2005), pp. 199–221.

Shevtsova, L., *Russia: lost in transition* (Washington, DC: Carnegie Endowment, 2007).

Shimshon, G., 'Corruption, institutions and development in Central Asia'. MA thesis (University of Leiden, 2004).

Shlapentokh, V., *The new Russian diaspora: Russian minorities in the former Soviet Republics* (New York: M.E. Sharpe, 1994).

'Russia's acquiescence to corruption makes the state machine inept', *Communist and Post-Communist Studies* 36:2 (2003), 151–61.

Siemaszko, A., 'Central and Eastern European victimisation rates: to compare or not to compare?', in A. Alvazzi del Frate, U. Zvekic and J. Van Dijk (eds.), *Understanding crime: experiences of crime and crime control* (Rome: UNICRI, 1993), pp. 87–92.

Simons, T.W., *Eurasia's new frontiers: young states, old societies, open futures* (Ithaca, NY: Cornell University Press, 2008).

Skocpol, T., 'Bringing the state back in: strategies of analysis in current research', in P. Evans, D. Rueschemeyer and T. Skocpol (eds.), *Bringing the state back in* (Cambridge University Press, 1984), pp. 3–37.

States and social revolutions: a comparative analysis of France, Russia and China (Cambridge University Press, 1979).

Smirnov, A., 'Georgia threatens to play the rebel card in the North Caucasus', *Chechnya Weekly*, 22 May (2008).

Smith, H., *On Clausewitz: a study of military and political ideas* (Basingstoke, UK: Palgrave MacMillan, 2005).

Smith, K.E., 'The outsiders: the European Neighbourhood Policy', *International Affairs* 81 (2005), 757–73.

Smith, M.A., *The Russian chronologies*, UK Department of Defence, Research and Assessment Branch (July–September 2009). Available at www.da.mod.uk/.../russian-chronologies/09(13)%20MAS3.doc.pdf

Smith, R., *The utility of force: the art of war in the modern world* (London: Allen Lane, 2005).

Snetkov, A., 'The securitisation versus post-structuralist debate in post-conflict environments: the Chechen case study'. Paper presented to the CREES Annual Conference, Cumberland Lodge, 8 June (2008).

Snow, D., *Distant thunder: patterns of conflict in the developing world* (London: M.E. Sharpe, 1997).

Snyder, J., *From voting to violence: democratisation and nationalist conflict* (New York: W.W. Norton, 2000).

Socor, V., 'Russia resumes gas imports from Turkmenistan', *Asia Times Online*, 6 January (2010). Available at /www.atimes.com/atimes/Central_Asia/LA06Ag02.html

Solovev, V., 'Moskva ustupila Vashingtonu' *Nezavisimaia gazeta*, 3 November (2001).

Souleimanov, E., and Ditrych, O., 'The internationalisation of the Russian-Chechen conflict: myths and reality', *Europe-Asia Studies* 60 (September 2008), 1199–222.

Sovetskaya rossiya, 22 April (1997), p. 1.

'Spain raids "major Russian gang"', *BBC News*, 13 June (2008). Available at http://news.bbc.co.uk/2/hi/europe/7453388.stm

Spector, B., Winbourne, S., O'Brien, J., and Rudenshiold, E., *Corruption assessment: Ukraine – final report*, 10 February 2006 (Washington, DC: Management Systems International/USAID, 2006).

Spector, R.A., *The transformation of Askar Akaev, president of Kyrgyzstan* (Berkeley Program in Soviet and Post-Soviet Studies, 2004). Available at http://repositories.cdlib.org/iseees/bps/2004 02-spec

Sperling, V., 'Introduction: the domestic and international obstacles to state-building in Russia', in V. Sperling (ed.), *Building the Russian state: institutional crisis and the quest for democratic governance* (Boulder, CO: Westview, 2000), pp. 1–23.

Spiegle, P., 'Biden says weakened Russia will bend to the US', *Wall Street Journal*, 25 July (2009), p. A1.

'Srednyaya velichina vzyatki povysilas' do 27 tysyach rubley', *Kommersant*, 27 July (2009). Available at www.kommersant.ru/doc.aspx?DocsID=1211294&ThemesID=239

Starostin, D., 'FSB bespokoit osmiy', *Online Vremya Novostei*, 27 September 2002. Available at www.vremya.ru/2002/178/4/27502.html

Steinmeier, F.W., 'We face new threats and challenges', *Der Spiegel*, 2 April (2009). Available at www.spiegel.de/international/europe/0.1518.619969.00.html

Sterling, C., *Crime without frontiers* (London: Warner, 1995).

Stockholm International Peace Research Institute, *SIPRI Yearbook, 2010* (Stockholm: SIPRI, 2010).

Storey, I., 'China's "Malacca dilemma"', *Jamestown Foundation China Brief* 6 (2006). Available at www.jamestown.org/programs/chinabrief/single/?tx_ ttnews%5Btt_news%5D=31575&tx_ttnews%5BbackPid%5D=196&no_ cache=1

'Strategiya dlya Rossii', *Nezavisimaya gazeta*, 22 April (1993), pp. 1, 3.

Sultanova, A., 'Pipelines to speed flow of Caspian oil to West', *Miami Herald*, 25 May (2005), p. 18A.

Suny, R.G., 'Living in the hood: Russia, empire, and old and new neighbours', in R. Legvold (ed.), *Russian foreign policy in the twenty-first century and the shadow of the past* (New York: Columbia University Press, 2007), pp. 33–76.

'Supporters of Batasuna will launch a new party', *Spain Review*, 7 February (2011). Available at www.spainreview.net/index.php/2011/02/07/supporters-of-batasuna-will-launch-a-new-political-party

Surtees, R., *Trafficking of men – a trend less considered: the case of Belarus and Ukraine* (Geneva: International Organisation for Migration, 2008).

Sussex, M., 'Beslan's lessons: is pre-emption better than cure?', *Australian Journal of International Affairs* 58 (2004), 414–18.

'The strategic implications of Russian resource diplomacy', in R.E. Kanet and M.R. Freire (eds.), *Russia and its neighbours* (New York: Routledge, in press).

Synovitz, R., 'Russia suspends participation in key arms treaty', Radio Free Europe/Radio Liberty (RFE/RL), 14 July (2007).

'Tajikistan wants Russia to pay for military base', *RIA Novosti*, 30 July (2009). Available at http://en.rian.ru/world/20090730/155672919.html

Talalayev, G. 'Boris Yeltsin addresses all-Russia conference on problems of the fight against organized crime and corruption: full text of speech', Moscow, ITAR-TASS, 12 February (1993).

Taylor, B., 'Putin's "historic mission": state-building and the power ministries in the North Caucasus', *Problems of Post-Communism* 54 (2007), 3–16.

Tilly, C., *Coercion, capital, and European states, AD 990–1990* (Oxford, UK: Blackwell, 1990).

'Reflections on the history of European state-making', in C. Tilly (ed.), *The formation of national states in Western Europe* (Princeton University Press, 1975), pp. 3–83.

Timoshenko, Y., 'Containing Russia', *Foreign Affairs* 86 (2007), 65–82.

Tishkov, V., *Ethnicity, nationalism and conflict in and after the Soviet Union: the mind aflame* (London: Sage, 1997).

Toal, G., 'Russia's Kosovo: a critical geopolitics of the August war over South Ossetia', *Défense nationale et sécurité collective* (October 2008). Available at www.colorado.edu/geography/class_homepages/geog_4712_ f08/ToalSouthOssetia.pdf

Tolz, V., 'Forging the nation: national identity and nation-building in postcommunist Russia', *Europe-Asia Studies* 50 (1998), 993–1022.

Torbakov, I., 'Russia seeks to use energy abundance to increase political leverage', *Eurasia Insight*, 19 November (2003).

'Russian policymakers air notion of "liberal empire" in Caucasus, Central Asia', *Eurasia Insight*, 27 October (2003).

Transparency International, 'Corruption perceptions index 2010' (2010). Available at www.transparency.org/policy_research/surveys_indices/cpi/2010/results

Sharpening the responses against global corruption (Berlin: Transparency International, 1996).

Treisman, D., 'Deciphering Russia's federal finance: fiscal appeasement in 1995 and 1996', *Europe-Asia Studies* 50 (1998), 893–906.

'Fiscal redistribution in a fragile federation: Moscow and the regions in 1994', *British Journal of Political Science* 28 (1998), 185–200.

Trenin, D., *Getting Russia right* (Washington, DC: Carnegie Endowment, 2007).

'Russia leaves the West', *Foreign Affairs* 85 (2006), 87–9.

'Russia reborn: reimagining Moscow's foreign policy', *Foreign Affairs* 88 (2009), 64–78.

Trenin, D., and Malashenko, A., with Lieven, A., *Russia's restless frontier: the Chechnya factor in post-Soviet Russia* (Washington, DC: Carnegie Endowment for International Peace, 2004).

Truscott, P., *Russia first: breaking with the West* (London: I.B. Tauris, 1997).

Tsygankov, A.P., 'Modern at last? Variety of weak states in the post-Soviet world', *Communist and Post-Communist Studies* 40 (2007), 423–39.

Russia's foreign policy: change and continuity in national identity (Lanham, MD: Rowman & Littlefield, 2006).

Tsypkin, M., *Russia's security and the war on terror* (London: Routledge, 2007).

Tyuryukanova, E., *Forced labour in the Russian Federation today: irregular migration and trafficking in human beings* (Geneva: International Labour Office: 2005).

'Ukaz Prezidenta Rossiyskoy Federatsii ot 19 maya 2008g N 815 "O merax po protivodeystoju korruptsii"', *Rossiyskaya Gazeta*, 22 May (2008).

Ukraine country economic memorandum (New York: World Bank, 2009).

United Nations, *A more secure world: our shared responsibility*. Report of the High-Level Panel on Threats, Challenges, and Change (New York: UN Department of Public Information, 2004). Available at www.un.org/secureworld/report2.pdf

United Nations Development Program, *Human development report, 1999* (New York: Oxford University Press, 1999).

United Nations General Assembly, 63rd Session, *Implementing the Responsibility to Protect*, Report of the Secretary General, 12 January (2009).

United Nations Office on Drugs and Crime, *Results of a pilot survey of forty selected organised criminal groups in sixteen countries* (Vienna: UNODC, 2002).

United Nations Security Council, *Resolution 1674*, 28 April (2006).

US Senate, Committee on Foreign Relations, 'Ballistic missiles: threat and response: hearings before the Committee on Foreign Relations United States Senate', One Hundred Sixth Congress, First Session (Washington, DC: Government Printing Office, 1999).

Van Creveld, M., *The changing face of war: combat from the Marne to Iraq* (New York: Random House, 2007).

The transformation of war (New York: Free Press, 1991).

van de Walle, N., 'The economic correlates of state failure: taxes, foreign aid, and policies', in R. Rotberg (ed.), *When states fail: causes and consequences* (Princeton University Press, 2004), pp. 94–115.

Van Dijk, J., 'Mafia markers: assessing organised crime and its impact upon societies', *Trends in Organised Crime* 10:4 (2007), 39–56.

Vasileva, O., *Georgia as a model of postcommunist transformation* (Moscow: s.n, 1993).

Vreeland, J.R., 'The effect of political regime on civil war: unpacking anocracy', *Journal of Conflict Resolution* 52 (2008), 401–25.

VTsIOM, 'Obshchestvennaya povestka dnya: bor'ba s korruptsiey i preodolenie krizisa', *Press-vypusk* 1099, 21 November (2008). Available at http://wciom.ru/arkhiv/tematicheskiiarkhiv/item/single/11021.html?no_cache=1&cHash=dee60cc421

Wagstyl, S., 'The year Russia flexed its diplomatic muscle', *Financial Times*, 17 December (2007).

Walzer, M., *Just and unjust war: a moral argument with historical illustrations* (New York: Basic Books, 2006).

Washington Post, 17 September (2004), p. A27.

Webber, M., *The international politics of Russia and the successor states* (Manchester University Press, 1996).

Weber, M., *From Max Weber: essays in sociology*, trans. and ed. H.H. Gerth and C.W. Mills (London: Routledge, 1991).

Webster, W. (ed.), *Russian organised crime: global organised crime project* (Washington, DC: Center for Strategic and International Studies, 1997).

Weenink, A., and van der Laan, F., 'The search for the Russian Mafia: Central and Eastern European criminals in the Netherlands, 1989–2005', *Trends in organised crime* 10:4 (2007), 57–76.

Weinert, M.S., 'From state security to human security', in P. Hayden (ed.), *The Ashgate research companion to ethics and international relations* (Farnham, UK: Ashgate, 2009), pp. 151–65.

Weir, F., 'Hilary Clinton slams Russia over Georgia: why Russia shrugs', *Christian Science Monitor*, 6 July (2010). Available at www.csmonitor.com/World/Europe/2010/0706/Hillary-Clinton-slams-Russia-over-Georgia-Why-Russia-shrugs

'Mass protests in Georgia aim to unseat Saakashvili', *Christian Science Monitor*, 8 April (2009).

Welt, C., 'The thawing of a frozen conflict: the internal security dilemma and the 2004 prelude to the Russo-Georgia war', *Europe-Asia Studies* 62 (2010), 63–97.

Wheatley, J., 'Managing ethnic diversity in Georgia: one step forward, two steps back', *Central Asian Survey* 28 (2009), 119–34.

Wheeler, C., 'Putin was set to do deal for Beslan children, says aide', *Guardian Unlimited*, 17 September (2004). Available at www.guardian.co.uk/world/2004/sep/17/chechnya.russia1

Wilson, J., *Strategic partners: Russian-Chinese relations in the post-Soviet era* (New York: M.E. Sharpe, 2004).

Wittig, T., 'Financing terrorism along the Chechnya-Georgia border, 1999–2002', *Global Crime* 10:3 (2009), 251–2.

Wolin, S., *Democracy incorporated: managed democracy and the spectre of inverted totalitarianism* (Princeton University Press, 2008).

World Bank, 'Russia: BEEPS at-a-glance', (2009). Available at http://siteresources.worldbank.org/INTECAREGTOPANTCOR/Resources/BAAGREV20060208Russia.pdf

World Bank in Russia, *Russian Economic Report* 16 (2008).

Yablokova, O., 'Levada leaves VTsIOM for VTsIOM', *Moscow Times*, 10 September (2003), p. 6.

Yeltsin, B., 'On priority measures for reforming the Russian Federation armed forces and improving their structure', *Rossiskaya gazeta*, 19 July (1997), p. 5.

    'Speech of Boris Yeltsin to members of Civic Union', ITAR-TASS, 1 March (1993).

Zhirinovsky, V.V., *Plevok na Zapad* (Moscow: Liberal'no-demokraticheskaia partiia Rossii, 1995).

    S tankami i pushkami ili bez tankov i pushek (Moscow: Liberal'no-demokraticheskaia partiia Rossii, 1995).

Ziegler, C.E., 'Energy in the Caspian Basin and Central Asia', in R.E. Kanet (ed.), *The new security environment: the impact on Russia, Central and Eastern Europe* (Aldershot, UK: Ashgate, 2005), pp. 210–18.

    'NATO, the United States and Central Asia: challenging sovereign governance'. Unpublished paper presented at the II WISC Conference, Ljubljana, Slovenia, 5–6 July (2008).

Zimmerman, W., *The Russian people and foreign policy: Russian elite and mass perspectives, 1993–2000* (Princeton University Press, 2002).

Zvekic, U., *Criminal victimisation in countries in transition* (Rome: UNICRI, 1998).

Zvelev, I., *Russia and its new diasporas* (Washington, DC: US Institute of Peace Press, 2000).

Index